The *Observer's* series was launched in 1937 with the publication of *The Observer's Book of Birds*. Today, over fifty years later, paperback *Observers* continue to offer practical, useful information on a wide range of subjects, and with every book regularly revised by experts, the facts are right up-to-date. Students, amateur enthusiasts and professional organisations alike will find the latest *Observers* invaluable.

'Thick and glossy, briskly informative' – *The Guardian*

'If you are a serious spotter of any of the things the series deals with, the books must be indispensable' – *The Times Educational Supplement*

O B S E R V E R S

SOCCER

Albert Sewell

BLOOMSBURY BOOKS
LONDON

PENGUIN BOOKS

Published by the Penguin Group
Penguin Books Ltd, 27 Wrights Lane, London W8 5TZ, England
Penguin Books USA Inc., 375 Hudson Street, New York, New York 10014, USA
Penguin Books Australia Ltd, Ringwood, Victoria, Australia
Penguin Books Canada Ltd, 10 Alcorn Avenue, Toronto, Ontario, Canada M4V 3B2
Penguin Books (NZ) Ltd, 182-190 Wairau Road, Auckland 10, New Zealand

Penguin Books Ltd, Registered Offices: Harmondsworth, Middlesex, England

Published by
Frederick Warne (Publishers) Ltd, London, England

First Edition 1972
Second Edition 1974
Third Edition 1976
Fourth Edition 1978
Fifth Edition 1980
Sixth Edition 1984

This edition published by Bloomsbury Books, an imprint of
The Godfrey Cave Group, 42 Bloomsbury Street, London, WC1B 3QJ,
under licence from Penguin Books Limited, 1993

1 3 5 7 9 10 8 6 4 2

Originally published as *The Observer's Book of Soccer*
in small hardback format

Printed and bound in Great Britain by
BPCC Hazell Books Ltd

Member of BPCC Ltd

ISBN 1 85471 184 9

CONTENTS

The History of the Game

It is impossible to say exactly when football began, because its origins are lost, literally, in the mists of time. Some say men (and women) first began kicking 'an object' around as far back as the twelfth century. Perhaps they did, but it took a long time for the game to become organized.

The first real stirrings were in the middle of last century, when boys at established English public schools, and at universities such as Cambridge, began to play a form of soccer which at least bore some resemblance to our modern game. It is surprising that a game thought of mainly as a working man's pastime should have originated in the very bastions of the so-called privileged classes.

However, such was the popularity of football that it was not long before it appealed to a wider audience. The oldest Football League club was founded in 1862 — 26 years before the formation of the League itself — Notts County, who came into existence three years before their arch-rivals Nottingham Forest.

The following year, 1863, saw the formation of the Football Association — in a public house in central London. This was the world's first organized attempt at controlling the game at national level, and it was from the new body's title that Association football, or soccer, got its name.

Many people north of the Border believe that Scotland, not England, gave football to the world. With due respect to the Scots, who have contributed so much to the game, this is not so. The first Scottish club, the famous and once powerful Queen's Park, did not appear on the field until 1867, and the Scottish Football Association waited until 1873 for its inception.

England-Scotland Rivalry

Brazil, West Germany, Hungary may come and go. England and Scotland go on for ever in the international soccer sense, despite misguided attempts in the past to belittle the annual clash between these two. The first match was played in November 1872, in Glasgow, and resulted in a goalless draw (it was to be 98 years before the next similar result).

As for Wales, they reached their centenary in 1976 with prospects brighter than at any time in their history. By beating Austria 1–0 at Wrexham, they qualified for the first time for the European Championship quarter-finals, as Britain's lone hopes. They dominated a qualifying group that also included Hungary, and won five of the six games. This finest achievement by Wales since their participation in the 1958 World Cup quarter-finals came at a time when England were still searching for the right formula.

The violent political climate of the seventies deepened Ireland's soccer problems, which have long included a need to supply players for two international sides — Northern Ireland and the Republic — and the recurring loss of promising players to Football League clubs. But season 1974–75 gave Irish soccer a welcome uplift — the visit of Yugoslavia in April was the first international staged in Belfast since October 1971, and a few weeks later Home Championship football returned to the province after a four-year boycott.

The Home Championship was first played for in season 1883–84 and Scotland had a clean sweep, winning all three matches. In 1885 professionalism was legalized in English soccer, and a year later Arbroath carved their own slice of history by winning a Scottish Cup tie 36–0 against the luckless, and long-since defunct Bon Accord. This remains the highest score in any official senior football match in Britain. The present-day off-side law and the system of early-round elimination of weak teams both help to ensure that this kind of farce will never be seen again.

In October 1887, Preston North End made a brave effort to challenge Arbroath's feat when they annihilated Hyde 26–0 in an FA Cup match.

First League in the World

The Football League was formed in 1888 and for those who wonder why it should be honoured with the title *The* Football League, and not the English Football League, the answer is that it was the first such body in the world.

How many of today's soccer followers can reel off the names of those famous twelve clubs which formed the basis of what has become the world's greatest league competition? They were Accrington, Aston Villa, Blackburn Rovers, Bolton Wanderers, Burnley, Derby County, Everton, Notts County, Preston North End, Stoke City, West Bromwich Albion and Wolverhampton Wanderers. Of that number only Accrington are not still members; they left the League in March 1962, after struggling through the years since the Second World War as Accrington Stanley.

In 1970 two other founder members, Aston Villa and Preston, were relegated to Division Three for the first time in their history. The following year Blackburn Rovers went down for the first time, along with Bolton, another of the famous originals. Such is the swing of fortune in soccer across the decades.

Modern fans think of Tottenham Hotspur in 1961 and Arsenal ten years later as the 'double clubs', i.e. those which have won both the League Championship and the FA Cup in the same season. But as long ago as 1888–89, the year in which the League began, Preston won the Cup without conceding a goal, and the Championship without losing a game. This was a remarkable achievement, even if competition was a lot less fierce in those days, and Aston Villa were the only other side before Tottenham, in 1960–61, to win both trophies in one season. They did it in the season 1896–97.

Floodlights are now part of every club's equipment. But how many people realize that matches were being played under artificial light long before the end of last century? The first reference to a 'floodlit' game is found in records dated 1887, which tell of a game being played at Sheffield by *candlelight*!

As the nineteenth century drew to a close, the game continued to boom. Attendances rose each year, and while there was no sign yet of international competition against foreign opponents, soccer was slowly being introduced abroad.

It is not known precisely when football was first taught to other countries — to the Brazilians for example — but we do know that British sailors had a lot to do with it. The British Navies, Royal and Merchant, were at the height of their power and influence in the fifty years between 1875 and 1925, and it was during this half century that the game was taken round the world. Sailors on leave abroad often played football among themselves, local inhabitants watched with interest, learned quickly, and soon challenged the soccer 'missionaries' and sometimes beat them.

28 Goals on First Tour

The first international match between England and a foreign country took place on 6 June 1908. England met Austria in Vienna and won handsomely 6–1. Two days later the teams met again at the same venue and this time the Austrians were beaten 11–1. England then went on to Budapest, and crushed Hungary 7–0, before moving finally to Prague and soundly defeating Bohemia (now Czechoslovakia) 4–0 to end a highly successful first professional tour abroad.

The following year the Austrians invited England back, no doubt hoping for revenge. This time they lost 8–1, so in three games in twelve months against the Austrians, all of them in Vienna, England piled up an aggregate of 25 goals and lost only three. However, and significantly in terms of the improvement in soccer standards abroad, when the teams next met, in May 1930 — again in Vienna — there was a goalless draw, and when Austria first played here (at Chelsea in December 1932) England only just scraped home 4–3.

Despite that 1908 England tour, international football with overseas countries competing did not become established until the early thirties. The First World War had much to do with that, and throughout the twenties, the total of matches played abroad by England was no more than sixteen.

It was not until the summer of 1950 that any British country played a team from the Americas. This was when England participated in the World Cup for the first time. They beat Chile 2–0 on their opening match of the final series in Brazil, but 29 June marked the most embarrassing day in the entire playing history of British soccer. From Belo Horizonte came what must rate as the most astonishing scoreline in the international game: England 0, USA 1. It was a result which rocked the football world. Perhaps the least excited country was the United States itself, so little interest did they show in the game of Association Football at that time. To the North Americans soccer was a minority sport, and that freak result was as unlikely as, say, England beating the USA at baseball. But it happened!

Rangers-Celtic Dominance

This match belongs, however, to soccer's comparatively modern history, and there is reason here to go back to the turn of the century. In the season 1898–99 a feat occurred which almost certainly will never be repeated in British soccer. Rangers, over the years Scotland's most successful club until the dominance of Celtic, took the Scottish League title in a canter. They won every one of the 18 games they played in the competition, and even allowing for the relatively low standard of Scottish club soccer, it was a tremendous achievement.

The overall standards of play in Scotland are certainly low. A look at past winners of the Scottish League Championship tells the tale. In 1932 Motherwell won the title for the first and only time. Apart from that year, the championship was shared between Rangers and Celtic from 1904, when it was won by Third Lanark, to 1948 when Hibernian took it. During those years the title went to Rangers no fewer than 20 times, and to Celtic 15. Indeed Motherwell's surprise victory in 1932 prevented what would otherwise have been a run of eight consecutive successes for Rangers.

Rangers' Championship success in 1964 gave them a world record total of 34 League titles, but from season 1965–66 Celtic dominated, and when they triumphed yet again in 1974, they brought Scotland a share in another world record — 9 consecutive League Championships — previously held jointly by MTK Budapest, who won the Hungarian title from 1917–25 inclusive, and CDNA Sofia, when they were Champions of Bulgaria from 1954–62.

Celtic's long reign ended when Rangers returned to the top in 1975, at which point the Scottish League took one of its most ambitious steps by shaping itself into three sections, headed by a premier division of ten clubs.

FIFA Formed

If, in the past, Scottish football tended to stagnate because of the great strength of Rangers and Celtic, the game elsewhere grew in power. The development that was to make soccer a world game came in 1904, when FIFA — the Federation of International Football Associations — was founded in Paris. Seven countries — France, Belgium, Holland, Switzerland, Spain, Denmark and Sweden — were the original members. Today there are more than 150.

Amateur soccer, or rather a twentieth-century version of the original amateur game, came along in 1907 when the Amateur FA was formed and the following year Britain put a team in the Olympic Games and won the final at London's White City, beating Denmark 2–0.

The 1974 Amateur Cup Final, won at Wembley by Bishops Stortford, was the last. Ever-increasing infringement of amateur status by many players led to the Football Association, after years of deliberation, dispensing with the word 'amateur'. Its eradication meant the end of the Amateur Cup and Amateur internationals. All footballers became 'players', with the professionals contracted, the rest known as non-contract players.

In 1923 Wembley staged its first Cup Final, with an attendance of 126,000, many of whom stormed the gates and broke in. In 1926 Huddersfield Town won the League Championship for the third successive year, the first team to do so, and a feat emulated only by Arsenal in 1933–34–35 and, almost half a century later, by Liverpool in 1982–83–84.

In 1927 Cardiff City beat Arsenal 1–0 at Wembley and became the first, and only, side to take the FA Cup out of England. This feat is still reckoned to be the most outstanding in Welsh soccer, which has always had to take second place in popularity to rugby. In 1929 England lost for the first time on foreign soil, Spain triumphing 4–3 in Madrid, and the following year the World Cup was launched. Uruguay beat Argentina 4–2 in the Final, and South America was on the world soccer map. And so into the thirties.

The record individual number of goals in any British senior League or Cup match was set in April 1936 when Joe Payne, Luton Town centre-forward, scored ten in his club's 12–0 win against Bristol Rovers in a Division 3 match.

Record British Crowd

A year later the largest crowd ever to watch a match in Britain squeezed into Hampden Park for the Scotland–England International. The official attendance was 149,547, and unless some spectacular new stadium is built it is a British record which will never be broken. Still in Scotland, Celtic's Jimmy McGrory retired in 1938 after scoring an all-time record 550 goals in first-class soccer. This was a record for Britain; overseas players have scored more — Brazil's Pele topped the 1,000 mark.

If Scottish club soccer was often overshadowed on the field by its English counterpart, the largest crowds were to be found north of the Border. Manchester United and Arsenal set up the still-existing record for an English League match — 82,950. That was on 17 January 1948, at Maine Road (United were still using Manchester City's ground while their own at Old Trafford was being restored after bomb damage during the War). In March of the same year Rangers and Hibernian met in the Scottish Cup semi-final at Hampden Park in front of 143,570. Then, in the Final, nearly a quarter of a million fans saw the two matches Rangers needed to beat Greenock Morton. Those were the days of the great crowds, after years when people had been starved of top-class competition.

Coming more up to date — although that depends to a large extent on the age of the reader — in 1953 Stanley Mortensen scored a hat-trick in the Coronation Year FA Cup Final against Bolton Wanderers. He was the first man to achieve such a feat this century, but even his performance was overshadowed by that of his partner, Stanley (subsequently Sir Stanley) Matthews.

Bolton, led by Nat Lofthouse, were 3–1 ahead well into the second half. It seemed all over for Blackpool, and for the genius Matthews who had never won a Cup-winners' medal, and was playing in what was to be his last Final. Then the two Stanleys broke loose. Matthews mesmerized a Bolton side playing one short after injury — there were no substitutes then — and Blackpool triumphed 4–3 in one of the all-time classic Finals.

The 'Matthews Final' could be regarded as almost the end of an era in British football. Six months later, at Wembley in November 1953, came the 6–3 slaughter of England by Hungary — those magnificent Magyars — which led to a vast re-thinking on the game's tactics and economics.

Europe: A New Dimension

A new competitive dimension was brought to the game in 1955 with the launching of the European Cup, and both in that and the two other big European tournaments — the Cup-Winners' Cup and Fairs Cup (now the UEFA Cup) — British clubs have figured prominently among the honours, as will be seen from reference to the European section of this book.

One of the most important factors in the revolution within British football was the removal of the maximum wage in 1961. This ensured that our stars did not need to go to Italy to earn salaries commensurate with their skills, as world-class players like John Charles, Denis Law, Jimmy Greaves and others had done.

The long-overdue acceptance of substitutes in League football was at last approved in 1965. A year later came the greatest achievement of all for British soccer, with England's triumph at

Wembley as host nation in the World Cup. In Mexico in 1970 the world crown was taken by Brazil for the third time.

In 1974 West Germany, emulating England eight years before, became the second successive European host nation to take the World Cup, and the next World series, in Argentina in 1978, also went to the home country.

By the mid-seventies, soccer was at last beginning to take roots across the Atlantic, with the growth of the North American League, while Europe threw down a big-money challenge to Britain's top stars. Kevin Keegan led the trail when he left Liverpool for SV Hamburg in a £500,000 transfer in June 1977; in June 1979 Laurie Cunningham, the coloured West Bromwich and England winger, was lured into Spanish football in a £950,000 move to Real Madrid, and five months later another England International was lost to home football when Nottingham Forest striker Tony Woodcock joined FC Cologne for £650,000.

But it was not all one-way movement of star players away from Britain. In July 1978 Tottenham astonished the football world by bringing to White Hart Lane two members of that year's triumphant Argentina World Cup squad — Osvaldo Ardiles and Ricardo Villa.

First Million-Pound Transfer

Transfer fees kept pace with rocketing inflation. In February 1979 Nottingham Forest manager Brian Clough paid Britain's first million-pound fee (£1,180,000) for Trevor Francis, the Birmingham and England striker, and seven months later the headlines carried two more million-pound deals in the space of four days. Wolves were involved in both, selling midfield player Steve Daley to Manchester City for £1,450,000 and then setting yet another British record with the signing of Scottish international striker Andy Gray from Aston Villa for £1,469,000.

Freedom of contract brought greater bargaining power to Britain's stars and increased the risk of unemployment to lesser players. England's 'team of the seventies' was unquestionably Liverpool. With continuity in the camp maintained by the appointment of Bob Paisley as manager when Bill Shankly retired in July 1974, the Anfield club reached new levels of achievement in that decade with four League Championship successes (giving them a record 11 First Division titles), two in the UEFA Cup, one FA Cup triumph and, best of all, European Cup conquests in consecutive years 1977 and 1978. In 1980 Liverpool were League Champions yet again, and by the end of season 1983–84 — Joe Fagan's first as Bob Paisley's successor — the First Division title had gone to Anfield seven times in nine seasons.

Next to Liverpool, Nottingham Forest were the principal prize-winners of that period. From the time they won promotion from the

12

Second Division in 1977 (when they just squeezed into third place), honours were earned season by season by Brian Clough and his men: League Champions in 1978. League Cup Winners in 1978 and 1979, and a record third successive appearance at Wembley in that competition in 1980; and they were successors to Liverpool also in 1979 as Britain's European Cup-holders.

The Eighties

The achievements of Liverpool, Forest and, to a lesser extent, a few other clubs, did not disguise the fact that, at the start of the eighties, there were problems within the game in urgent need of discussion and solution if British football was to progress long-term on the right lines.

For a time, insanity continued in the transfer market, with clubs spending fortunes they did not possess on players who, with few exceptions, were ridiculously overpriced. It could not last, of course, and the £1.5m paid by Manchester United to West Bromwich Albion for Bryan Robson in October 1981 looked like remaining indefinitely the record British fee when, two years later, the Football League introduced a rule whereby 50 per cent of all transfer fees had to be paid at the time players were signed and the balance within 12 months.

In 1980 Northern Ireland celebrated their centenary by winning the British Championship for the first time since 1914. In 1981, the Football League changed its points system to three for a win, hoping that the extra incentive would produce more exciting football and halt the slide in attendances.

Sponsorship at high level was just around the corner. In 1982 the League Cup became the Milk Cup, and for the next two years the new prize remained in old hands, Liverpool's. Season 1983–84 brought two of the most revolutionary changes in the game's history.

A three-year deal worth £3.2m with a Japanese camera and business equipment company turned the Football League competition into the Canon League, and a controversial new agreement with television brought live coverage of ten League matches (five shown on Friday nights by BBC, five on Sunday afternoons by ITV), plus two FA Cup ties on each channel (rounds 3–6 inclusive), with the Milk Cup Final switched to Sunday for live transmission. Acceptance of shirt advertising was essential to both deals.

Football had sold its independence for many pieces of gold, to compensate for attendances having dropped, by season 1982–83, to a post-war 'low' of 18,788,822 — considerably less than half the all-time record 'high' of 41,271,414 spectators who paid to watch League soccer in season 1948–49.

Guide to the 92 Football League Clubs in England and Wales

As at 31 May, 1984

Aldershot

Recreation Ground, High Street, Aldershot
Tel: 0252-20211 **Colours:** *Red & Blue*

The years of the Second World War provided Aldershot with the most colourful teams in their history. Many of the game's best names were on military service in the garrison town and appeared as guests for the club. Among them were Frank Swift, Tommy Lawton, Matt Busby, Denis Compton, and the full England half-back line of that era, Cliff Britton, Stan Cullis and Joe Mercer.

In more settled times Aldershot rarely achieved much of distinction until, by attaining fourth place in Division Four in season 1972–73, they won promotion for the first time. Before that, their most successful season was in 1969–70 when they were sixth in Division Four. That was the season too, when they attracted their record attendance to the Recreation Ground, 19,138 watching their fourth round FA Cup replay against Carlisle.

Aldershot can claim a share of at least one record — that of the quickest goal. Albert Mundy scored six seconds after the kick-off at Hartlepool on 25 October 1958.

A further distinction for the club who came into the Football League in 1932 when displacing Thames F.C., is that they are the only members of the League who play in a public park.

Record attendance: 19,138 v Carlisle (FA Cup), January 1970.
Modern Capacity: 16,000. **Nickname:** 'Shots'.
Entered Football League: 1932 — Div. 3 (South).
Biggest win: 8-1 v Gateshead (Div. 4), September 1958.
Heaviest defeat: 0–9 v Bristol City (Div. 3 South), December 1946.
Highest final League position: 4th in Div. 4, 1972–73.
Best in FA Cup: 5th Round, 1932–33, 1978–79.
Best in League/Milk Cup: 2nd Round, 1960–61, 1962–63, 1963–64, 1965–66, 1966–67, 1970–71, 1971–72, 1981–82, 1983–84.
Pitch measurements: 117½ x 76 yd.
Highest League Scorer in Single Season: John Dungworth — 26 in 1978–79 (Div. 4).
Transfers —
  Highest fee paid: £45,000 — Colin Garwood (from Portsmouth), February 1980.
  Highest fee received: £100,000 — John Dungworth (to Shrewsbury), October 1979.

Arsenal

Arsenal Stadium, Highbury, London N5 1BU
Tel: 01-226 0304   **Colours:** *Red & White*

By performing the League Championship-FA Cup double in 1971, Arsenal not only caught up with their illustrious past — they exceeded it. They became the first club to win the Championship eight times, and the 'double' was signalled by Bertie Mee being voted 'Manager of the Year' and captain Frank McLintock winning the 'Footballer of the Year' award.

Arsenal have been constant members of Division One since 1919, and their greatest era until the seventies occurred during the 1930s when they 'came to power' under the managership of Herbert Chapman. They were League Champions in 1931, 1933, 1934, 1935 and 1938, and won the FA Cup in 1930 and 1936.

After the war, under Tom Whittaker, they won the First Division title in 1948 and 1953, and the FA Cup again in 1950. But then came a long period of non-success from which the way back to former glory followed two losing appearances in the League Cup Final.

In the 1970 Fairs Cup they won their first European prize and a year later they completed the double. They ended the seventies by winning the FA Cup in 1979 for the fifth time.

A year later Arsenal made Wembley history when playing in a third successive FA Cup Final and also earned the chance of dual Cup honours in the same season by reaching the Cup-Winners' Cup Final. But they finished with neither.

The Double (League Champions, FA Cup Winners): 1970–71.
League Champions: 1930–31, 1932–33, 1933–34, 1934–35, 1937–38, 1947–48, 1952–53, 1970–71.
FA Cup Winners: 1929–30, 1935–36, 1949–50, 1970–71, 1978–79.
European Fairs Cup Winners: 1969–70.
Record attendance: 73,295 v Sunderland (League), March 1935.
Modern Capacity: 60,000. **Nickname:** 'Gunners'.
Entered Football League: 1893 — Div. 2.
Biggest wins: 12–0 v Loughborough T. (Div. 2), March 1900, and 12–0 v Ashford United (FA Cup), 1893–94.
Heaviest defeat: 0–8 v Loughborough T. (Div. 2), December 1896.
Best in League Cup/Milk Cup: Runners-up 1967–68, 1968–69.
Pitch measurements: 110 x 71 yd.
Highest League Scorer in Single Season: Ted Drake — 42 in 1934–35 (Div. 1).
Highest transfer fee paid: £1,350,000 — Kenny Sansom (from Crystal Palace), August 1980.
Highest transfer fee received: £1,250,000 — Clive Allen (to Crystal Palace), August 1980.

Aston Villa

Villa Park, Birmingham B6 6HE
Tel: 021-327-6604 **Colours:** *Claret & Blue*

Aston Villa revived old glories by winning the First Division for the seventh time in 1981 (71 years after their last Championship triumph), and a year later manager Tony Barton's team achieved further distinction by taking the European Cup to Villa Park. In the Final in Rotterdam they beat Bayern Munich 1–0 (Peter Withe).

One of Britain's most distinguished clubs, Villa were among the 12 founder members of the Football League in 1888. They were Champions six times between 1894 and 1910, and in 1897 completed the 'double' of League title and FA Cup — a feat previously achieved only by Preston in 1888–89.

Villa's 128 League goals in 1930–31 (when Championship runners-up) is still the highest total by any club in the First Division, and they share with Tottenham the FA Cup record of seven successes.

Triumph over Barcelona in the European Super Cup in 1983 meant that Villa had achieved distinction for a third successive season — a level of performance that would not be easy to maintain in an era of increasingly fierce competition, both on the field and in the commercial sense.

The 'Double' (League Champions, F.A. Cup Winners): 1896–97.
League Champions: 1893–94, 1895–96, 1896–97, 1898–99, 1899–1900, 1909–10, 1980–81.
European Cup Winners: 1981–82.
European Super Cup Winners: 1982–83.
Division 2 Champions: 1937–38, 1959–60.
Division 3 Champions: 1971–72.
FA Cup Winners: 1886–87, 1894–95, 1896–97, 1904–05, 1912–13, 1919–20, 1956–57.
League Cup Winners: 1960–61, 1974–75, 1976–77.
Record attendance: 76,588 v Derby County (F.A. Cup 6th Rd), March 1946. **Modern capacity:** 48,000. **Nickname:** Villans.
Year Formed: 1874. **Entered Football League:** 1888 (Div. 1).
Biggest win: 13–0 v Wednesday Old Ath. (FA Cup 1st Rd) 1886–87.
Heaviest defeat: 1–8 v Blackburn R. (FA Cup 3rd Rd) 1888–89.
Pitch measurements: 115 x 75 yd.
Highest League scorer in one season: T. ('Pongo') Waring — 49 in 1930–31 (Div. 1).
Highest transfer fee paid: £500,000 — Peter Withe (from Newcastle), May 1980.
Highest transfer fee received: £1,469,000 — Andy Gray (to Wolves), September 1979.

Barnsley

Oakwell Ground, Barnsley
Tel: 0226-295353   **Colours:** *Red & White*

Ever since their formation, Barnsley have known the extremes of fortune. Often, it must be said, the emphasis has been on the struggle to make ends meet. Yet there have been great occasions such as winning the FA Cup as a Second Division side in 1912 after herculean efforts in the Final against West Bromwich Albion.   The teams met first at the old Crystal Palace in a goalless draw, and Barnsley snatched victory by the only goal during extra time in the replay at Bramall Lane, Sheffield. This was deserved compensation for their 2-0 defeat, by Newcastle, in the Final two years earlier, when a second match was also required to decide the outcome.

One of their biggest disappointments was missing promotion to Division One in 1922 on goal average. Three times Barnsley were Third Division North Champions: in 1933-34, when they scored 118 goals; in 1938-39, when they won 30 and drew 7 of their 42 League games; and in 1954-55.

Like other clubs living in the shadows of better-known neighbours, Barnsley have discovered many stars, among them Eric Brook and Fred Tilson, who together played in Manchester City's 1934 FA Cup-winning team; George Hunt, Wilf Copping, Dick Spence, Danny Blanchflower and Tommy Taylor, who lost his life in the Munich air disaster involving Manchester United in February 1958.

After a seven-year spell (1972-79) in the Fourth Division, Barnsley achieved two promotion successes in three seasons, returning to Division Two in 1981.

FA Cup Winners: 1911-12.
Division 3 (North) Champions: 1933-34, 1938-39, 1954-55.
Record attendance: 42,056 v Stoke (FA Cup), February 1936.
Modern capacity: 35,000. **Nickname:** 'Tykes'.
Entered Football League: 1898 — Div. 2.
Biggest wins: 9-0 v Loughborough T. (Div. 2), January 1899 and 9-0 v Accrington Stanley (Div. 3 North), February 1934.
Heaviest defeat: 0-9 v Notts County (Div. 2), November 1927.
Best in League/Milk Cup: 5th Round, 1981-82.
Pitch measurements: 110 x 74 yd.
Highest League Scorer in Single Season: Cecil McCormack — 33 in 1950-51 (Div 2).
Highest transfer fee paid: £95,000 — Ian Evans (from Crystal Palace), March 1980; £95,000 — Alan Birch (from Wolves), February 1982.
Highest transfer fee received: £200,000 — Mick McCarthy (to Manchester City), December 1983.

Birmingham City

St Andrew's, Birmingham B9 4NH
Tel: 021-772 0101/2689 **Colours:** *Blue & White*

Although the League Championship, FA Cup and European prizes still elude them, Birmingham City have seldom been short of class players in one or more key positions. Their speciality has been goalkeepers of international calibre, among them Dan Tremelling, Harry Hibbs, Gil Merrick and Jim Herriot.

As Small Heath, the club were founder members of Division Two in 1892. They stepped into Division One in 1894, but slipped back two years later. Promotion came once more in 1901, but this time they lasted only one season. They climbed again in 1903; the name Small Heath was dropped in favour of Birmingham in 1905, and a year later they moved to their present St Andrew's home.

Since the last war, as Birmingham City, they have been FA Cup Finalists (1956), Fairs Cup Finalists twice (1960, 1961), League Cup Winners (1963) and promoted four times to the First Division — in 1948, 1955, 1972 and 1980.

That latest promotion was achieved through the wise spending by manager Jim Smith of the £1,180,000 received in February 1979 from the transfer of Trevor Francis to Nottingham Forest.

His successor, Ron Saunders, who moved across from Villa Park in February 1982, became the first man to have been in charge of both clubs in the second city. But for Birmingham's 13th post-war manager, team-strengthening prospects in the transfer market were not helped by accounts showing the club was £1.87 m. in debt at the end of season 1982–83.

Division 2 Champions: 1892–93, 1920–21, 1947–48, 1954–55.
League Cup Winners: 1962–63.
Record attendance: 66,844 v Everton (FA Cup), February, 1939.
Modern capacity: 41,000. **Nickname:** 'Blues'.
Entered Football League: 1892 — Div. 2.
Biggest wins: 12–0 v Walsall Town Swifts (Div. 2), December 1892 and 12–0 v Doncaster Rovers (Div.2), April 1903.
Heaviest defeats: 1–9 v Blackburn Rovers (Div.1), January 1895 and 1–9 v Sheffield Wednesday (Div.1), December 1930.
Best in FA Cup: Final 1930–31, 1955–56.
Pitch measurements: 115 x 74 yd.
Highest League Scorer in Single Season: Joe Bradford — 29 in 1927–28 (Div. 1).
Highest transfer fee paid: £350,000 — David Langan (from Derby County), June 1980.
Highest transfer fee received: £1,180,000 — Trevor Francis (to NottinghamForest), February 1979.

Blackburn Rovers

Ewood Park, Nuttall Street, Blackburn BB2 4JF
Tel: 0254-55432 **Colours:** *Blue & White*

The FA Cup was almost the exclusive property of Blackburn Rovers during the latter part of the last century. They won the trophy in three successive years, 1884–86, and again in 1890 and 1891, then had to wait 37 years to win it for the sixth time.

Rovers were original members of the Football League in 1888 and carried off the First Division Championship in 1912 and 1914. They remained continuously in the top flight until 1936. Since then, however, they have had varying spells in the Second Division and their fortunes slumped to a new low in 1970–71 when they dropped into Division Three.

Many chroniclers of the game — and certainly those old enough to remember — maintain that Bob Crompton was the finest full-back of any era. In the early part of the century he was capped 41 times for England and played for Rovers for 23 years.

Since the Second World War Rovers most-capped players, both for England, have been winger Bryan Douglas (36 Internationals) and half-back Ronnie Clayton (35), who established what is still the club's record of 580 League appearances between 1950 and 1969.

Blackburn's FA Cup hat-trick in 1884–85–86 is commemorated to this day by a special shield proudly displayed in one of football's most welcoming boardrooms, and while many clubs nowadays show lessening respect for traditional colours, Rovers have stayed true to their famous blue and white halves. Margaret Thatcher is honorary vice-president.

League Champions: 1911–12, 1913–14.
Division 2 Champions: 1938–39.
Division 3 Champions: 1974–75.
FA Cup Winners: 1883–84, 1884–85, 1885–86, 1889–90, 1890–91, 1927–28.
Record attendance: 61,783 v Bolton (FA Cup), March 1929.
Modern capacity: 23,500. **Entered Football League**: 1888 — Div. 1.
Biggest win: 11–0 v Rossendale United (FA Cup), 1884–85.
Heaviest defeat: 0–8 v Arsenal (Div. 1), February 1933.
Best in League/Milk Cup: Semi-final 1961–62.
Pitch measurements: 116 x 72 yd.
Highest League Scorer in Single Season: Ted Harper — 43 in 1925–26 (Div. 1).
Highest transfer fee paid: £80,000 — Duncan McKenzie (from Chelsea), March 1979.
Highest transfer fee received: £357,000 — Kevin Hird (to Leeds), February 1979.

Blackpool

Bloomfield Road, Blackpool FY1 6JJ
Tel: 0253-404331 **Colours:** *Tangerine & White*

Their appearance at Wembley in the years immediately after the Second World War will remain treasured memories for all associated with the Blackpool club. They went down 4-2 to Manchester United in the 1948 FA Cup Final, which belongs among Wembley's finest games; then they lost 2-0 to Newcastle in 1951 and finally came their memorable 4-3 triumph over Bolton in 1953. That was the match in which Stanley Matthews inspired his team-mates to snatch victory and Stanley Mortensen scored a hat-trick.

Blackpool came closest to taking the First Division title in 1956 when they finished runners-up. They continued as a power through the fifties when much of the credit was due to their astute manager Joe Smith, the former England and Bolton inside-forward.

After being relegated in 1967, they bounced back again in 1970, but their comeback lasted only one season as they finished bottom of Division One —a sad ending to the career of one of their finest ever players, Jimmy Armfield, who made 568 League appearances for the club and was capped 43 times at full-back for England, another Blackpool record.

From the glories of the early post-war years, Blackpool's fortunes slipped to their lowest level in recent times, with relegation to the Third Division in 1978 and to the Fourth in 1981. The ultimate humiliation for one of the game's once-great clubs came in 1983, when they had to apply for re-election. Against the threat of liquidation, players had to be sold that summer, and collection-boxes went round local pubs to help keep Blackpool afloat.

FA Cup Winners: 1952-53.
Division 2 Champions: 1929-30.
Record attendance: 39,118 v Man. Utd (League), April 1952.
Modern Capacity: 18,000. **Nickname:** 'Tangerines'.
Entered Football League: 1896 — Div. 2.
Biggest win: 8-4 v Charlton Ath. (Div. 1), September 1952.
Heaviest defeats: 1-10 v Small Heath (Div. 2), March 1901, and 1-10 v Huddersfield Town (Div. 1), December 1930.
Best in League/Milk Cup: Semi-final 1961-62.
Pitch measurements: 111 x 73 yd.
Highest League Scorer in Single Season: Jimmy Hampson — 45 in 1929-30 (Div. 2).
Highest transfer fee paid: £150,000 — Colin Morris (from Southend), December 1979.
Highest transfer fee received: £325,000 — Mick Walsh (to Everton), August 1978.

Bolton Wanderers

Burnden Park, Bolton BL3 2QR
Tel: 0204-389200   **Colours:** *White & Navy Blue*

Three times between 1923 — the first Wembley FA Cup Final — and 1929, Bolton Wanderers won the game's most coveted domestic trophy. They did so without conceding a goal at Wembley. Five Wanderers players took part in each of those successive Finals —against West Ham in 1923 (2-0), Manchester City 1926 (1-0) and Portsmouth 1929 (2-0). They were Pym in goal, Haworth, Nuttall, Seddon and Butler.

Curiously, for all their Cup-fighting prowess and as founder-members of the Football League, Bolton have never won the Championship. Relegated in 1964, they sank into Division Three in 1971, but two years later began the climb back as Third Division Champions. In 1978 they returned to the top section as Second Division Champions, only to fall again at the end of season 1979-80.

Three years later Wanderers finished bottom of Division Two, and the opening match of 1983-84, against Wimbledon, attracted only 3,992 to a ground that had once held nearly 70,000. The attendance of 3,266 against Plymouth the following April was their lowest in the League for 51 years.

Bolton's individual League scoring record for a season (38 goals by Joe Smith) has stood longer than that of any other club — since 1920-21.

Tragedy struck Burnden Park on 9 March 1946, when crush barriers broke at an FA Cup-tie between Bolton and Stoke City. Thirty-three people were killed and more than four hundred injured in the worst football disaster ever known in England.

FA Cup Winners: 1922-23, 1925-26, 1928-29, 1957-58.
Division 2 Champions: 1908-09, 1977-78.
Division 3 Champions: 1972-73.
Record attendance: 69,912 v Manchester City (FA Cup), February 1933. **Modern Capacity:** 43,000. **Nickname:** 'Trotters'.
Entered Football League: 1888 — Div. 1.
Biggest win: 13-0 v Sheffield United (FA Cup), February 1890.
Heaviest defeat: 0-7 v Manchester City (Div. 1), March 1936.
Best in League/Milk Cup: Semi-final 1976-77.
Pitch measurements: 112½ x 76 yd.
Highest League Scorer in Single Season: Joe Smith — 38 in 1920-21 (Div. 1).
Highest transfer fee paid: £350,000 — Len Cantello (from WBA), May 1979.
Highest transfer fee received: £340,000 — Neil Whatmore (to Birmingham), August 1981.

AFC Bournemouth

Dean Court, Bournemouth, Dorset BH7 7AF
Tel: 0202-35381 **Colours:** *Red & White*

No era has been more exciting or rewarding for Bournemouth than the early seventies. Their promotion from the Fourth Division in 1971 was followed by three more good seasons, in each of which they challenged for a Second Division place.

Centre-forward Ted MacDougall broke several Bournemouth goalscoring records, among them most goals in a season, previously held by Ron Eyre with 32 in season 1928–29. During the successful 1970–71 season MacDougall was the Football League's highest scorer with 42, and the following season scored nine goals in a match — a new FA Cup record — when Bournemouth beat Margate 11–0 in the first round, their record victory.

But eventually the club was unable to hold him any more than opposing defences could, and in September 1972 sold their shooting star to Manchester United for £220,000.

In December 1982 the club made history of the wrong sort, suffering their worst-ever defeat by 9–0 on a frozen pitch away to Third Division leaders Lincoln City.

Harry Redknapp, then coach, was Bournemouth's manager when, 13 months later, they revived memories of FA Cup glories against Tottenham and Wolves in the mid-fifties. Drawn at home to Manchester United in the 3rd Round, they beat the holders 2–0 — 27 years after a previous Cup visit by United had set the all-time crowd record at Dean Court.

The club was originally known simply as Boscombe, but when elected to the Third Division (South) in 1923, Bournemouth was incorporated in the title. In 1972 they 'went Continental' by changing their name to AFC Bournemouth.

Record attendance: 28,799 v Manchester United (FA Cup), March 1957. **Modern Capacity:** 19,000. **Nickname:** 'Cherries'.
Entered Football League: 1923 — Div. 3 (South).
Biggest win: 11–0 v Margate (FA Cup), November 1971.
Heaviest defeat: 0–9 v Lincoln City (Div. 3), December 1982.
Highest final League position: 2nd in Div. 3 South, 1947–48.
Best in FA Cup: 6th Round 1956–57.
Best in League/Milk Cup: 4th Round 1961–62, 1963–64.
Pitch measurements: 115 x 75 yd.
Highest League Scorer in Single Season: Ted MacDougall — 42 in 1970–71 (Div. 4).
Highest transfer fee paid: £70,000 — Brian Clark (from Cardiff), October 1972.
Highest transfer fee received: £220,000 — Ted MacDougall (to Manchester United), September 1972.

Bradford City

Valley Parade, Bradford BD8 7DY
Tel: 0274-306062   **Colours:** *Claret & Amber*

Bradford City have succeeded in keeping first-class Association football alive in the area since neighbours Bradford Park Avenue lost their membership of the Football League in 1970.

Yet most of City's glories belong to the past. They were in Division One between 1908 and 1922, and became the first holders of the present FA Cup in 1911 when they defeated Newcastle United 1–0 at Old Trafford, after a goalless draw at the old Crystal Palace. During seasons 1910–11 and 1911–12, Bradford City played 12 consecutive FA Cup ties without conceding a goal.

When they won the Third Division North title in season 1928–29, City scored 128 goals and obtained 63 points, by far their best statistics in League football.

Not surprisingly in an area noted for the handling game, Bradford City FC developed in 1903 from a Rugby club - Manningham. Since then a number of fine players have worn City's colours, among them Sam Barkas, Tommy Cairns, Arthur Whitehurst (who scored seven goals v Tranmere in 1929), Willie Watson and Trevor Hockey.

In the seventies, City changed status three times between Divisions 3 and 4, and in 1980 they missed promotion back to the Third on goal difference. Two years later they did move up.

In the summer of 1983, City narrowly survived the threat of bankruptcy, and it was December before they achieved their first home win of the following season. Then, having won only one of 15 games in the Third Division, player-manager Trevor Cherry, the former Leeds and England defender, and his men broke the club record with ten successive League wins in which 36 goals were scored.

FA Cup Winners: 1910–11.
Division 2 Champions: 1907–08.
Division 3 (North) Champions: 1928–29.
Record attendance: 39,146 v Burnley (FA Cup), March 1911.
Modern Capacity: 16,000. **Nickname:** 'Paraders'.
Entered Football League: 1903 — Div. 2.
Biggest win: 11–1 v Rotherham (Div. 3 North), August 1928.
Heaviest defeat: 1–9 v Colchester Utd (Div. 4), December 1961.
Best in League/Milk Cup: 5th Round 1964–65.
Pitch measurements: 112 x 71 yd.
Highest League Scorer in Single Season: David Layne — 34 in 1961–62 (Div. 4).
Highest transfer fee paid: £30,000 — David McNiven (from Leeds), February 1978; £30,000 — Billy Ingham (from Burnley), August 1980.
Highest transfer fee received: £50,000 — Steve Baines (to Walsall), June 1980.

Brentford

Griffin Park, Braemar Road, Brentford, Middlesex
Tel: 01-560-2021   **Colours:** *Red, White & Black*

Formed in 1888, when by one vote they decided against setting up as a Rugby club, Brentford turned professional in 1900, and after successes in the Southern League became founder members of the Third Division in 1920.

Among their achievements was to win all 21 home League matches in the Third Division (South) in season 1929-30 — no club has since won every home game in a season — but, curiously, they failed to win promotion that year, finishing runners-up. In 1932-33 they took the title and added the Second Division crown two seasons later.

After the Second World War, Brentford slipped from First to Fourth Division. In January 1967 they were near to going out of existence, but they resisted a take-over bid by Queens Park Rangers, and by November 1971 they had cleared a debt of £104,000.

Among their post-war managers have been the Bill Dodgins, father and son, and it was under 'young Bill' that Brentford went up to the Third Division again in 1978 after three spells in Div. 4.

They have since been a mostly mid-table club, and in February 1984 Frank McLintock, former Arsenal and Scotland defender, became the club's 15th post-war manager. His immediate task was to keep Brentford in Division Three; the next to try to achieve what had eluded so many before him and turn Griffin Park's First Division potential into modern reality.

Division 2 Champions: 1934-35.
Division 3 (South) Champions: 1932-33.
Division 4 Champions: 1962-63.
Record attendance: 39,626 v Preston NE (FA Cup), March 1938.
Modern Capacity: 38,000. **Nickname:** 'Bees'.
Entered Football League: 1920 — Div. 3.
Biggest win: 9-0 v Wrexham (Div. 3), October 1963.
Heaviest defeats: 0-7 v Swansea (Div. 3 South), November 1924; 0-7 v Walsall (Div. 3 South), January 1957.
Best in FA Cup: 6th Round 1937-38, 1945-46, 1948-49.
Best In League/Milk Cup: 4th Round 1982-83.
Pitch measurements: 114 x 75 yd.
Highest League Scorer in Single Season: Jack Holliday — 36 in 1932-33 (Div. 3 South).
Highest transfer fee paid: £65,000 — Alan Whitehead (from Bury), July 1981.
Highest transfer fee received: £60,000 — Andy McCulloch (to Sheffield Wednesday), June 1979.

Brighton & Hove Albion

Goldstone Ground, Hove, Sussex BN3 7DE
Tel: 0273-739535 **Colours:** *Blue & White*

In 1983, Brighton came within one kick of producing one of the greatest shocks in FA Cup Final history. Having achieved the incongruous double of relegation and a first appearance at Wembley — beating Newcastle, Manchester City, Liverpool, Norwich and Sheffield Wednesday on the way — they continued to do the unexpected by travelling to the Final by helicopter.

So, literally, 'Seagulls' flew over Wembley that afternoon, and when they landed they gave their aristocratic opponents, Manchester United, heavy odds-on favourites, the fright of their lives. In the last seconds of extra time, with the score 2–2, the Scot Gordon Smith had only Gary Bailey to beat, but the shot was blocked.

Through the post-war years, Brighton have had a series of 'name' managers, among them Don Welsh, Billy Lane, Archie Macaulay, Brian Clough (for eight months in season 1973–74), Peter Taylor, Alan Mullery (who lifted the club from Third Division to First between 1977 and 1979) and Mike Bailey, whose successor Jimmy Melia took the team to Wembley.

Five months later, Melia had gone, but for a lot of people the memories of Brighton's thrilling FA Cup run all the way to the 1983 Final will remain indelible. Not least the astonishing Sunday in February, when the bottom team in the First Division went North to play the Champions Liverpool, and beat them 2–1, with the winning goal by former Anfield favourite Jimmy Case.

Division 3 (South) Champions: 1957–58.
Division 4 Champions: 1964–65.
Record attendance: 36,747 v Fulham (League), December 1958.
Modern Capacity: 32,500. **Nickname:** 'Seagulls'.
Entered Football League: 1920 — Div. 3.
Biggest win: 10–1 v Wisbech (FA Cup), November 1965.
Heaviest defeat: 0–9 v Middlesbrough (League), August 1958.
Best in FA Cup: Final 1982–3.
Best in League/Milk Cup: 5th Round 1978–79.
Pitch measurements: 112 x 75 yd.
Highest League Scorer in Single Season: Peter Ward — 32 in 1976–77 (Div. 3).
Highest transfer fee paid: £400,000 — Gordon Smith (from Glasgow Rangers), June 1980; £400,000 — Michael Robinson (from Man. City), July 1980; £400,000 — Jimmy Case (from Liverpool), August 1981.
Highest transfer fee received: £900,000 — Mark Lawrenson (to Liverpool), August 1981.

Bristol City

Ashton Gate, Bristol BS3 2EJ
Tel: 0272-632812   **Colours:** *Red & White*

The return of First Division football to Ashton Gate in 1976, after an absence of 65 years, brought joy to the West Country that was, sadly, short-lived. When 1980 dawned, Bristol City were still in Division One, but by 1982 they had sunk to the Fourth Division — a 2½-year decline without parallel. Such were the financial problems that the club was wound up and re-floated as 'Bristol City (1982)'.

In October 1983 they made Terry Cooper, former Leeds and England full-back, football's first player-manager-director. At the age of 39 he was the Football League's senior player (mostly as substitute) in a side that took the club up to Division Three in 1984.

In their first season in Division One, in 1906-07, Bristol City finished runners-up to Newcastle, and two years later reached the FA Cup Final for the only time in their history. First Division status was surrendered in 1911 and they alternated between Divisions Two and Three during the next 60 years with seasons of occasional brilliance.

City's most celebrated international was centre-half Billy Wedlock, who played 26 times for England from 1907-12. Another England cap, John Atyeo, holds the club's records for most League appearances (597) and most League goals (315) between 1951 and 1966. He also scored 35 Cup goals.

Division 2 Champions: 1905-06.
Division 3 (South) Champions: 1922-23, 1926-27, 1954-55.
Record attendance: 43,335 v Preston NE (FA Cup), Feb. 1935.
Modern capacity: 31,000. **Nickname:** 'Robins'.
Entered Football League: 1901 — Div. 2.
Biggest win: 11-0 v Chichester (FA Cup), November 1960.
Heaviest defeat: 0-9 v Coventry City (League), April 1934.
Best in FA Cup: Final 1908-09.
Best in League/Milk Cup: Semi-final 1970-71.
Pitch measurements: 115 x 78 yd.
Highest League Scorer in Single Season: Don Clark — 36 in 1946-47 (Div. 3 South).
Highest transfer fee paid: £250,000 — Tony Fitzpatrick (from St Mirren), July 1979.
Highest transfer fee received: £350,000 — Garry Collier (to Coventry), May 1979.

Bristol Rovers

Ground: Eastville. Offices: Filton Road, Hambrook, Bristol BS16 1JG
Tel: 0272-573687 **Colours:** *Blue & White*

Although twice in the 1950s Bristol Rovers finished sixth in Division Two, most of their existence has been spent in Third Division company, but season 1973–74 raised hopes of a shining new era at Eastville. From kick-off day in August, Rovers were unbeaten in 27 League games until 1 February, a sequence stretched to 32 by five matches without defeat at the end of the previous season.

On the strength of such a run, which was highlighted by the free scoring of Alan Warboys and Bruce Bannister, Rovers set up a long lead in the Third Division. The 8–2 win at Brighton on 1 December was the biggest victory in their history, and with City doing great deeds in the FA Cup, Bristol became a region of intense football interest in 1973–74. It ended with Rovers promoted on goal average as runners-up to Oldham.

On a Sunday afternoon in August 1980, fire destroyed Rovers' main stand, and for five home matches they shared City's ground at Ashton Gate. The season ended with both clubs relegated to Division Three, both heavily in debt and Bristol's football fortunes at a desperate level.

Moves to make the ground-sharing arrangement permanent fell down. Eastville remains Rovers home, but only for playing purposes; the administration is handled from mobile huts at the Hambrook training ground.

Debts of £500,000 at the time of the fire were inherited by a new board and virtually wiped out by the end of 1983–84, under Rovers' first player-manager David Williams, at 29 the youngest team boss in the Football League.

Division 3 (South) Champions: 1952–53.
Record attendance: 38,472 v Preston NE (FA Cup), January 1960.
Modern Capacity: 15,000. **Nickname:** 'Pirates'.
Entered Football League: 1920 — Div. 3.
Biggest win: 8–2 v Brighton (Div. 3), December 1973.
Heaviest defeat: 0–12 v Luton Town (Div. 3 South), April 1936.
Best in FA Cup: 6th Round 1950–51, 1957–58.
Best in League/Milk Cup: 5th Round 1970–71, 1971–72.
Pitch measurements: 110 x 70 yd.
Highest League Scorer in Single Season: Geoff Bradford — 33 in 1952–53 (Div. 3 South).
Highest transfer fee paid: £100,000 — Stewart Barrowclough (from Birmingham), July 1979.
Highest transfer fee received: £175,000 — Steve White (to Luton), December 1979.

Burnley

Turf Moor, Burnley, Lancs. BB10 4BX
Tel: 0282-27777 & 38021   **Colours:** *Claret, Blue & White*

The winning of the League Championship by a small-town team, as Burnley did for the second time in 1960, stands as a remarkable achievement in a competition almost totally dominated in its history by big-city clubs. Chairman Bob Lord presided over Burnley's post-war eminence, and his memory is perpetuated in the naming of the Turf Moor stand after him.

In the years when the transfer market thrived, Burnley used it shrewdly, not only to survive in the shadow of the Manchester glamour clubs, but to challenge them, too. The policy was to find youthful talent, groom it and eventually sell it to keep the club solvent.

Such outstanding discoveries included Leighton James (sold to Derby), Martin Dobson (Everton), Willie Morgan (Man. United), Ralph Coates (Tottenham), Steve Kindon (Wolves), Dave Thomas (QPR), Geoff Nulty (Newcastle), Brian Flynn (Leeds), Terry Cochrane (Middlesbrough) and Tony Morley (Aston Villa).

Burnley were one of the League's 12 founder members in 1888. On the way to their first Championship success in 1920–21, they played 30 consecutive First Division matches without defeat (21 wins, 9 draws, goals 68–17) between 6 September and 25 March. That stood as a Football League record until 1969–70, when Leeds went 34 matches before losing.

League Champions: 1920–21, 1959–60.
Division 2 Champions: 1897–98, 1972–73.
Division 3 Champions: 1981–82.
FA Cup Winners: 1913–14.
Record attendance: 54,775 v Huddersfield Town (FA Cup), February 1924. **Modern Capacity:** 21,000. **Nickname:** 'Clarets'.
Entered Football League: 1888 — Div. 1.
Biggest League wins: 9–0 v Darwen (Div. 1), January 1892; 9–0 v Crystal Palace (FA Cup), 1908–09; 9–0 v New Brighton (FA Cup), January 1957.
Heaviest League defeats: 0–10 v Aston Villa (Div. 1), August 1925; 0–10 v Sheffield Utd (Div. 1), January 1929.
Best in League/Milk Cup: Semi-final 1960–61, 1968–69.
Pitch measurements: 115½ x 73 yd.
Highest League Scorer in Single Season: George Beel — 35 in 1927–28 (Div. 1).
Highest transfer fee paid: £165,000 — Leighton James (from QPR), September 1978.
Highest transfer fee received: £325,000 — Trevor Steven (to Everton),June 1983.

Bury

Gigg Lane, Bury BL9 9HR
Tel: 061-764 4881/2 **Colours:** *White & Royal Blue*

'The Shakers' have certainly shocked the football world in their time, starting from season 1894–95, when they won the Second Division Championship in their first year as League members. Five years later they defeated Southampton 4–0 in the FA Cup Final at the old Crystal Palace, and in 1903 they caused an even bigger stir by winning the trophy again without conceding a goal in any of their ties. They trounced Derby County on the same ground by six goals to nil — which remains the biggest winning margin in the Final.

Bury stayed in Division 1 for seventeen seasons; they dropped to the Second Division in 1912 and regained higher status in 1924, but this time they survived for only five seasons. Since then they have achieved occasional periods of glory such as winning the Division Three title in 1960–61 by a margin of six points. They reached the semi-final of the Football League Cup in season 1962–63, losing 4–3 on aggregate to Birmingham City, the eventual winners of the trophy. Bury showed their tenacity as Cup fighters in 1955 when they played Stoke City for a record 9 hours 22 minutes, in five meetings in the FA Cup third round before Stoke won 3–2 at Old Trafford.

Since their formation in 1885, Bury have known no other home but Gigg Lane. They are one of the few clubs whose individual scoring record was achieved in modern times — 35 Fourth Division goals by Craig Madden in 1981–82, beating the 31 by Norman Bullock (Div. 1) in 1925–26.

FA Cup Winners: 1899–1900, 1902–03.
Division 2 Champions: 1894–95.
Division 3 Champions: 1960–61.
Record attendance: 35,000 v Bolton Wanderers (FA Cup), January 1960.
Modern Capacity: 35,000. **Nickname:** 'Shakers'.
Entered Football League: 1894 — Div. 2.
Biggest win: 12–1 v Stockton (FA Cup), 1896–97.
Heaviest defeats: 0–10 v Blackburn Rovers (FA Cup), 1887–88; 0–10 v West Ham (Milk Cup) 1983–84.
Best in League/Milk Cup: Semi-final 1962–63.
Pitch measurements: 116 x 80 yd.
Highest League Scorer in Single Season: Craig Madden — 35 in 1981–82 (Div. 4).
Highest transfer fee paid: £35,000 — David Gregory (from Stoke), September 1978.
Highest transfer fee received: £150,000 — Neville Southall (to Everton), July 1981.

Cambridge United

Abbey Stadium, Newmarket Road, Cambridge CB5 8LL
Tel: 0223-241237   **Colours:** *Amber & Black*

Cambridge United won the Southern League Championship in successive years, 1968–69 and 1969–70, and so impressed Football League clubs that at the annual meeting, in June 1970, they were elected to the Fourth Division in place of Bradford Park Avenue.

The first season in the League was very much one of trial and error. United finished 20th, only one place clear of the re-election zone, but in 1972 they improved to tenth and a year later third place in the final table took them up to Division Three. They dropped again to the Fourth in 1974, but the set-back was temporary.

A new manager, Ron Atkinson, really put the club on the map, taking them from Fourth to Second Division in successive seasons (1976–77, 1977–78). From non-League football to Division Two in eight years was a remarkable achievement.

His successor, John Docherty, achieved wonders in keeping the club in the middle of that division for five seasons, but in 1983–84, with gates down to 2,000, United struck their worst spell as a League club.

The season ended in relegation, and with an unwanted place in the records. For starting in October, Cambridge went 31 matches in Division 2 without a win (21 defeats, 10 draws) — the longest sequence without victory by any club in Football League history.

Division 4 Champions: 1976–77.
Record attendance: 14,000 v Chelsea (Friendly), May 1970.
Modern capacity: 12,000.
Entered Football League: 1970 — Div. 4.
Biggest League win: 6–0 v Darlington (Div. 4), September 1971.
Heaviest defeats: 0–6 v Aldershot (Div. 3), April 1974; 0–6 v Darlington (Div. 4), September 1974; 0–6 Chelsea (Div. 2), January 1983.
Best in FA Cup: 5th Round 1982–83.
Best in League/Milk Cup: 4th Round 1980–81.
Pitch measurements: 112 x 75 yd.
Highest League Scorer in Single Season: Alan Biley — 21 in 1977–78 (Div. 3)
Highest transfer fee paid: £180,000 — George Reilly (from Northampton), November 1979.
Highest transfer fee received: £350,000 — Alan Biley (to Derby), January 1980.

Cardiff City

Ninian Park, Cardiff CF1 8SX
Tel: 0222-398636 **Colours:** *Blue & White*

The most memorable event in Cardiff City's history occurred in 1927, when they became the first non-English club to win the FA Cup. They beat Arsenal 1-0 at Wembley and the drama was heightened by the fact that the Arsenal goalkeeper, Dan Lewis, whose error allowed Cardiff to triumph, was himself a Welshman.

Three years earlier another mistake — this time by a City player — cost Cardiff the First Division Championship. They needed two points from their final match against Birmingham, but missed a penalty late in the game and could only draw.

In the Cardiff goal, during their First Division days of the 1920s, was Tom Farquharson, still in the records as their longest-serving player. He made 445 League appearances between 1922 and 1935.

Cardiff's star waned, however, and the club slipped into the Second Division in 1929 and the Third (South) two seasons later, but re-emerged as Southern Section Champions in 1947. Since the last war they have had two spells totalling seven years in the First Division, from 1952-57 and 1960-62, but at the end of 1974-75, after narrowly escaping relegation for three seasons, they dropped into Division Three. They won promotion first time, as they did when relegated again in 1982.

As frequent Welsh Cup winners, Cardiff have made eleven appearances in the European Cup-Winners' Cup and in 1967-68 they reached the semi-finals.

FA Cup Winners: 1926-27.
Division 3 (South) Champions: 1946-47.
Record attendance: 61,566 Wales v England (International), October 1961.
Modern Capacity: 43,000. **Nickname:** 'Bluebirds'.
Entered Football League: 1920 — Div. 2.
Biggest win: 9-2 v Thames (Div. 3 South), February 1932.
Heaviest defeat: 2-11 v Sheffield United (Div. 1), January 1926.
Best in League/Milk Cup: Semi-final 1965-66.
Pitch measurements: 112 x 76 yd.
Highest League Scorer in Single Season: Stan Richards — 31 in 1946-47 (Div. 3. South).
Highest transfer fee paid: £180,000 — Godfrey Ingram (from San José Earthquakes, USA), September 1982.
Highest transfer fee received: £110,000 — John Toshack (to Liverpool), November 1970.

Carlisle United

Brunton Park, Carlisle CA1 1LL
Tel: 0228-26237 **Colours:** *Blue*

Carlisle United's progress was unspectacular following their formation in 1903. In 1928 they were elected to Division Three (North) in place of Durham City and finished eighth in their first campaign. But they had to seek re-election in 1934–35.

They were third in 1951, but when Division Four was formed from the bottom 12 clubs of each section of the Third in 1958, Carlisle were among them. They gained promotion in 1962, dropped straight back the following season, but immediately went up again, with Hugh McIlmoyle scoring 39 out of a grand total of 113 League goals.

Carlisle, situated so close to the Border that at one time there was speculation about their joining the Scottish League, swept on into Division Two in 1965, just twelve months after leaving the Fourth Division. In 1974 they at last brought top-division football to their north-west outpost by finishing third in Division Two — a wonderful achievement for a club of their size.

Life in the First Division began astonishingly, with 1–0 wins in the first three games, at Chelsea, at Middlesbrough and at home to Tottenham. But they could not play above themselves indefinitely, and for Carlisle it proved a one-season stay in top company.

Two years later they were back in Division Three, but by season 1983–84 manager Bob Stokoe had turned them into surprise contenders for a return to Division One.

Division 3 Champions: 1964–65.
Record attendance: 27,500 v Birmingham City (FA Cup), January 1957; 27,500 v Middlesbrough (FA Cup), February 1970.
Modern capacity: 25,000. **Nickname:** 'Cumbrians'.
Entered Football League: 1928 — Div. 3 (North).
Biggest wins: 8–0 v Hartlepool (Div. 3 North), September 1928; 8–0 v Scunthorpe United (Div. 3 North), December 1952.
Heaviest defeat: 1–11 v Hull City (Div. 3 North), January 1939.
Best in FA Cup: 6th Round 1974–75.
Best in League/Milk Cup: Semi-final 1969–70.
Pitch measurements: 117 x 78 yd.
Highest League Scorer in Single Season: Jimmy McConnell — 42 in 1928–29 (Div. 3 North).
Highest transfer fee paid: £120,000 — Gordon Staniforth (from York), October 1979.
Highest transfer fee received: £250,000 — Peter Beardsley (to Vancouver Whitecaps), March 1982.

Charlton Athletic

The Valley, Floyd Road, Charlton, London SE7 8AW
Tel: 01-853-0444 **Colours:** *Red & White*

After nearly two years of escalating financial problems, Charlton
Athletic were dramatically saved from closure in the High Court in
London on 8 March, 1984. Debts of £1.6m had put the club in the
hands of the receiver, and after repeated court adjournments of a
winding-up petition, only half an hour of the deadline set by the
Football League remained when Mr Justice Mervyn Davies approved
a rescue deal presented by the Sunley property group.

Charlton was a name to conjure with between 1935 and 1947
when the club distinguished themselves in League and Cup. They
came within touching distance of a memorable League hat-trick
after winning the Division Three (South) Championship in 1935.
The following season they gained promotion to Division One, and
twelve months later they were runners-up for the Championship.

Beaten in extra time in the FA Cup Final of 1946 by Derby,
Charlton returned to Wembley the following season and beat
Burnley 1-0 after extra time. But after the glories of the forties came
the slump with Charlton falling into Division Two in 1957 and then,
in 1972, to Division Three, which they had left in 1935. They
returned to the Second Division in 1975, and again in 1981, but
those up-and-down experiences did not compare with the traumas
of 1983-84.

In December 1957 Charlton staged one of the most amazing
recoveries in football history. With 20 minutes left in a Second
Division match at home to Huddersfield, they were losing 5-1 and
reduced by injury to ten men — yet finished winners by 7-6, with
Johnny Summers scoring five of the goals.

FA Cup Winners: 1946-47.
Division 3 (South) Champions: 1928-29, 1934-35.
Record attendance: 75,031 v Aston Villa (FA Cup), February 1938.
Modern capacity: 25,000. **Nickname:** 'Robins'.
Entered Football League: 1921 — Div. 3 (South).
Biggest win: 8-1 v Middlesbrough (Div. 1), September 1953.
Heaviest defeat: 1-11 v Aston Villa (Div. 2), November 1959.
Best in League/Milk Cup: 4th Round 1962-63, 1964-65, 1978-79.
Pitch measurements: 114 x 73 yd.
Highest League Scorer in Single Season: Ralph Allen — 32 in
1934-35 (Div. 3 South).
Highest transfer fee paid: £325,000 — Allan Simonsen (from
Barcelona), November 1972.
Highest transfer fee received: £650,000 — Mike Flanagan (to
Crystal Palace), August 1979.

Chelsea

Stamford Bridge Grounds, Fulham Park, London SW6 1HS
Tel: 01-385 5545/6   **Colours:** *Royal Blue & White*

For the first fifty years of their existence Chelsea did not win a single prize. Then they celebrated their golden jubilee by taking the League Championship of 1954–55 under the managership of Ted Drake. Under his successor, Tommy Docherty, they won the League Cup in 1964–65 and, guided by Dave Sexton, they collected two more trophies in successive seasons.

In 1970 Chelsea at last lifted the FA Cup, dramatically beating Leeds 2–1 in extra time at Old Trafford in the first replayed Final since 1912. That victory qualified them for the Cup-Winners' Cup, and led them a year later to their first European prize, Real Madrid being beaten in the replayed Final in Athens. In 1972 they reached their third successive Final — this time in the League Cup — but Stoke beat them 2–1.

At that point the club embarked on spectacular plans to create a stadium worthy of the team, but things went drastically wrong. The Chelsea side disintegrated, the new stand created debts of more than £3m., managers came and went and, with stability desperately needed on and off the field, the worst blow of all came in 1979 with relegation for the third time in 17 years.

By 1982 Chelsea were drifting towards oblivion, but new, all-action chairman Ken Bates breathed fresh life into the camp. While the club battled in court for a future at Stamford Bridge, John Neal's team — driven on by player-coach John Hollins on his return from Arsenal — took Chelsea back to the First Division in 1984.

League Champions: 1954–55.
Division 2 Champions: 1983–84.
FA Cup Winners: 1969–70.
League Cup Winners: 1964–65.
Winner of European Cup-Winners' Cup: 1970–71.
Record attendance: 82,905 v Arsenal (League), October 1935.
Modern Capacity: 36,000. **Nickname:** 'Blues'.
Entered Football League: 1905 — Div. 2.
Biggest win: 13–0 v Jeunesse Hautcharage, Luxembourg (European Cup-Winners' Cup), September 1971.
Heaviest defeat: 1–8 Wolves (Div. 1), September 1953.
Pitch measurements: 114 x 71½ yd.
Highest League Scorer in Single Season: Jimmy Greaves — 41 in 1960–61 (Div. 1).
Highest transfer fee paid: £225,000 — David Hay (from Celtic), July 1974.
Highest transfer fee received: £750,000 — Ray Wilkins (to Manchester United), August 1979.

Chester City

Sealand Road, Chester CH1 4LW
Tel: 0244-371376 **Colours:** *Blue & White*

The club was formed in 1884 — four years before the Football League began — but did not gain election to the old Third Division North until 1931, when they replaced Nelson.

A number of international players, among them Tommy Lawton and Don Welsh, assisted the club while on military service during the Second World War. On the resumption of peace-time League football in 1946–47, Chester creditably filled third place but a succession of managers, including Frank Brown, Louis Page and John Harris, were unable to bring the Cheshire club much success.

It came, however, in season 1974–75, in their finest-ever effort in knock-out football. Chester dismissed First Division giants Leeds 3–0 and Newcastle 1–0 (after drawing 0–0 away) to reach the League Cup semi-final. Aston Villa then stopped them 5–4 on aggregate, but consolation was only weeks away — a place in Division Three, the first time promotion had been won in Chester's history, albeit by four-hundredths of a goal.

For a time at the beginning of 1980 Chester challenged for a place in the Second Division and although eventually disappointed in that direction, they received handsome compensation in the transfer market. They sold 18-year-old Welsh Youth international striker Ian Rush, at the end of his first season in senior football, to Liverpool for £300,000, easily a record for Chester.

How Sealand Road's dwindling support must have yearned for a player of Rush's ability in 1983–84, when the club finished last in the Canon League — an inauspicious end to the season in which 'City' was appended to the club's title.

Record attendance: 20,500 v Chelsea (FA Cup), January 1952.
Modern Capacity: 20,000. **Nickname:** 'Seals'.
Entered Football League: 1931 - Div. 3 (North).
Biggest win: 12–0 v York City (Div. 3 North), February 1936.
Heaviest defeat: 2–11 v Oldham Athletic (Div. 3 North), January 1952.
Highest final League position: 2nd in Div. 3 (North), 1935–36.
Best in FA Cup: 5th Round 1976–77, 1979–80.
Best in League/Milk Cup: Semi-final 1974–75.
Pitch measurements: 114 x 75 yd.
Highest League Scorer in Single Season: Dick Yates — 36 in 1946–47 (Div. 3 North).
Highest transfer fee paid: £45,000 — Trevor Phillips (from Hull, March 1980; £45,000 — Steve Ludlam (from Carlisle), June 1980.
Highest transfer fee received: £300,000 — Ian Rush (to Liverpool), May 1980.

Chesterfield

Recreation Ground, Saltergate, Chesterfield S40 4SX
Tel: 0246-32318 **Colours:** *Blue & White*

Membership of Chesterfield FC in their formation year of 1866 cost a couple of shillings or ten new pence. Exactly 100 years later the club's most distinguished product, Gordon Banks, kept goal for England in their World Cup Final victory over West Germany at Wembley. Banks, later of Leicester City and Stoke City, always acknowledged the value of his early days with Chesterfield. He was one of two outstanding goalkeepers developed post-war by the club. The other was Ray Middleton, who became a Justice of the Peace following his work for local youth organizations. Other well-known players in the town of the Crooked Spire have included members of the Milburn family, 'Legs' Linacre, Tommy Capel and Gordon Dale.

Chesterfield played in Division Two between 1899 and 1909 but then dropped out of the League until 1921, when they re-entered as members of Division Three (North), a section which they won in 1931 and 1936.

They have spent two separate periods in Division Two since those early days, and in 1947 finished fourth — the highest final placing they have attained in the Football League. Fourth Division Champions in 1970, they have finished fifth twice since and fourth in 1980 in a bid to win back the Second Division place they last held in 1951.

Centre-half Dave Blakey set the club's League appearance record (613) between 1948–67, and a rare trophy came Chesterfield's way in 1980–81, when they won the Anglo-Scottish Cup. They beat Rangers in the second round and Notts County in the final.

Division 3 (North) Champions: 1930–31, 1935–36.
Division 4 Champions: 1969–70.
Record attendance: 30,968 v Newcastle (League), April 1939.
Modern Capacity: 20,000. **Nickname:** 'Blues'.
Entered Football League: 1899 — Div. 2.
Biggest win: 10–0 v Glossop NE (Div. 2), January 1903.
Heaviest defeat: 1–9 v Port Vale (Div. 2), September 1932.
Best in FA Cup: 5th Round 1932–33, 1937–38, 1949–50.
Best in League/Milk Cup: 4th Round 1964–65.
Pitch measurements: 114 x 73 yd.
Highest League Scorer in Single Season: Jimmy Cookson — 44 in 1925–26 (Div. 3 North).
Highest transfer fee paid: £150,000 — Phil Bonnyman (from Carlisle), March 1980.
Highest transfer fee received: £150,000 — Alan Birch (to Wolves), August 1981.

Colchester United

Layer Road, Colchester CO2 7JJ
Tel: 0206-574042   **Colours:** *Royal Blue & White*

Colchester United first made an impact on soccer in 1948, when they achieved a series of astonishing FA Cup giant-killing acts. While still members of the Southern League, they knocked out Huddersfield Town and Bradford (who had previously defeated Arsenal) before finally falling at Blackpool in the fifth round. Their manager then was Ted Fenton, who later guided West Ham back to the First Division.

Not surprisingly after such impressive evidence of their talents, Colchester were elected to the Football League in 1950. And 21 years later, in the fifth round of season 1970–71, they celebrated their 'coming of age' with another incredible Cup triumph. This time they defeated Leeds United 3–2 at Layer Road, and by now even Wembley seemed a possibility for manager Dick Graham's team of Fourth Division enthusiasts, but in the quarter-finals Colchester were drawn away to Everton and beaten 5–0.

Three times in the sixties Colchester lost their place in Division Three, but they returned again at the end of season 1973–74 on the strength of magnificent home form and the scoring power of 24-goal Bobby Svarc. At the start of the eighties United were bidding strongly to win a Second Division place for the first time, but finished fifth. A year later (1981) they dropped back into Division Four.

In February 1984, Micky Cook played his 600th League game (a record) for the club he joined 15 years earlier.

Record attendance: 19,072 v Reading (FA Cup), November 1948.
Modern Capacity: 16,000. **Nickname:** 'U's.'
Entered Football League: 1950 — Div. 3 (South).
Biggest win: 9–1 v Bradford City (Div. 4), December 1961.
Heaviest defeats: 0–7 v Leyton Orient (Div. 3 South), January 1952; 0–7 v Reading (Div. 3 South), September 1957.
Highest final League position: 2nd in Div. 4, 1961–62.
Best in FA Cup: 6th Round 1970–71.
Best in League/Milk Cup: 5th Round 1974–75.
Pitch measurements: 110 x 74 yd.
Highest League Scorer in Single Season: Bobby Hunt — 37 in 1961–62 Div. 4).
Highest transfer fee paid: £25,000 — Roger Osborne (from Ipswich), February 1981.
Highest transfer fee received: £90,000 — Trevor Lee (to Gillingham), January 1981.

Coventry City

Highfield Road, Coventry CV2 4FW
Tel: 0203-57171 **Colours:** *Sky Blue*

The rise of Coventry City from the obscurity of the Fourth Division in 1959, to the glamour of the First Division eight years later, is one of the success stories of post-war soccer.

From the old Southern League, they gained admission to the Football League in 1919 and just avoided relegation from the Second Division in their first season. They dropped down to the Third Division in 1925 and took eleven seasons to get back into the Second, finishing 1935–36 as Third Division South Champions.

Coventry slipped again in 1952 and became founder members of the Fourth Division in 1958. After only one season in the Fourth, however, the new-look City gained promotion and began the thrilling climb that took them into the First Division in 1967. Thus they became the only club to have played in six divisions of the Football League (3N, 3S, 4, 3, 2, 1).

That ebullient manager, Jimmy Hill, led the Sky Blue revolution of the sixties and having reached the First Division for the first time, City had to survive a two-season threat of relegation before they could breathe more comfortably in the top section. Then, caught up in the car industry's depression in the mid-seventies, Coventry found the need to sell players at big fees and buy modestly.

In season 1980–81 Highfield Road became England's first all-seater football stadium (capacity 20,500), but admission prices were too steep for gates to remain healthy.

Division 2 Champions: 1966–67.
Division 3 (South) Champions: 1935–36.
Division 3 Champions: 1963–64.
Record attendance: 51,455 v Wolves (League), April 1967.
Modern Capacity: 20,500. **Nickname:** 'Sky Blues'.
Entered Football League: 1919 — Div. 2.
Biggest win: 9–0 v Bristol City (Div. 3 South), April 1934.
Heaviest defeat: 2–10 v Norwich City (Div. 3 South), Mar. 1930.
Best in FA Cup: 6th Round 1962–63, 1972–73, 1981–82, (also reached the last eight in old 4th Round 1909–10).
Best in League Cup/Milk Cup: Semi-final 1980–81.
Pitch measurements: 110 x 72 yd.
Highest League Scorer in Single Season: Clarrie Bourton — 49 in 1931–32 (Div. 3 South).
Highest transfer fee paid: £350,000 — Garry Collier (from Bristol City). May 1979.
Highest transfer fee received: £1,250,000 — Ian Wallace (to Nottingham Forest), July 1980.

Crewe Alexandra

Gresty Road, Crewe CW2 6EB
Tel: 0270-213014 **Colours:** *Red & White*

For more than a century, Crewe has been better known as the town with Britain's biggest railway junction than for the achievements of its soccer team. The club owed its origin to the game of cricket — in 1876 the local side formed a football section, and the unique title 'Crewe Alexandra' derived from the name of the town and that of a pub used by locomotive workers there.

Few realise that the 1887 FA Cup semi-final (Aston Villa 3, Glasgow Rangers 1) was played on Crewe's ground, and a year later Alexandra's own team of amateurs reached the semi-final.

They turned professional in 1893, the year after becoming a founder member of Division Two of the Football League. Unhappily, they were not re-elected in 1896 and remained in comparative obscurity until re-entering the League.

Since then the story of Crewe has been one of mostly hard struggle. Promotion from Division Four in 1962–63, when they were third, and again in 1967–68 (fourth) provided brief periods of reward, and another was the club's remarkable 2-1 FA Cup third round win at Chelsea in January 1961.

The most melancholy period in Crewe's long history occurred during 1956–57, when, from September until April, they played 30 consecutive League matches without a win.

One of the finest players produced by Crewe was Frank Blunstone, who moved to Chelsea as a boy winger in February 1953 and went on to gain five caps for England.

Record attendance: 20,000 v Tottenham (FA Cup), January 1960.
Modern Capacity: 17,000. **Nickname:** 'Railwaymen'.
Entered Football League: 1892 — Div. 2.
Biggest win: 8–0 v Rotherham United (Div. 3 North), October 1932.
Heaviest defeat: 2–13 v Tottenham (FA Cup), February 1960.
Highest final League position: 3rd in Div. 4, 1962–63.
Best in FA Cup: Semi-final 1887–88.
Best in League/Milk Cup: 3rd Round 1960–61, 1974–75, 1975–76, 1978–79.
Pitch measurements: 112 x 75 yd.
Highest League Scorer in Single Season: Terry Harkin — 34 in 1964–65 (Div. 4).
Highest transfer fees paid: £10,000 — Colin Chesters (from Derby), September 1979; £10,000 — Micky Guy (from Sheffield United), September 1979.
Highest transfer fee received: £40,000 — Paul Bowles (to Port Vale), October 1979.

Crystal Palace

Selhurst Park, London SE25 6PU
Tel: 01-653-4462 **Colours:** *Royal Blue & Red*

The progress of Crystal Palace to First Division status became more than a dream from April 1966, when they appointed Bert Head manager. He joined them from Bury, but first made his mark in football management at Swindon, where he built a star-studded team from nothing. By 1969 Palace completed the astonishing climb from Fourth Division to First in only eight years.

Selhurst Park was redeveloped to match proudly-won status, but despite enormous spending in the transfer market Palace were always struggling to stay in top company. In March 1973 the flamboyant Malcolm Allison took over, but he could not save the club from relegation that season or the next.

In 1975-76 Palace approached Christmas seven points clear in the Third Division and, with remarkable wins away to Leeds, Chelsea and Sunderland, they reached the FA Cup semi-final for the first time. But their decline was even more spectacular, and after losing the semi-final to Southampton they faded to fifth in the final table.

The appointment of Terry Venables to succeed Allison revitalized the club. In 1977 they earned promotion from Division Three and two years later they won the Second Division championship. With Palace fielding one of the youngest and most talented sides in the country, the potential seemed unlimited, but relegation soon followed Venables' departure and 'team of the eighties' talk was quickly forgotten.

Division 2 Champions: 1978-79.
Division 3 Champions: 1920-21.
Record attendance: 51,801 v Burnley (League), May 1979.
Modern Capacity: 38,000. **Nickname:** 'Eagles'.
Entered Football League: 1920 — Div. 3.
Biggest win: 9-0 v Barrow (Div. 4), October 1959.
Heaviest defeat: 4-11 v Manchester City (FA Cup), February 1926.
Best in FA Cup: Semi-final 1975-76.
Best in League/Milk Cup: 5th Round 1968-69, 1970-71.
Pitch measurements: 110 x 75 yd.
Highest League Scorer in Single Season: Peter Simpson — 46 in 1930-31 (Div. 3 South).
Highest transfer fee paid: £1,250,000 — Clive Allen (from Arsenal) August 1980.
Highest transfer fee received: £1,350,000 — Kenny Sansom (to Arsenal), August 1980.

Darlington

Feethams Ground, Darlington, Co. Durham DL1 5JB
Tel: 0325-465097 **Colours:** *White & Black*

Eighty pounds would not buy a set of team kit today. Yet in season 1924–25 Darlington won the Third Division North title with a team assembled for just that modest sum. They finished five points ahead of the next two clubs, Nelson and New Brighton.

Darlington are one of the comparatively few League clubs to have used only one ground — Feethams — since their formation in 1883. They rent it from the cricket club 'next door'. In their early years they played in the Northern League and became professional in 1908, when they joined the North-Eastern League. The club became one of the original members of the old Division Three North in 1921.

They remained there until Division Four was created in 1958, and in season 1965–66 they delighted their supporters by finishing runners-up with the same number of points (59) as the champions, Doncaster Rovers. A year later, however, they were relegated, and they have been in Division Four ever since, and five times during this period they have had to seek re-election.

Darlington's best-known players have included centre-forward David Brown (74 League goals in 97 matches from 1923–26) and Ken Furphy, who went on to manage Workington, Watford, Blackburn and Sheffield United.

The club's transfer record was almost trebled in May 1982, when they sold striker David Speedie to Chelsea for £70,000. He was spotted by the London club's manager, John Neal, when he scored three goals in a friendly match Southampton played at Feethams to raise desperately-needed funds for Darlington.

Division 3 (North) Champions: 1924–25.
Record attendance: 21,023 v Bolton Wanderers (League Cup), November 1960.
Modern Capacity: 15,000. **Nickname:** 'Quakers'.
Entered Football League: 1921 — Div. 3 (North).
Biggest win: 13–1 v Scarborough (FA Cup), 1886.
Heaviest defeat: 0–10 v Doncaster (Div. 4), January 1964.
Best in FA Cup: 5th Round 1957–58.
Best in League/Milk Cup: 5th Round 1967–68.
Pitch measurements: 110 x 74 yd.
Highest League Scorer in Single Season: David Brown — 39 in 1924–25 (Div. 3 North).
Highest transfer fee paid: £20,000 — Eric Probert (from Notts County), October 1978.
Highest transfer fee received: £70,000 — David Speedie (to Chelsea), May 1982.

Derby County

The Baseball Ground, Derby DE3 8NB
Tel: 0332-40105   **Colours:** *White & Dark Blue*

In recent years, several Football League clubs have been in danger of closure, and for none has the threat been more serious than to Derby County. History shows them as founder members of the League in 1888, FA Cup winners in 1946 and twice Champions.

But such a background counted for little when, in 1984, Derby found themselves in a worse position off the field than on it, where they were fighting to stay in the Second Division. With debts of £1.4m., they faced a winding-up petition.

With one survival package rejected, chief executive Stuart Webb and the directors were given seven days to produce another. In a desperate race against time, Derby's day of salvation proved to be Monday, 2 April, 1984.

County had thrived on the arrival of Brian Clough in May 1967. Under his inspiring managership (and, on the field, rallied by the captaincy and playing skill of Dave Mackay) Derby roared back to the First Division two years later.

In season 1971–72 they became League Champions for the first time, but in October 1973 Clough sensationally quit the club, and the task of restoring calm after a major upheaval fell upon Mackay, who left Nottingham Forest to return to Derby. He did it with maximum effect, for by the end of the following season (1974–75) County were Champions again. But a long period of instability followed, and it so nearly ended in extinction in 1984. The next worst thing did happen, though, with Derby relegated to Division Three.

League Champions: 1971–72, 1974–75.
Division 2 Champions: 1911–12, 1914–15, 1968–69.
Division 3 (North) Champions: 1956–57.
FA Cup Winners: 1945–46.
Record attendance: 41,826 v Tottenham (League), September 1969. **Modern Capacity:** 30,500. **Nickname:** 'Rams'.
Entered Football League: 1888 — Div. 1.
Biggest win: 12–0 v Finn Harps (UEFA Cup), September 1976.
Heaviest defeat: 2–11 v Everton (FA Cup), 1889–90.
Best in League/Milk Cup: Semi-final 1967–68.
Pitch measurements: 110 x 71 yd.
Highest League Scorers in Single Season: Jack Bowers — 37 in 1930–31 (Div. 1); Ray Straw — 37 in 1956–57 (Div. 3 North).
Highest transfer fee paid: £400,000 — David Swindlehurst (from Crystal Palace), April 1980.
Highest transfer fee received: £400,000 — Charlie George (to Southampton), December 1978.

Doncaster Rovers

Belle Vue Ground, Doncaster DN4 5HT
Tel: 0302-535281 **Colours:** *Red & White*

Doncaster Rovers' past is crowded with players of distinction: the Keetley brothers, Frank, Harold, Joe and Tom (who still holds the club record for the most League goals — 178); Fred Emery, later manager; Sam Cowan who won England caps with Manchester City; Jack Lambert, Arsenal's centre-forward in the 1930 and 1932 FA Cup Finals; Peter Doherty, rated by many as the most skilful inside-forward of his era: Clarrie Jordan (42 League goals in 1946–47); Manchester United and Northern Ireland goalkeeper Harry Gregg; and England Under-23 forward Alick Jeffrey, who, with 36 goals, was the League's top scorer in 1964–65.

The Belle Vue ground is opposite Doncaster racecourse and no more notable performances have been achieved on it than in 1946–47. That season Rovers took the old Third Division North title with 33 wins — a Football League record — and the astonishing total of 72 points from 42 League matches, including 37 from away games. That points tally remained a League record for 29 years — until beaten by Lincoln City in 1975–76.

Under Billy Bremner, former Leeds and Scotland star, they went up in 1981, back to the Fourth Division two years later and were promoted again in season 1983–84. The 16 post-war managers of Doncaster include Lawrie McMenemy, who was with the club from 1968–71, taking them to the Fourth Division championship in 1969.

Division 3 (North) Champions: 1934–35, 1946–47, 1949–50.
Division 4 Champions: 1965–66, 1968–69.
Record attendance: 37,149 v Hull (League), October 1948.
Modern Capacity: 21,150.
Entered Football League: 1901 — Div. 2.
Biggest win: 10–0 v Darlington (Div. 4), January 1964.
Heaviest defeat: 0–12 v Small Heath (Div. 2), April 1903.
Best in FA Cup: 5th Round 1951–52, 1953–54, 1954–55, 1955–56.
Best in League/Milk Cup: 5th Round 1975–76.
Pitch measurements: 112 x 77 yd.
Highest League Scorer in Single Season: Clarrie Jordan — 42 in 1946–47 (Div. 3 North).
Highest transfer fee paid: £70,000 — John Philliben (from Stirling Albion), March 1984.
Highest transfer fee received: £70,000 — Mike Elwiss (to Preston), February 1974; £70,000 — Dennis Peacock (to Bolton), March 1980.

Everton

Goodison Park, Liverpool L4 4 EL
Tel: 051-521 2020 **Colours:** *Blue & White*

Twice during Harry Catterick's managership, in 1963 and 1970, Everton won the Championship, making seven League titles in all for the Goodison Park club, and in 1966 they took the FA Cup for the third time.

Everton broke all British transfer records in February 1974 when, in a part-exchange deal with Birmingham City, they paid the equivalent of £350,000 for striker Bob Latchford. Six months later they set a new British cash record of £300,000 when signing Martin Dobson from Burnley.

Despite such big signings, Everton failed to shift the power of Merseyside football from Anfield, although in April 1976 they became the first club in Football League history to reach the milestone of 3,000 First Division points.

Their all-time record scorer was the legendary Bill ('Dixie') Dean with a career total of 349 League goals for the club (1925-37), including the Football League record of 60 in season 1927-28. Dean died on 1 March, 1980, aged 72, while watching the Everton-Liverpool 'derby'. His ashes were scattered at Goodison Park.

Howard Kendall, who won a Championship medal at wing-half in the Everton side of 1970, returned as manager in May 1980. An extensive turnover of players quickly followed, but the silverware continued to go to the club next door.

The 1984 Milk Cup competition produced Wembley's first all-Merseyside Final. Beaten in a replay at Maine Road, Manchester, Everton then went back to Wembley for the FA Cup Final against Watford, and were worthy winners, 2-0.

League Champions: 1890-91, 1914-15, 1927-28, 1931-32, 1938-39, 1962-63, 1969-70.
Division 2 Champions: 1930-31.
FA Cup Winners: 1905-06, 1932-33, 1965-66, 1983-84.
Record attendance: 78,299 v Liverpool (League), September 1948.
Modern Capacity: 53,000. **Nickname:** 'Toffees'.
Entered Football League: 1888 — Div. 1.
Biggest win: 11-2 v Derby County (FA Cup), 1889-90.
Heaviest defeat: 4-10 v Tottenham (Div. 1), October 1958.
Best in League Cup/Milk Cup: Finalists 1976-77, 1983-84.
Pitch measurements: 112 x 75 yd.
Highest League Scorer in Single Season: Bill ('Dixie') Dean — 60 in 1927-28 (Div. 1).
Highest transfer fee paid: £700,000 — Adrian Heath (from Stoke City), January 1982.
Highest transfer fee received: £400,000 — Mickey Thomas (to Brighton), November 1981.

Exeter City

St James's Park, Exeter EX4 6PX
Tel: 0392-59466   **Colours:** *Red, White & Black*

No one would suggest that life has been easy for the City club which has never journeyed above the Third Division. Nevertheless, a number of distinguished players began their careers at St James's Park. They include left-winger Cliff Bastin, who became an England international and collected FA Cup-winning and First Division Championship medals with Arsenal before he was 20; and Dick Pym, Bolton's goalkeeper in three successive Cup Finals at Wembley in the 1920s.

Who among Exeter's older supporters will forget the wonderful Cup run in 1931? After fighting through to the competition proper, they beat First Division Derby 3-2 at Exeter; next they won 2-1 at Bury and then, in front of their own followers again, defeated Leeds United 3-1. That victory put Exeter in the last eight for the first time, and after a 1-1 draw at Sunderland, City's record crowd saw them lose the replay 4-2.

It was another 50 years before Devon saw such excitement again. Then, in 1980-81, Exeter once more reached the quarter-finals. On the way they beat Leatherhead, Millwall, Maidstone, and next First Division Leicester 3-1 (after 1-1 away). Then came a 1-1 draw at St. James' Park, Newcastle, against one of the giants of FA Cup history, followed by an amazing 4-0 replay triumph at St. James's Park, Exeter. Six of City's goals in the Cup run came from Tony Kellow (who scored 33 in the season), but the dream ended 2-0 at Tottenham in Round 6.

Record attendance: 20,984 v Sunderland (FA Cup), March 1931.
Modern Capacity: 17,500. **Nickname:** 'Grecians'.
Entered Football League: 1920 — Div. 3.
Biggest wins: 8-1 v Coventry City (Div. 3 South), December 1926; 8-1 v Aldershot (Div. 3 South), May 1935.
Heaviest defeats: 0-9 v Notts County (Div. 3 South), October 1948; 0-9 v Northampton (Div. 3 South), April 1958.
Highest final League position: Runners-up Div. 3 (South) 1932-33. Runners-up Div. 4 1976-77.
Best in FA Cup: 6th Round 1930-31, 1980-81.
Best in League/Milk Cup: 4th Round 1973-74, 1979-80.
Pitch measurements: 115 x 75 yd.
Highest League Scorer in Single Season: Fred Whitlow — 34 in 1932-33 (Div. 3 South).
Highest transfer fee paid: £70,000 — Tony Kellow (from Blackpool), March 1980.
Highest transfer fee received: £125,000 — Tony Kellow (to Blackpool), November 1978.

Fulham

Craven Cottage, Stevenage Road, London SW6 6HH
Tel: 01-736-6561 **Colours:** *White & Black*

For years Fulham have been known as 'London's friendliest club', but few took them seriously as contenders for prizes until 1975, when they reached Wembley for the first time after four FA Cup semi-final disappointments. After Sunderland in 1973, they became the second Second Division finalists in three seasons, and although beaten 2-0 by West Ham, Fulham's appearance at Wembley reflected enormous credit on the club, on manager Alec Stock and on captain Alan Mullery, who was voted 'Footballer of the Year'.

In 1961 Fulham had made their England captain, Johnny Haynes, Britain's first £100-a-week footballer. In 1966 they supplied right-back George Cohen to England's triumphant World Cup team; in March 1974 they paid West Ham £25,000 for that World Cup-winning captain, Bobby Moore, at the end of his record 108-cap international career. A year later Moore was back in familiar surroundings at Wembley, playing against his old club in the Cup Final.

Haynes remains the Fulham player with most League appearances (594 from 1952-70), most England caps (56) and, arguably, more class than any other footballer in the club's history.

In 1982, by which time Rugby League was also being played at Craven Cottage, the enthusiastic management of Malcolm Macdonald inspired Fulham's promotion from Division 3, and a year later they missed a return to the First Division by only one place.

Division 2 Champions: 1948-49.
Division 3 (South) Champions: 1931-32.
Record attendance: 49,335 v Millwall (League), October 1938.
Modern Capacity: 25,000. **Nickname:** 'Cottagers'.
Entered Football League: 1907 — Div. 2.
Biggest win: 10-1 v Ipswich (Div. 1), December 1963.
Heaviest defeat: 0-9 v Wolves (Div. 1), September 1959.
Best in FA Cup: Runners-up 1974-75.
Best in League/Milk Cup: 5th Round 1966-68, 1970-71.
Pitch measurements: 110 x 75 yd.
Highest League Scorer in Single Season: Frank Newton — 41 in 1931-32 (Div. 3 South).
Highest transfer fee paid: £150,000 — Peter Kitchen (from Orient), February 1979; £150,000 — Teddy Maybank (from Brighton), December 1979.
Highest transfer fee received: £350,000 — Richard Money (to Liverpool), May 1980.

Gillingham

Priestfield Stadium, Gillingham, Kent ME7 4DD
Tel: 0634-51854 **Colours:** *Blue & White*

When Gillingham were voted out of the Football League in 1938 and replaced by Ipswich Town, their existence as a senior club seemed to be over. But after the war, under an energetic and far-seeing management, they became a force in the Southern League. In 1950, the Football League decided to increase membership from 88 to 92 clubs, by extending each Third Division section (North and South) from 22 to 24 teams, and the 'Gills' were re-admitted.

The club started life as New Brompton Excelsior, changing their name to Gillingham in 1913. The subsequent playing years until they left the League provided little of distinction. In fact, the club had to wait until season 1963-64 for their first major success — the Championship of the Fourth Division. They lost only nine of their 46 matches and beat Carlisle United to the title on goal average, each club obtaining 60 points.

Gillingham were relegated in 1971, but returned to the Third Division in 1974 as the season's highest-scoring team with 90 goals. Their sharpshooter was Brian Yeo, whose 31 League goals equalled the club record set 19 years earlier by Ernie Morgan.

The Fourth Division title in 1964 remains the only honour won, but in 1979 Gillingham came within one place and one point of reaching the Second Division for the first time. That remains the target of the Medway town club after a current spell of ten mainly mid-table years in Division Three.

Division 4 Champions: 1963-64.
Record attendance: 23,002 v Queen's Park Rangers (FA Cup), January 1948.
Modern Capacity: 22,000. **Nickname:** 'Gills'.
Entered Football League: 1920 — Div. 3.
Biggest win: 10-1 v Gorleston (FA Cup), November 1957.
Heaviest defeat: 2-9 v Nottingham Forest (Div. 3 South), November 1950.
Best in FA Cup: 5th Round 1969-70.
Best in League/Milk Cup: 4th Round 1963-64.
Pitch measurements: 114 x 75 yd.
Highest League Scorers in Single Season: Ernie Morgan — 31 in 1954-55 (Div. 3 South); Brian Yeo — 31 in 1973-74 (Div. 4).
Highest transfer fee paid: £90,000 — Trevor Lee (from Colchester), January 1981.
Highest transfer fee received: £65,000 — Dick Tydeman (to Charlton), December 1976.

Grimsby Town

Blundell Park, Cleethorpes, S. Humberside DN35 7PY
Tel: 0472-697111   **Colours:** *Black & White*

In the period between the two wars Grimsby Town, whose ground is situated in the town of Cleethorpes, played in four sections of the Football League — the Third Division and Third North, as well as the First and Second Divisions.

They were still in Division One immediately after the Second World War, but finished bottom in 1948, and after ups and downs between Divisions Two and Four, they found themselves having to seek re-election through finishing 91st on the League ladder in season 1968–69. Three years later they were Fourth Division champions. They went down again in 1977, but within two years were back in the Third Division, and as champions of that section in 1980, they completed the climb from Fourth Division to Second in successive seasons.

The club was founded as Grimsby Pelham in 1878, but after a year dropped the name of Pelham. They won the Division Two Championship in 1901 and again in 1934. Two years later they lost to Arsenal by the only goal in the semi-final of the FA Cup. They again reached the last four in 1939, this time crashing 5-0 to Wolverhampton Wanderers.

Grimsby have produced many first-class forwards, none better than Ernest (Pat) Glover, who scored 42 League goals in 1933–34.

Two men destined to reach the top in football management have been among Grimsby's 17 post-war managers: Bill Shankly and Lawrie McMenemy.

Division 2 Champions: 1900-01, 1933-34.
Division 3 (North) Champions: 1925-26, 1955-56.
Division 3 Champions: 1979-80.
Division 4 Champions: 1971-72.
Record attendance: 31,650 v Wolves (FA Cup), February 1937.
Modern Capacity: 22,000. **Nickname:** 'Mariners'.
Entered Football League: 1892 — Div. 2.
Biggest win: 9-2 v Darwen (Div. 2), April 1899.
Heaviest defeat: 1-9 v Arsenal (Div. 1), January 1931.
Best in FA Cup: Semi-final 1935-36, 1938-39.
Best in League/Milk Cup: 5th Round 1965-66, 1979-80.
Pitch measurements: 111 x 74 yd.
Highest League Scorer in Single Season: Pat Glover — 42 in 1933-34 (Div. 2).
Highest transfer fee paid: £70,000 — Phil Bonnyman (from Chesterfield), August 1982.
Highest transfer fee received: £75,000 — Terry Donovan (to Aston Villa), July 1979.

Halifax Town

Shay Ground, Halifax, W. Yorkshire, HX1 2YS
Tel: 0422-53423   **Colours:** *Blue & White*

The seasons of reward have been strictly limited for Halifax Town since their early days in the Yorkshire Combination and Midland League. So there was understandable excitement in 1971 when the club made a sustained bid to bring Second Division football to The Shay for the first time, but they had to be content with third place.

Two seasons earlier Town had won their way into the Third Division as runners-up to Doncaster Rovers after an unbroken sequence as members of the Third Division (North) and then the Fourth Division. In those bleak days Halifax had to seek re-election seven times, and it says much for their perseverance that they were repeatedly voted back.

The Shay bulged at its sides one February day in 1953, when nearly 37,000 turned up to watch Tottenham Hotspur in the FA Cup fifth round. Halifax had made the most of their luck in being drawn at home in every tie, and after dealing with Ashton and Southport, they put out First Division 'giants' Cardiff and Stoke. But they went down 3-0 to Spurs.

The Halifax pitch, surrounded by a speedway track, is one of the smallest in the League. In the Big Freeze winter of 1962–63, when Town went months without match income, they opened the gates for ice-skaters to use the frozen pitch. Those same turnstiles admitted only 911 spectators to the Fourth Division match against Chester on 14 February, 1984. It was the smallest crowd in Halifax history.

Record attendance: 36,885 v Tottenham (FA Cup), February 1953.
Modern Capacity: 16,500.
Entered Football League: 1921 — Div. 3 (North). ·
Biggest win: 7-0 v Bishop Auckland (FA Cup), January 1967.
Heaviest defeat: 0-13 v Stockport County (Div. 3 North), January 1934.
Highest final League position: Runners-up Div. 3 (North) 1934–35; runners-up Div. 4 1968–69.
Best in FA Cup: 5th Round 1932-33, 1952-53.
Best in League/Milk Cup: 4th Round 1963-64.
Pitch measurements: 110 x 70 yd.
Highest League Scorer in Single Season: Albert Valentine — 34 in 1934–35 (Div. 3 North).
Highest transfer fee paid: £25,000 — Kevin Johnson (from Huddersfield), August 1978.
Highest transfer fee received: £50,000 — Mick Kennedy (to Huddersfield), August 1980.

Hartlepool United

Victoria Ground, Clarence Road, Hartlepool, Cleveland
Tel: 0429-222077   **Colours:** *Blue & White*

Overshadowed throughout their existence by their powerful north-eastern neighbours, Newcastle and Sunderland, the Hartlepool club have known more of life's struggles than success. Indeed, they have had to apply 14 times for re-election.

They joined the old Division Three North on its formation in 1921, and stayed in this section until they moved into the newly created Fourth Division in 1958. They did finish runners-up in 1956-57, but in those days only one club gained promotion from each Third Division section. They scored 90 League goals that season.

They had to wait another 11 years, until 1968, before they experienced promotion. Then they took third place in Division Four behind Luton and Barnsley. Unfortunately, at the end of the following season they were relegated.

The club where Brian Clough began in management has lived almost permanently on the breadline and, with gates falling below 1,000, they were saved from extinction in February 1984 by a local businessman.

In the same season Hartlepool signed the man with more medals than any other English player in the game's history — Ray Kennedy, on a free transfer from Swansea. In his hey-day he helped Arsenal do the 'double', won League Championship and European honours galore with Liverpool, and 17 caps for England.

All that must have seemed like another world to Kennedy as he pulled on a Hartlepool shirt, but the Geordie miner's son was back in his native North-east — at 33 still playing football and running a local pub with his wife.

Record attendance: 17,426 v Man. United (FA Cup), January 1957.
Modern Capacity: 18,000. **Nickname:** 'Pool'.
Entered Football League: 1921 — Div. 3 (North).
Biggest win: 10-1 v Barrow (Div. 4), April 1959.
Heaviest defeat: 1-10 v Wrexham (Div. 4), March 1962.
Highest final League position: Runners-up Div. 3 (North) 1956-57.
Best in FA Cup: 4th Round 1954-55, 1977-78.
Best in League/Milk Cup: 4th Round 1974-75.
Pitch measurements: 113 x 76 yd.
Highest League Scorer in Single Season: Bill Robinson — 28 in 1927-28 (Div. 3 North).
Highest transfer fee paid: £10,000 — Ambrose Fogarty (from Sunderland), November 1963.
Highest transfer fee received: £60,000 — Malcolm Poskett (to Brighton), February 1978.

Hereford United

Edgar Street, Hereford HR4 9JU
Tel: 0432-276666 **Colours:** *White & Navy Blue*

After striving for years for Football League membership, Southern League Hereford United so captured the public imagination with spectacular deeds in the 1971–72 FA Cup that, four months later, they were voted into the Fourth Division, displacing Barrow.

By knocking out Newcastle United (six times winners of the FA Cup) 2–1 in the third round after drawing 2–2 at St James's Park, Hereford became the first non-League club to dismiss First Division opponents since Yeovil in 1949. The success story continued on their entry to the Football League, for their first season ended with promotion as Fourth Division runners-up.

Of United's 64 Third Division goals in 1974–75, Dixie McNeil scored 31, a record for the club in his first season with them, and there was another milestone in 1975–76 which ended with Hereford runaway champions — and promoted to the Second Division four years after leaving the Southern League.

Their stay lasted only one year, however, and after two successive seasons of relegation Hereford found themselves back in Division Four in 1978. Three times in the next four seasons they had to apply for re-election, but there was considerable improvement on the field in 1983–84, though attendances remained at a worrying level.

Hereford's pitch, 80 yards across, is the widest in the Football League. One of the best players reared on it was Kevin Sheedy, transferred in July 1978 for £80,000 to Liverpool and subsequently a Republic of Ireland international with Everton.

Division 3 Champions: 1975–76.
Record attendance: 18,114 v Sheffield Wednesday (FA Cup), January 1958.
Modern Capacity: 17,500.
Entered Football League: 1972 — Div. 4.
Biggest win: 11–0 v Thynnes (FA Cup), September 1947.
Heaviest defeat: 2–9 v Yeovil Town (S. League), September 1955.
Best in FA Cup: 4th Round 1971–72, 1973–74, 1976–77, 1981–82.
Best in League/Milk Cup: 3rd Round 1974–75.
Pitch measurements: 111 x 80 yd.
Highest League Scorer in Single Season: Dixie McNeil — 35 in 1975–76 (Div. 3).
Highest transfer fee paid: £25,000 — David Cunningham (from Aston Villa), August 1979.
Highest transfer fee received: £100,000 — Steve Emery (to Derby), September 1979.

Huddersfield Town

Leeds Road, Huddersfield HD1 6PE
Tel: 0484-20335 **Colours:** *Blue & White*

In the mid-twenties Huddersfield reigned supreme as First Division Champions for three successive years (1924–25-26), the finest era in their history. It followed worrying periods of financial crisis.

The appointment of Herbert Chapman as manager (1922-25) heralded the club's dominant period. In that great team of the twenties which Chapman created were the captain Clem Stephenson, who had played for Aston Villa, winger Billy Smith, who made nearly 500 appearances in 15 years, full-backs Roy Goodall and Sam Wadsworth.

Having won the FA Cup for the first time in 1922, Town went on to their Championship treble, the first in League history, and since equalled by Arsenal in 1933-34-35 and Liverpool in 1982-83-84.

Town stayed in Division One until 1952, then won back their place first time. In 1956 they dropped again and spent 14 years in the Second Division. Their return as Division Two champions was but a fleeting revival, for by 1973 Huddersfield had tumbled for the first time into the Third Division.

Two years later, they fell even further but, under Mick Buxton, they began the climb back as Fourth Division champions with 101 League goals in 1979-80, and a decade in the doldrums ended with a return to Division Two in 1983, when top scorer Mark Lillis had a unique sponsorship arrangement. A local butcher offered him a T-bone steak for every goal he scored, and Lillis's total for the season was 20 free steaks.

League Champions: 1923-24, 1924-25, 1925-26.
Division 2 Champions: 1969-70.
Division 4 Champions: 1979-80.
FA Cup Winners: 1921-22.
Record attendance: 67,037 v Arsenal (FA Cup), February 1932.
Modern Capacity: 48,000.
Entered Football League: 1910 — Div. 2.
Biggest win: 10-1 v Blackpool (Div. 1), December 1930.
Heaviest defeat: 0-8 v Middlesbrough (Div. 1), September 1950.
Best in League/Milk Cup: Semi-final 1967-68.
Pitch measurements: 116 x 76 yd.
Highest League Scorers in Single Season: Sam Taylor — 35 in 1919-20 (Div. 2), George Brown — 35 in 1925-26 (Div. 1).
Highest transfer fee paid: £120,000 — Terry Austin (from Mansfield Town), December 1980.
Highest transfer fee received: £100,000 — Trevor Cherry (to Leeds), June 1972.

Hull City

Boothferry Park, Hull HU4 6EU
Tel: 0482-51119 **Colours:** *Amber, Black & Red*

The modern story of Hull City is one of survival and revival. Between 1978 and 1981 the Humberside team dropped from Second to Fourth Division; in February 1982 the receiver was called in and the club put up for sale.

Then, under the new leadership of chairman Don Robinson and manager Colin Appleton, both from non-League Scarborough, City's fortunes soared. First, Mr Robinson talked the players into a wage cut, then he sold the huge car-park for re-development, and debts of £1.2m were cleared within a year.

On the field, a bold target was set — to emulate the rapid rise of Swansea and Watford from Fourth Division to First. Immediate promotion was followed by another determined push towards the Second Division in 1984. They missed by one place.

Hull remains the biggest city in England yet to stage First Division football. If and when it comes, they already have the ground and facilities of the required standard.

Hull were formed as an amateur club in 1904 and gained admission to the Second Division in 1905. Four times up to 1960 they dropped into the Third Division, then regained their status in the higher grade as Third Division Champions in 1966.

They came closest to promotion to Division One in 1910 when Oldham Athletic pipped them for second place by .286 of a goal. During the Second World War Hull's ground in Anlaby Road was hit by enemy bombs, and in 1946 the club was re-formed and acquired their present impressive home, Boothferry Park, which since January 1951 has had its own railway station.

Division 3 (North) Champions: 1932–33, 1948–49.
Division 3 Champions: 1965–66.
Record attendance: 55,019 v Manchester United (FA Cup), February 1949. **Modern Capacity:** 30,600. **Nickname:** 'Tigers'.
Entered Football League: 1905 — Div. 2.
Biggest win: 11–1 v Carlisle (Div. 3 North), January 1939.
Heaviest defeat: 0–8 v Wolves (Div. 2), November 1911.
Best in FA Cup: Semi-final 1929–30.
Best in League/Milk Cup: 4th Round 1973–74, 1975–76, 1977–78.
Pitch measurements: 113 x 73 yd.
Highest League Scorer in Single Season: Bill McNaughton — 39 in 1932–33 (Div. 3 North).
Highest transfer fee paid: £150,000 — Mick Tait (from Carlisle), September 1979.
Highest transfer fee received: £200,000 equivalent (£170,000 plus a player) — Stuart Pearson (to Manchester United), May 1974.

Ipswich Town

Portman Road, Ipswich 1P1 2DA
Tel: 0473-219211 **Colours:** *Blue & White*

Football fame first came to Ipswich in 1962 when they won the Championship in their first season in Division One. Under Alf Ramsey the club had a remarkable rise. He took over as manager in August 1955, after Town had gone down to the Third Division. Two years later they were back in the Second Division. They won promotion to the First as Champions after four more seasons, and the following year won the League title itself.

In 1978, three years after losing in the semi-final, the FA Cup dream came true when Ipswich reached Wembley for the first time and beat Arsenal by the only goal, scored by Roger Osborne.

Three years later, they put their name on the list of European prize-winners, beating the Dutch team AZ Alkmaar in the UEFA Cup Final. It was one more remarkable achievement by a comparatively small, but sensibly-run, 'family' club with whom the influential name Cobbold has long been synonymous.

Both in 1981 and 1982 Ipswich finished second in the Championship. Then they lost Bobby Robson to England, just as they had lost Alf Ramsey before. A costly new stand went up at Portman Road, Ipswich went more than £1.5m in the red, and they could not afford to buy replacements for departing Internationals of the calibre of Dutch stars Arnold Muhren and Frans Thijssen, strikers Alan Brazil and Paul Mariner, and high-scoring midfield player, John Wark.

League Champions: 1961–62.
Division 2 Champions: 1960–61, 1967–68.
Division 3 (South) Champions: 1953–54, 1956–57.
FA Cup Winners: 1977–78.
UEFA Cup Winners: 1980–81.
Record attendance: 38,010 v Leeds (FA Cup), March 1975.
Modern Capacity: 37,000. **Nickname:** 'Blues'.
Entered Football League: 1938 — Div. 3 (South).
Biggest win: 10–0 v Floriana, Malta (European Cup), September 1962.
Heaviest defeat: 1–10 v Fulham (Div. 1), December 1963.
Best in League Cup/Milk Cup: Semi-final 1981–82.
Pitch measurements: 112 x 75 yd.
Highest League Scorer in Single Season: Ted Phillips — 41 in 1956–57 (Div. 3 South).
Highest transfer fee paid: £250,000 — Kevin O'Callaghan (from Millwall). January 1980.
Highest transfer fees received: £450,000 — Brian Talbot (to Arsenal), January 1979; £450,000 — Alan Brazil (to Tottenham), March 1983.

Leeds United

Elland Road, Leeds LS11 0ES
Tel: 0532-716037 **Colours:** *White, Blue & Yellow*

From the late sixties, Leeds established a reputation as one of the most consistent and powerful clubs in Europe. Between 1964 and 1975 they won seven major prizes: Second Division, League Cup, two League Championships, the Fairs Cup twice and the FA Cup. Over the same period they were runners-up eleven times in domestic and European competitions.

In 1969 they set a new First Division points record (67) and under Don Revie they became a major all-international force.

In July 1974 Revie left Elland Road to manage England. His successor, Brian Clough, was sacked after 44 days and replaced by Jimmy Armfield from Bolton. The season ended with Leeds only the third British club to reach the European Cup Final, but they lost 2-0 to Bayern Munich and were banned from Europe because of misconduct by supporters at the Final in Paris.

Three times League Leeds have been close to completing the League Championship-FA Cup double (1965, 1970, 1972). Though the Cup was at last won in 1972, this competition has provided United's biggest upsets, with odd-goal defeats from Fourth Division Colchester (1971), Second Division Sunderland (in the 1973 Final), another Second Division side, Bristol City, in 1974 and Third Division Crystal Palace in 1976. An 18-year spell of First Division membership ended in 1982.

Jack Charlton holds the club's League appearances record (629 from 1953-73) and Billy Bremner is the most-capped Leeds player (54 for Scotland).

League Champions: 1968-69, 1973-74.
Division 2 Champions: 1923-24, 1963-64.
FA Cup Winners: 1971-72. **League Cup Winners:** 1967-68.
European Fairs Cup Winners: 1967-68, 1970-71.
Record attendance: 56,892 v Sunderland (FA Cup), March 1967.
Modern Capacity: 44,000.
Entered Football League: 1905 — Div. 2 (as Leeds City).
Biggest win: 10-0 v Lyn Oslo (European Cup), September 1969.
Heaviest defeat: 1-8 v Stoke City (Div. 1), August 1934.
Pitch measurements: 115 x 76 yd.
Highest League Scorer in Single Season: John Charles — 42 in 1953-54 (Div. 2).
Highest transfer fee paid: £930,000 — Peter Barnes (from WBA), August 1981.
Highest transfer fee received: £500,000 — Frank Gray (to Nottingham Forest), July 1979.

Leicester City

Filbert Street, Leicester, LE2 7FL
Tel: 0533-555000 **Colours:** *Blue & White*

A dozen old boys of Wyggeston School paid ninepence each to buy a football and start a soccer team in 1884. They called themselves Leicester Fosse. At first they used the Leicester rugby ground, but in 1889 moved to Filbert Street and five years later they were elected to the Second Division.

The name was changed from Fosse to City in 1919. By then they were a well-established Second Division club. They have won the Division Two Championship six times and got their first taste of First Division football in 1925. They have played in the FA Cup Final four times — thrice in the sixties — and never won it.

Two Arthurs have been principal goalscoring heroes of Leicester. Arthur Chandler achieved a total of 262 between 1923 and 1935 — his feat of scoring in 16 consecutive matches in season 1924–25 (Div. Two) remains a British record — and Arthur Rowley scored 44 League goals in the 1956–57 season.

Goalkeepers, too, have thrilled the fans at Filbert Street. In 1967 City transferred England's World Cup-winning 'keeper Gordon Banks to Stoke and replaced him with Peter Shilton. He followed Banks into the England team . . . and to Stoke in November 1974.

At the beginning of the eighties, Leicester moved yo-yo-like to and from the First Division: Second Division champions in 1980, relegated in 1981 and up again in 1983 when, with a 15-match unbeaten run (8 wins, 7 draws) over the season's last three months, they surprised everyone — most of all Fulham — by snatching third promotion place by a point.

Division 2 Champions: 1924–25, 1936–37, 1953–54, 1956–57, 1970–71, 1979–80.
League Cup Winners: 1963–64.
Record attendance: 47, 298 v Tottenham (FA Cup), February 1928.
Modern Capacity: 32,000. **Nickname:** 'Filberts'.
Entered Football League: 1894 — Div. 2 (as Leicester Fosse).
Biggest win: 10-0 v Portsmouth (Div. 1), October 1928.
Heaviest defeat: 0-12 v Nottingham Forest (Div. 1), April 1909.
Best in FA Cup: Runners-up 1948–49, 1960–61, 1962–63, 1968–69.
Pitch measurements: 112 x 75 yd.
Highest League Scorer in Single Season: Arthur Rowley — 44 in 1956–57 (Div. 2).
Highest transfer fee paid: £250,000 — Jim Melrose (from Partick), July, 1980.
Highest transfer fee received: £340,000 — Peter Shilton (to Stoke), November 1974.

Lincoln City

Sincil Bank, Lincoln LN5 8LD
Tel: 0522-22224 **Colours:** *Red & White*

If Lincoln City had won away to Fulham in the final match of 1981–82, they would have climbed to the Second Division from the Fourth in successive seasons. Instead, a 1–1 draw took Fulham up.

By the following January, Colin Murphy, working miracles on a shoe-string, had taken the 'Imps' to the top of Division Three, but the limitations of a professional staff no more than 14 strong undermined another promotion effort.

Differences between boardroom and dressing-room did not help, but Lincoln City council eased the club's financial problems by buying the Sincil Bank ground for £250,000.

The cathedral city, though never a hot-bed of soccer interest, has staged League football since 1892, when Lincoln became founder-members of the Second Division.

The club's honours list is restricted to three championship successes in the old Third Division Northern Section and the Fourth Division title in 1976. That was won under an impressive young manager named Graham Taylor, who, a year later, moved on to achieve great things with Watford.

In their 1976 triumph, Lincoln set what was then a new record for any division of the Football League with 74 points, and their 111 League goals was the first century by any club since QPR's in the Third Division in 1966–67.

Andy Graver, who had two spells with the club, totalled 144 League goals for Lincoln through the 1950s and for rapid scoring, no one in League history has bettered Frank Keetley's six goals in 21 minutes at home to Halifax (Div. 3 North) in January 1932.

Division 3 (North) Champions: 1931–32, 1947–48, 1951–52.
Division 4 Champions: 1975–76.
Record attendance: 23,196 v Derby County (League Cup), November 1967. **Modern Capacity:** 16,225. **Nickname:** 'Imps'.
Entered Football League: 1892 — Div. 2.
Biggest win: 11–1 v Crewe Alexandra (Div. 3 North), Sept. 1951.
Heaviest defeat: 3–11 v Manchester City (Div. 2), March 1895.
Best in FA Cup: 4th Round 1953–54, 1960–61, 1975–76.
Best in League/Milk Cup: 4th Round 1967–68.
Pitch measurements: 110 x 75 yd.
Highest League Scorer in Single Season: Alan Hall — 42 in 1931–32 (Div. 3 North).
Highest transfer fee paid: £38,000 — George Shipley (from Southampton), January 1980.
Highest transfer fee received: £150,000 — Mick Harford (to Newcastle), December 1980.

Liverpool

Anfield Road, Liverpool L4 0TH
Tel: 051-263 2361   **Colours**: *All Red*

When Bill Shankly stunned the football world in July 1974 by announcing that he was retiring from football management, Liverpool did not need to look far for his replacement — just across the famous Anfield boot-room, in fact. Bob Paisley, player, trainer and assistant-manager at the club he joined in 1939, started his first team talk with the words: "I never really wanted this job, anyway...". Nine years later, he moved into the boardroom with the most astonishing honours list ever achieved by any British manager — 19 major prizes.

It was one of the most emotional moments Wembley has known when, the Milk Cup having been won for the third successive year, the Liverpool players pushed Bob Paisley ahead of them up the famous steps to receive the trophy on his farewell appearance there. He bowed out as Manager of the Year for the sixth time.

His successor was 62-year-old Joe Fagan (25 years at Anfield) and in one respect he at once exceeded even the glories of Shankly and Paisley. Liverpool won the Milk Cup for the fourth consecutive year, completed the League Championship hat-trick and won their fourth European Cup — the first English club to take three major prizes in one season.

League Champions: 1900–01, 1905–06, 1921–22, 1922–23, 1946–47, 1963–64, 1965–66, 1972–73, 1975–76, 1976–77, 1978–79, 1979–80, 1981–82, 1982–83, 1983–84.
Division 2 Champions: 1893–94, 1895–96, 1904–05, 1961–62.
FA Cup Winners: 1964–65, 1973–74.
League/Milk Cup Winners: 1980–81, 1981–82, 1982–83, 1983–84.
European Cup Winners: 1976–77, 1977–78, 1980–81 1983–84.
UEFA Cup Winners: 1972–73, 1975–76.
European Super Cup Winners: 1977–78.
Record attendance: 61,905 v Wolves (FA Cup), February 1952.
Modern Capacity: 45,000. **Nickname:** 'Reds'.
Entered Football League: 1893 — Div. 2.
Biggest win: 11–0 v Stromsgodset (Cup-Winners' Cup), September 1974.
Heaviest defeat: 1–9 v Birmingham (Div. 2), December 1954.
Pitch measurements: 110 x 75 yd.
Highest League Scorer in Single Season: Roger Hunt — 41 in 1961–62 (Div 2).
Highest transfer fee paid: £900,000 — Mark Lawrenson (from Brighton), August, 1981.
Highest transfer fee received: £500,000 — Kevin Keegan (to SV Hamburg). June 1977.

Luton Town

Kenilworth Road, Luton, Beds, LU1 1DH
Tel: 0582-411622   **Colours:** *White & Orange*

In modern times few teams outside the First Division have played as excitingly as Luton Town did in winning the Second Division championship in 1982. Twenty-one of their 86 goals came from Brian Stein, and on their return to the top division after a seven-year absence, manager David Pleat declared: "We shall carry on attacking. That is our strength."

Worthy sentiments that were almost to Luton's peril. They went to the final League game of season 1982–83 needing victory at Maine Road to stay up. They got it by the only goal, scorer Raddy Antic in the closing minutes, and their opponents, Manchester City, went down instead.

As a small-town club, Luton have lived for years in the face of financial difficulties. In December 1975, with debts of £724,000, they were saved from liquidation by transferring forward Peter Anderson to the Belgian club, Royal Antwerp, for £80,000. In the middle of season 1983–84 the club announced that, because of road-building plans affecting Kenilworth Road in 1985, they would be forced to move and planned to set up home 23 miles along the M1 at Milton Keynes. There were protest marches by supporters.

Back in the Thirties, emergency centre-forward Joe Payne put Luton in the headlines, and himself in the record books, by scoring TEN goals in a 12–0 win at home to Bristol Rovers. That was in a Third Division (Southern Section) match on Easter Monday 1936. His feat has never been equalled in League or FA Cup.

Division 2 Champions: 1981–82.
Division 3 (South) Champions: 1936–37.
Division 4 Champions: 1967–68.
Record attendance: 30,069 v Blackpool (FA Cup), March 1959.
Modern Capacity: 22,500. **Nickname:** 'Hatters'.
Entered Football League: 1897 — Div. 2.
Biggest win: 12–0 v Bristol Rovers (Div. 3 South), April 1936.
Heaviest defeat: 1–9 v Swindon Town (Div. 3 South), August 1920.
Best in FA Cup: Runners-up 1958–59.
Best in League/Milk Cup: 5th Round 1978–79.
Pitch measurements: 112 x 72 yd.
Highest League Scorer in Single Season: Joe Payne — 55 in 1936–37 (Div. 3 South).
Highest transfer fee paid: £400,000 — Paul Walsh (from Charlton in part-exchange), July 1982.
Highest transfer fee received: £700,000 — Paul Walsh (to Liverpool), May 1984.

Manchester City

Maine Road, Moss Side, Manchester M14 7WN
Tel: 061-226 1191/2 **Colours:** *Sky Blue*

Following their return from the Second Division in 1966, Manchester City became one of Britain's most formidable sides under the dual influence of Joe Mercer as manager and Malcolm Allison, coach. In three seasons they won four of the game's top prizes — the League Championship in 1968, the FA Cup in 1969 and, in 1970, the League Cup and Cup-Winners' Cup.

Allison returned to Maine Road in January 1979, and over the next 15 months City were involved in an extraordinary transfer turnover of £7½ million, signing ten players for £4½ million and selling 13 for £3 million. The arrivals included two million-pound players: Steve Daley (£1,450,000 from Wolves) and Kevin Reeves (£1,250,000 from Norwich). At the end of it all, City finished season 1979–80 modestly in 17th place.

In 1981 they shared the 100th FA Cup Final with Tottenham. That did not disguise the fact that they had over-reached themselves in their earlier transfer extravaganza. The team suddenly fell apart, and defeat at home to Luton in the last match of season 1982-83 sent City into the Second Division.

In the early 1930s City overshadowed United in Manchester's battle for soccer prestige and in 1937 they won their first League Championship. The following season they were relegated in unique circumstances — as First Division top scorers with 80 goals.

League Champions: 1936-37, 1967-68.
Division 2 Champions: 1898–99, 1902–03, 1909–10, 1927–28, 1946–47, 1965–66.
FA Cup Winners: 1903–04, 1933–34, 1955–56, 1968–69.
League Cup Winners: 1969–70, 1975–76.
Winners of European Cup-Winners' Cup: 1969–70.
Record attendance: 84,569 v Stoke (FA Cup), March 1934.
Modern Capacity: 52,000.
Entered Football League: 1892 — Div. 2 (as Ardwick).
Biggest win: 11-3 v Lincoln City (Div. 2), March 1895.
Heaviest defeat: 1-9 v Everton (Div. 1), September 1906.
Pitch measurements: 117 x 79 yd.
Highest League Scorer in Single Season: Tom Johnson — 38 in 1928-29 (Div. 1).
Highest transfer fee paid: £1,450,000 — Steve Daley (from Wolves), September 1979.
Highest transfer fee received: £900,000 — Trevor Francis (to Sampdoria, Italy), July 1982.

Manchester United

Old Trafford, Manchester M16 ORA
Tel: 061-872 1661/2 **Colours:** *Red & White*

Manchester United's is a history of two clubs, not one. The first died on 6 February 1958, when the aircraft bringing them home from a European Cup-tie crashed in snow on take-off from Munich. Eight players were among the 23 people killed.

The life of manager Matt Busby was also in the balance, and by the time he was able to return to Old Trafford, a new Mancester United team had been born. Less than three months later they played Bolton in the most emotionally-charged FA Cup Final of all. In 1963 they returned to Wembley and won the Cup for the third time; they became League Champions again in 1965 and 1967 and at Wembley, a year later, on 29 May 1968, they defeated Benfica 4–1 to become England's first holders of the European Cup.

Over the next 15 years United experienced relegation (1974), immediate promotion, and two successes in the FA Cup. They were achieved under Tommy Docherty in 1977 and Ron Atkinson in 1983, when the prize was collected for United by Britain's costliest player — Bryan Robson. It was the perfect present for father-figure Sir Matt Busby, now President, on his 74th birthday.

League Champions: 1907-08, 1910-11, 1951-52, 1955-56, 1956-57, 1964-65, 1966-67.
Division 2 Champions: 1935-36, 1974-75.
FA Cup Winners: 1908-09, 1947-48, 1962-63, 1976-77, 1982-83.
European Cup Winners: 1967-68.
Record attendance: 76, 692 — Wolves v Grimsby (FA Cup Semi-final), March 1939. (Record crowd for a League match in England is 82,950 for Manchester United v Arsenal, January 1948 — played on Manchester City's ground.)
Modern capacity: 58,000.
Entered Football League: 1892 — Div. 1 (as Newton Heath).
Biggest win: 10–0 v Anderlecht, Belgium (European Cup), September 1956.
Heaviest defeat: 0–7 v Aston Villa (Div. 1), December 1930.
Best in League Cup/Milk Cup: Finalists 1982-83.
Pitch measurements: 116 x 76 yd.
Highest League Scorer in Single Season: Dennis Viollet — 32 in 1959-60 (Div. 1).
Highest transfer fee paid: £1,500,000 — Bryan Robson (from WBA) October 1981.
Highest transfer fee received: £1,500,000 — Ray Wilkins (to AC Milan), May 1984.

Mansfield Town

Field Mill Ground, Quarry Lane, Mansfield, Notts
Tel: 0623-23567 **Colours:** *Yellow & Blue*

The name of Mansfield Town was on many people's lips one February night in 1969 — and no wonder. The Third Division club had astounded the football world by beating West Ham United — who included three World Cup players, Bobby Moore, Geoff Hurst and Martin Peters — 3-0 in the FA Cup fifth round.

Forty years earlier, in 1929, Mansfield, then a non-League club, produced an equally remarkable Cup result by winning 1-0 away to Second Division Wolves in the third round. That performance was a factor in Mansfield being accepted into the Football League two years later, when Newport County dropped out of the Third Division Southern Section for one season.

Such days of spectacular deeds helped to compensate followers of Mansfield for seasons of comparatively unexciting activity until the club gained promotion to the Second Division for the first time in 1976-77. But they lasted there for only one season.

They missed the Second Division by one place in 1951 and 1965. In 1975 Town won the Fourth Division Championship by six points.

Roy Goodall, Freddie Steele, Charlie Mitten, Sam Weaver, Raich Carter, Tommy Cummings and Billy Bingham are among illustrious names who as managers tried to bring a higher standard to Mansfield's football.

Though the club did not join the Football League until 1931, Field Mill has been their home since 1905, when they bought the ground from the Duke of Portland.

Division 3 Champions: 1976-77.
Division 4 Champions: 1974-75.
Record attendance: 24,467 v Nottingham Forest (FA Cup), January 1953.
Modern Capacity: 23,500. **Nickname:** 'Stags'.
Entered Football League: 1931 — Div. 3 (South).
Biggest wins: 9-2 v Rotherham (Div. 3 North), December 1932; 9-2 v Hounslow Town (FA Cup), November 1962.
Heaviest defeat: 1-8 v Walsall (Div. 3 North), January 1933.
Best in FA Cup: 6th Round 1968-69.
Best in League/Milk Cup: 5th Round 1975-76.
Pitch measurements: 115 x 72 yd.
Highest League Scorer in Single Season: Ted Harston — 55 in 1936-37 (Div. 3 North).
Highest transfer fee paid: £75,000 — Steve Taylor (from Luton), July 1979.
Highest transfer fee received: £200,000 — Mike Saxby (to Luton), July 1979.

Middlesbrough

Ayresome Park, Middlesbrough, Cleveland T51 4PB
Tel: 0642-819659 **Colours:** *Red & White*

Former Leeds and England centre-half Jack Charlton's first season as a manager ended triumphantly in 1974 with Middlesbrough returning to the First Division after an interval of 20 years. Charlton instilled Leeds-type efficiency into 'Boro's play, and they led the field from the start to give the North-east a second successive year of triumph following Sunderland's FA Cup victory in 1973.

After four years in charge, Charlton left the club, and Boro' remained in the First Division until 1982, when they paid the price for selling good players. Another new manager, Malcolm Allison, pulled them clear of further relegation in 1982-83, but a worsening financial position thwarted his plans to keep the talent needed if Middlesbrough were to challenge for First Division status again.

Middlesbrough twice won the Amateur Cup (1895, 1898), and they caused a sensation in 1905, when they paid Sunderland the game's first transfer fee of £1,000 for Alf Common.

During their early years, Middlesbrough set several records. Two came in 1926-27 when, after the change in the offside law, they scored what is still the Division Two record of 122 goals. Local-born centre-forward George Camsell contributed 59, another unbeaten record for the same division. In 1927-28, Middlesbrough and Tottenham shared a less enviable record — the highest points totals (37 and 38) for teams relegated from the First Division.

Division 2 Champions: 1926-27, 1928-29, 1973-74.
FA Amateur Cup Winners: 1894-95, 1897-98.
Record attendance: 53,596 v Newcastle United (League), December 1949.
Modern Capacity: 42,500. **Nickname:** 'Boro'.
Entered Football League: 1899 — Div. 2.
Biggest win: 10-3 v Sheffield United (Div. 1), November 1933.
Heaviest defeat: 0-9 v Blackburn (Div. 2), November 1954.
Best in FA Cup: 6th Round 1935-36, 1946-47, 1969-70, 1974-75, 1976-77, 1977-78, 1980-81. (Also reached last eight — old 3rd Round — in 1900-01, 1903-04.)
Best in League/Milk Cup: Semi-final 1975-76.
Pitch measurements: 115 x 75 yd.
Highest League Scorer in Single Season: George Camsell — 59 in 1926-27 (Div. 2).
Highest transfer fee paid: £375,000 — Irving Nattrass (from Newcastle), July 1979.
Highest transfer fee received: £600,000 — David Armstrong (to Southampton), August 1981.

Millwall

The Den, Cold Blow Lane, London SE14 5RH
Tel: 01-639-3143   **Colours:** *Blue & White*

Between 1964 and 1967 Millwall established a League record that will not easily be beaten. They played 59 consecutive home matches without defeat, a sequence that started in the Fourth Division on 24 August 1964 and ended in a Second Division match against Plymouth Argyle on 14 January 1967. A much earlier Millwall record was their aggregate of 127 goals in winning the Third Division (South) Championship of 1927-28.

The club was among the original members of the Third Division in 1920. In 1937 they became the first Third Division club to reach the FA Cup semi-finals, beating First Division opponents Chelsea, Derby County and Manchester City at The Den, before falling 2-1 to Sunderland at the last hurdle before Wembley.

A year later Millwall were back in Division Two, but after the war their fortunes slumped and they dropped from Second Division to Third and then through the trapdoor to the Fourth. They climbed back to the Second in successive seasons (1964-65-66), but were once more relegated in 1975. A tremendous late run took them up again twelve months later for another Second Division stay.

Between 1966 and 1971, midfield player Eamonn Dunphy was capped 22 times by the Republic of Ireland while with Millwall (a record for London's dockland club), and on 20 January, 1974 The Den staged the first Sunday match in Football League history (Millwall 1, Fulham 0).

Division 3 (South) Champions: 1927-28, 1937-38.
Division 4 Champions: 1961-62.
Record attendance: 48,672 v Derby County (FA Cup), February 1937.
Modern Capacity: 32,000. **Nickname:** 'Lions'.
Entered Football League: 1920 — Div. 3.
Biggest wins: 9-1 v Torquay United (Div. 3 South), August 1927; 9-1 v Coventry City (Div. 3 South), November 1927.
Heaviest defeat: 1-9 v Aston Villa (FA Cup), January 1946.
Best in FA Cup: Semi-final 1899-1900, 1902-03, 1936-37.
Best in League/Milk Cup: 5th Round 1973-74, 1976-77.
Pitch measurements: 110 x 72½ yd.
Highest League Scorer in Single Season: Dick Parker — 37 in 1926-27 (Div. 3 South).
Highest transfer fee paid: £150,000 — Trevor Aylott (from Barnsley), August 1982.
Highest transfer fee received: £250,000 — Kevin O'Callaghan (to Ipswich), January 1980.

Newcastle United

St James's Park, Newcastle-upon-Tyne NE1 4ST
Tel: 0632-328361 **Colours:** *Black & White*

When Newcastle lured 31-year-old Kevin Keegan to the North-east in a £100,000 transfer from Southampton in August 1982, Tyneside welcomed its first football hero since the days of Malcolm Macdonald. Attendances soared, and Keegan responded to the adulation, the challenge and the captaincy with 21 goals in his first season at St. James's Park.

They were not enough to take United to a higher final position than fifth, but with Keegan, now cast aside by England, continuing to thrive in club football, he turned the promotion dream into reality with 27 goals in 1983-84. The celebrations, however, were tinged with sadness, for in mid-season Keegan had announced that he would be retiring from competitive football in May.

Geordie fans sang with great gusto at Wembley, in 1951 and 1952, when their club became the first this century to take the FA Cup in successive seasons. In 1955 they won it again, for the sixth time, but their 100 per cent Wembley record ended in 1974, when United lost 3-0 to Liverpool in their record eleventh FA Cup Final.

After the Second World War Tyneside roared to the sharpshooting of 'Wor Jackie' Milburn, who scored 178 League goals (the club aggregate record) from 1946-57. Together with full-back Bob Cowell and left-winger Bobby Mitchell, he played in the Cup-winning teams of 1951, 1952 and 1955.

League Champions: 1904-05, 1906-07, 1908-09, 1926-27.
Division 2 Champions: 1964-65.
FA Cup Winners: 1909-10, 1923-24, 1931-32, 1950-51, 1951-52, 1954-55.
European Fairs Cup Winners: 1968-69.
Record attendance: 68,386 v Chelsea (League), September 1930.
Modern Capacity: 38,000. **Nickname:** 'Magpies'.
Entered Football League: 1893 — Div. 2.
Biggest win: 13-0 v Newport County (Div. 2), October 1946.
Heaviest defeat: 0-9 v Burton Wanderers (Div. 2), April 1895.
Best in League/Milk Cup: Final 1975-76.
Pitch measurements: 115 x 75 yd.
Highest League Scorer in Single Season: Hughie Gallacher — 36 in 1926-27 (Div. 1).
Highest transfer fee paid: £250,000 — John Trewick (from WBA), December 1980.
Highest transfer fee received: £500,000 — Peter Withe (to Aston Villa), May 1980.

Newport County

Somerton Park, Newport, Gwent NPT OHZ
Tel: 0633-277543   **Colours:** *Amber & Black*

Supporters of Newport County still wonder what the club might have achieved but for the outbreak of the Second World War. Their speculation is understandable for in 1938-39, the last full League season before hostilities, Newport won the Division Three South Championship in confident style.

But when, after a seven-year wait, League football resumed in 1946-47, they faced the Second Division with a reshaped team and were promptly relegated. They finished bottom with only 23 points from the 42 fixtures, and conceded 133 goals. At Newcastle, on 5 October 1946, County crashed 13-0, and Len Shackleton scored six of them. That equalled what is still the heaviest Football League defeat (Stockport County 13, Halifax Town 0 in Division Three North on 6 January 1934).

From 1962 until 1980 they remained members of the Fourth Division. Then, managed by Len Ashurst, they played some of the best football in their history, and County's record run of ten successive League victories helped them finish third and win promotion for the first time since 1939.

For clubs such as Newport who are constantly beset by financial problems, a run in the FA Cup can be a boon. Unfortunately, such occasions have been rare, though in 1949 Newport reached the fifth round before losing, a little unluckily, 3-2 at Portsmouth.

In 1982-83, Newport possessed the highest scorer in the four divisions in Tommy Tynan, whose 31 goals comprised 25 League, 4 FA Cup and 2 Milk Cup. The following season John Aldridge scored 26 for County before his £70,000 transfer to Oxford in March.

Division 3 (South) Champions: 1938-39.
Record attendance: 24,268 v Cardiff City (League), October 1937.
Modern Capacity: 18,000. **Nickname:** 'Ironsides'.
Entered Football League: 1920 — Div. 3.
Biggest win: 10-0 v Merthyr Town (Div. 3 South), April 1930.
Heaviest defeat: 0-13 v Newcastle United (Div. 2), October 1946.
Best in FA Cup: 5th Round 1948-49.
Best in League/Milk Cup: 3rd Round 1962-63.
Pitch measurements: 110 x 75 yd.
Highest League Scorer in Single Season: Tudor Martin — 34 in 1929-30 (Div. 3 South).
Highest transfer fee paid: £80,000 — Alan Waddle (from Swansea), January 1981.
Highest transfer fee received: £70,000 — John Aldridge (to Oxford Utd.), March 1984.

Northampton Town

County Ground, Abington Avenue, Northampton NN1 4PS
Tel: 0604-31553 **Colours:** *Maroon & White*

Northampton Town are always assured of one significant entry in the history of the Football League. In 1965 they became the first club to rise from the Fourth to the First Division, a feat they achieved in five remarkable seasons. The tragedy was that their return to the lowest reaches of the League should be even swifter. They lasted only one season in Division One and, almost unbelievably, by 1969 were back in Division Four.

The club first tasted success as Southern League champions in 1909 and the man who guided them to that triumph was Herbert Chapman, later to win managerial fame with Huddersfield Town and Arsenal. Strangely, that was Northampton's only notable football prize until they took the Division Three title in 1962-63.

Dave Bowen, the former Wales and Arsenal wing-half, who managed the club through most of the vicissitudes to the 1970s, Cliff Holton, another previously with Arsenal, Ron Flowers and Jack English are just a few of the experienced players who have starred for the 'Cobblers', whose ground is also the home of Northamptonshire County Cricket Club.

That means Northampton have a three-sided ground, the only one of its kind in the four divisions since Yorkshire stopped sharing Bramall Lane with Sheffield United. Another distinction for Town is that their pitch is the longest in the Football League at 120 yards.

The previous highest fee Town had received for a player (£60,000 when future England full-back Phil Neal was transferred to Liverpool in October 1974) was trebled in November 1979, when Cambridge United paid £180,000 for striker George Reilly, a record for Div. 4.

Division 3 Champions: 1962-63.
Record attendance: 24,523 v Fulham (League), April 1966.
Modern Capacity: 17,000. **Nickname:** 'Cobblers'.
Entered Football League: 1920 — Div. 3.
Biggest win: 10-0 v Walsall (Div. 3 South), November 1927.
Heaviest defeat: 0-11 v Southampton (Southern League), December 1901.
Best in FA Cup: 5th Round 1933-34, 1949-50, 1969-70.
Best in League/Milk Cup: 5th Round 1964-65, 1966-67.
Pitch measurements: 120 x 75 yd.
Highest League Scorer in Single Season: Cliff Holton — 36 in 1961-62 (Div. 3).
Highest transfer fee paid: £50,000 — Steve Phillips (from Brentford), August 1980.
Highest transfer fee received: £180,000 — George Reilly (to Cambridge United), November 1979.

Norwich City

Carrow Road, Norwich NR1 1JE
Tel: 0603-612131   **Colours:** *Yellow & Green*

The seventies were the most significant years in Norwich City's history. In 1972 they reached Division One for the first time; in 1973 manager Ron Saunders took them to a first Wembley appearance (they lost the League Cup Final to Tottenham, 1–0); season 1973–74, during which Saunders moved to Manchester City, ended with the 'Canaries' dropping back into Division Two, and a year later, under John Bond, they were back in the top section.

Their greatest FA Cup run came in 1959 when, as a Third Division side, they knocked out Manchester United, Cardiff, Tottenham and Sheffield United before losing 1–0 to Luton after a 1–1 draw in the semi-final.

Norwich, given the nickname 'Canaries' when they adopted their green and yellow colours, and moved to a ground called 'The Nest' in 1908, were founder-members of Division Three (South) in 1920. They won promotion to Division Two in 1934, but were relegated in 1939 and stayed down until 1960.

In March 1980 the previous record transfer fee received by Norwich leapt from £175,000 to £1,250,000 when they transferred striker Kevin Reeves to Manchester City. Another £1m departure was Justin Fashanu to Nottingham Forest in August 1981.

That sale followed relegation at the end of Ken Brown's first season, but he never lost his smile. City looked remote promotion hopes at 13th place in mid-March, but they then produced a storming run of 11 wins in 13 games and snatched third place.

Division 2 Champions: 1971–72.
Division 3 (South) Champions: 1933–34.
League Cup Winners: 1961–62.
Record attendance: 43,984 v Leicester City (FA Cup), March 1963.
Modern Capacity: 30,000. **Nickname:** 'Canaries'.
Entered Football League: 1920 — Div .3.
Biggest win: 10–2 v Coventry (Div. 3 South), March 1930.
Heaviest defeat: 2–10 v Swindon Town (Southern League), September 1908.
Best in FA Cup: Semi-final 1958–59.
Pitch measurements: 114 x 74 yd.
Highest League Scorer in Single Season: Ralph Hunt — 31 in 1955–56 (Div. 3 South).
Highest transfer fee paid: £300,000 — Drazan Muzinic (from Hajduk Split, Yugoslavia), August 1980.
Highest transfer fee received: £1,250,000 — Kevin Reeves (to Man. City), March 1980.

Nottingham Forest

City Ground, Nottingham NG2 5FJ
Tel: 0602-822202   **Colours:** *Red & White*

Forest were founded in 1865, and are the third-oldest League club after Notts County and Stoke City. In various ways, they helped shape the game's early history. For instance, their England International Sam Widdowson was the first player to wear shinguards, in 1874. It was in a Forest game four years later that a referee used a whistle for the first time — previously signals were given by a handkerchief — and in 1891 the crossbar and nets made their first appearance in soccer, at the Forest ground.

All that is ancient Forest history. In modern times they have become one of Britain's most successful clubs under the management of Brian Clough. In successive seasons they won double honours — the League Championship and League Cup (both for the first time) in 1977-78 and a year later the European Cup and League Cup.

In February 1979, Forest made striker Trevor Francis the first million-pound footballer in Britain, when they paid Birmingham £1,180,000 for his transfer. Three months later he scored the goal that beat Malmo in Munich to retain for Britain the European Cup that Liverpool had held for two years.

Forest began the eighties by beating Barcelona to win the European Super Cup and they again emulated Liverpool by winning the European Cup for the second successive year.

League Champions: 1977-78.
Division 2 Champions: 1906-07, 1921-22.
Division 3 (South) Champions: 1950-51.
FA Cup Winners: 1897-98, 1958-59.
European Cup Winners: 1978-79, 1979-80.
League Cup Winners: 1977-78, 1978-79.
European Super Cup Winners: 1979-80.
Record attendance: 49,945 v Manchester United (League), October 1967. **Modern Capacity:** 35,000.
Entered Football League: 1892 — Div. 1.
Biggest win: 14-0 v Clapton (FA Cup), 1890-91.
Heaviest defeat: 1-9 v Blackburn Rovers (Div. 2), April 1937.
Pitch measurements: 115 x 78 yd.
Highest League Scorer in Single Season: Wally Ardron — 36 in 1950-51 (Div. 3 South).
Highest transfer fee paid: £1,250,000 — Ian Wallace (from Coventry City), July 1980.
Highest transfer fee received: £1,250,000 — Garry Birtles (to Manchester United), October 1980.

Notts County

Meadow Lane, Nottingham NG2 6AG
Tel: 0602-861155 **Colours:** *Black & White*

Notts County are the oldest club in the Football League, formed in 1862 and founder members of the League in 1888. Twice in the next six years they reached the final of the FA Cup. They lost 3–1 to Blackburn Rovers at Kennington Oval in 1891, but in 1894 they won the trophy by beating Bolton Wanderers 4–1 at Everton.

Few events in County's chequered history have caused greater comment than the sensational signing of centre-forward Tommy Lawton from Chelsea in November 1947 for £20,000, a figure which few clubs, let alone a Third Division side, could afford in those days.

Jackie Sewell went from Meadow Lane to Sheffield Wednesday in March 1951, for the then record fee of £34,500, after scoring nearly 100 League goals. Another remarkable County character was the 6ft 5in Albert Iremonger, rated by some as the finest goalkeeper never to play for England. He made 564 League appearances for the club from 1904–26.

From 1967–71 County were down in the Fourth Division. Ten years later they were back in the First after an absence of 55 seasons.

But with Forest only just across Trent Bridge, County struggled to survive — as much against public apathy as against opponents. With gates falling below 6,000 in 1984 and debts of £1m., relegation to Division Two surprised no-one.

Division 2 Champions: 1896–97, 1913–14, 1922–23.
Division 3 (South) Champions: 1930–31, 1949–50.
Division 4 Champions: 1970–71.
FA Cup Winners: 1893–94.
Record attendance: 47,301 v York (FA Cup), March 1955.
Modern Capacity: 23,500. **Nickname:** 'Magpies'.
Entered Football League: 1888 — Div. 1.
Biggest win: 11–1 Newport County (Div. 3 South), January 1949.
Heaviest defeats: 1–9 v Aston Villa (Div. 1) September 1888; 1–9 v Blackburn Rovers (Div. 1), November 1889; 1–9 v Portsmouth (Div. 2), April 1927.
Best in League/Milk Cup: 5th Round 1963–64, 1972–73, 1975–76.
Pitch measurements: 117 x 76 yd.
Highest League Scorer in Single Season: Tom Keetley — 39 in 1930–31 (Div. 3 South).
Highest transfer fee paid: £480,000 — John Chiedozie (from Orient), August 1981.
Highest transfer fee received: £150,000 — Mick Vinter (to Wrexham), June 1979.

Oldham Athletic

Boundary Park, Oldham, Lancs. OL1 2PA
Tel: 061-624-8110 **Colours:** *Blue & White*

It may not be generally appreciated by modern followers of the game that from 1910-23 Oldham Athletic played in the First Division and missed the League Championship title by only one point in 1915. In modern times, despite modest resources — with attendances below 4,000 on occasions — the club ended 1983-84 with the Second Division's longest current membership (ten seasons).

Eric Gemmell performed a notable goalscoring feat for Oldham in season 1951-52. Playing in a Third Division North match against Chester, he scored seven times in an 11-2 win.

In addition to developing goalscorers, Oldham have found a number of international goalkeepers, notably Jack Hacking, Ted Taylor, Albert Gray and Frank Moss, who was one of seven Arsenal players capped by England against Italy in 1934.

Season 1970-71 was special in two ways for Oldham. They earned promotion to Division Three and their players also won the one-season Ford Sporting League, bringing the club total prize money of £80,000 for the improvement of spectator facilities.

With a late-season flourish, Oldham snatched the Third Division Championship of 1973-74, returning to the Second Division after an interval of twenty years. Jimmy Frizzell was the successful manager, and he served the club for 27 years (15 as player) until he was replaced in June 1982 by Joe Royle, the former Everton and England striker.

Division 3 (North) Champions: 1952-53.
Division 3 Champions: 1973-74.
Record attendance: 47,671 v Sheffield Wednesday (FA Cup), January 1930.
Modern Capacity: 26,300.
Entered Football League: 1907 — Div. 2.
Biggest win: 11-0 v Southport (Div. 4), December 1962.
Heaviest defeat: 4-13 v Tranmere (Div. 3 North), December 1935.
Best in FA Cup: Semi-final 1912-13.
Best in League/Milk Cup: 3rd Round 1981-82, 1983-84.
Pitch measurements: 110 x 74 yd.
Highest League Scorer in Single Season: Tom Davis — 33 in 1936-37 (Div. 3 North).
Highest transfer fee paid: £200,000 — Ken Clements (from Man. City), September 1979.
Highest transfer fee received: £300,000 — Simon Stainrod (to QPR), November 1980.

Orient

Leyton Stadium, Brisbane Road, London E10 5NE
Tel: 01-539-2223 **Colours:** *All Red*

The club owe their name to the Orient Shipping Company. They
were formed in 1881 as Clapton Orient, became Leyton Orient in
1946 and dropped the prefix 'Leyton' in 1967. Orient made their
home at Brisbane Road in 1937, having previously shared Clapton
greyhound stadium, the Essex cricket ground at Leyton and the old
Lea Bridge speedway stadium.

Alec Stock, who had three spells in charge, took them to second
place in Division Three South in 1955 and up into Division Two as
Champions 12 months later. In 1962 they gained promotion with
Liverpool to Division One, but survived only one season.

In 1978, managed by Jimmy Bloomfield in his second spell with
the club, Orient had their finest FA Cup run, beating three First
Division sides before losing to Arsenal in the semi-final at Stamford
Bridge.

They just missed Wembley then, but had actually played two
home League games (against Brentford and Southend) there in
November 1930 when ground problems at Lea Bridge caused them
to seek temporary accommodation elsewhere.

Situated halfway between First Division West Ham and
Tottenham, Orient have struggled increasingly for support. In
1983-84 their gates fell to barely 2,000.

It was not the first time Orient's existence had been under threat.
In October 1970, with debts of £100,000 (an alarming figure in those
days), a public meeting was called, and a generous response, plus
the transfer of centre-half Tommy Taylor to West Ham for £100,000,
solved immediate difficulties.

Division 3 (South) Champions: 1955–56.
Division 3 Champions: 1969–70.
Record attendance: 34,345 v West Ham United (FA Cup), January
1964. **Modern Capacity:** 26,500. **Nickname:** 'O's'.
Entered Football League: 1905 — Div. 2 (as Clapton Orient).
Biggest wins: 9-2 v Aldershot (Div. 3 South), February 1934; 9-2 v
Chester (League Cup), October 1962.
Heaviest defeat: 0-8 v Aston Villa (FA Cup), January 1929.
Best in FA Cup: Semi-final 1977–78.
Best in League/Milk Cup: 5th Round 1962–63.
Pitch measurements: 110 x 80 yd.
Highest League Scorer in Single Season: Tom Johnston — 35 in
1957–58 (Div. 2).
Highest transfer fee paid: £150,000 — Peter Taylor (from
Tottenham), November 1980.
Highest transfer fee received: £480,000 — John Chiedozie (to Notts
County), August 1981.

Oxford United

Manor Ground, Headington, Oxford OX3 7RS
Tel: 0865-61503   **Colours:** *Yellow & Blue*

The early eighties have been notable for extraordinary happenings at the Manor Ground, rural home of one of League football's newer members. In 1981, Oxford United were saved from bankruptcy by millionaire publisher Robert Maxwell taking control, and in the spring of 1983 he announced that Oxford and Reading were to be merged into one club, to be known as Thames Valley Royals.

Amid protest marches in Oxford and fierce resistance from Reading, both clubs retained their identity, and Oxford's fortunes rocketed in 1983–84. While steadily mounting a promotion effort, they embarked on long runs in the two domestic cups.

First, in the Milk Cup, they knocked out Bristol City, Newcastle, Leeds and, after two replays, Manchester United, before losing in a fifth round replay away to Everton. Increased prices round by round meant that Oxford's receipts record was smashed at five successive home ties and an exciting FA Cup effort lasted until the fifth round.

Then, when all the cup excitement was over, manager Jim Smith and his men got back to the business of winning promotion back to the Second Division Oxford had left in 1976.

Oxford United were formed in 1896 as Headington United but did not turn professional until 1949. They took their present name in 1961 and, after Accrington Stanley withdrew from Division Four a year later, Oxford got the chance of League status, quickly proving themselves worthy of it. In 1964 they became the first Fourth Division side to reach the sixth round of the FA Cup, and in only six seasons of League membership they climbed two divisions.

Division 3 Champions: 1967–68, 1983–84.
Record attendance: 22,730 v Preston NE (FA Cup), February 1964.
Modern Capacity: 17,350.   **Entered Football League:** 1962 — Div. 4.
Biggest win: 7–0 v Barrow (Div. 4), December 1964.
Heaviest defeats: 0–5 v Cardiff (Div. 2), February 1969; 0–5 v Cardiff (Div. 2), September 1973; 0–5 v Nottingham Forest (League Cup), October 1978.   **Best in FA Cup:** 6th Round 1963–64.
Best in League/Milk Cup: 5th Round 1969–70, 1983–84.
Pitch measurements: 112 x 78 yd.
Highest League Scorer in Single Season: Colin Booth — 23 in 1964–65 (Div. 4).
Highest transfer fee paid: £70,000 — Andy McCulloch (from Cardiff), June 1974.
Highest transfer fee received: £100,000 — Les Taylor (to Watford), November 1980.

Peterborough United

London Road, Peterborough PE2 8AL
Tel: 0733-63947 **Colours:** *Blue & White*

When Peterborough United, an ambitious Southern League club with a splendidly appointed ground, won admission to the Football League in 1960-61, the cynics wondered whether they were really equipped to bridge the gap between the two grades of football. The 'Posh', as they are familiarly known, gave the best possible answer: they won the Fourth Division Championship at the first attempt, and in record-breaking style.

Terry Bly was the chief destroyer of defences in Peterborough's first season in League football. His tally of 52 goals in 46 games remains the highest for the division — no other player has topped 50 League goals for any club in post-war football — and the 134 goals obtained by Peterborough is a record for any division of the Football League. Will it ever be beaten?

In 1965, Peterborough reached the sixth round of the FA Cup, beating Salisbury, Queens Park Rangers, Chesterfield, Arsenal and Swansea before losing to Chelsea.

In terms of football progress, few clubs new to the League had advanced so far in such a short time, but in 1968 the club was demoted to the Fourth Division because of alleged irregularities in their books. At the end of his second season in 1974, manager Noel Cantwell had inspired another Peterborough promotion success as Fourth Division winners, but their next stay in Division Three lasted only five years.

They have finished well in the top half of the table in all five seasons since, without quite managing to get back among the promotion-winning teams at the finishing line.

Division 4 Champions: 1960-61, 1973-74.
Record attendance: 30,096 v Swansea (FA Cup), February 1965.
Modern Capacity: 28,000. **Nickname:** 'Posh'.
Entered Football League: 1960 — Div. 4.
Biggest win: 8-1 v Oldham Athletic (Div. 4), November 1969.
Heaviest defeat: 1-8 v Northampton (FA Cup), December 1946.
Best in FA Cup: 6th Round 1964-65.
Best in League/Milk Cup: Semi-final 1965-66.
Pitch measurements: 113 x 76 yd.
Highest League Scorer in Single Season: Terry Bly — 52 in 1960-61 (Div. 4).
Highest transfer fee paid: £60,000 — Bill Green (from West Ham), July 1978.
Highest transfer fee received: £135,000 — Bob Doyle (to Blackpool), July 1979.

Plymouth Argyle

Home Park, Plymouth PL2 1BQ
Tel: 0752-52561   **Colours:** *Green, Black & White*

For as long as Sir Francis Drake's statue looks out over Plymouth
Hoe, they will talk in Devon of Argyle's achievements in 1983-84,
when a team not sure of their Third Division place took the club
further than they had ever been in the FA Cup.

Wins against Southend, Barking, Newport and Darlington carried
Plymouth through the first four rounds. Then a solitary goal by
Tommy Tynan, away to First Division WBA, sent them into the
quarter-finals for the first time.

There, after a 0-0 draw at home to Derby — watched by Home
Park's biggest crowd (34,365) for nine years — a goal direct from
Andy Rogers' swerving corner-kick won the replay. Nobody enjoyed
that moment more than Plymouth's best-known supporter, former
Labour leader, Michael Foot.

So Argyle became only the sixth Third Division team to reach the
FA Cup semi-final, in which they lost by a solitary goal to Watford at
Villa Park.

Only six months before, John Hore (a former Argyle player) was
part-time manager of Bideford, in the Western League. Then Bobby
Moncur resigned at Home Park and Hore, a Cornishman, took
charge of his old club, launching them on their historic Cup run.

Plymouth achieved some extraordinary feats in their early days in
the old Southern Section of the Third Division. For six consecutive
years between 1921 and 1927 they finished runners-up, twice
missing promotion by a point and once on goal average. The
reward for consistency was finally earned in 1930 when Argyle took
the title with unmistakable authority, finishing seven points clear.

Division 3 (South) Champions: 1929-30, 1951-52.
Division 3 Champions: 1958-59.
Record attendance: 43,596 v Aston Villa (League), October 1936.
Modern Capacity: 38,000. **Nickname:** 'Pilgrims'.
Entered Football League: 1920 — Div. 3.
Biggest win: 8-1 v Millwall (Div. 2), January 1932.
Heaviest defeat: 0-9 v Stoke City (Div. 2), December 1960.
Best in FA Cup: Semi-final 1983-84.
Best in League/Milk Cup: Semi-final 1964-65, 1973-74.
Pitch measurements: 112 x 75 yd.
Highest League Scorer in Single Season: Jack Cock — 32 in
1925-26 (Div. 3 South).
Highest transfer fee paid: £75,000 — David Kemp (from Carlisle),
September 1979.
Highest transfer fee received: £250,000 — Gary Megson (to Everton),
February 1980.

Portsmouth

Fratton Park, Frogmore Road, Portsmouth
Tel: 0705-731204   **Colours:** *Blue & White*

Portsmouth spent 32 consecutive years in Division One after gaining promotion in 1927 on the strength of a goal average that was 1/250th of a goal better than Manchester City's. Elevation to football's top flight was to be the launching pad for a catalogue of League and Cup successes. Portsmouth were defeated in the 1929 and 1934 FA Cup Finals, but shocked Wolves in the 1939 Final.

With war then breaking out, they achieved the distinction (as still its once-only winners) of keeping the trophy in their possession for seven years — longer than any other club has ever held it.

The famous 'Pompey Chimes' rang out across Fratton Park as the League title was won in 1949, and Portsmouth successfully defended the following season, becoming only the eighth club in the history of the game to complete such a double.

Thus Portsmouth were the first former Third Division club to win the Championship, but their star waned dramatically. They dropped to Division Two in 1959 and to the Third two years later, but returned first time as Third Division Champions in 1962.

Between 1946 and 1965 Jimmy Dickinson, England half-back in 48 post-war internationals, set a then British record with 764 League appearances — all for Portsmouth.

In 1978 they dropped to Division Four, but two seasons later the 'Pompey Chimes' were heard again as Portsmouth clinched promotion and in 1983 they became the first club to win the Third Division championship twice.

League Champions: 1948–49, 1949–50.
Division 3 (South) Champions: 1923–24.
Division 3 Champions: 1961–62, 1982–83.
FA Cup Winners: 1938–39.
Record attendance: 51,385 v Derby County (FA Cup), February 1949. **Modern Capacity:** 40,000. **Nickname:** 'Pompey'.
Entered Football League: 1920 — Div. 3.
Biggest win: 9–1 v Notts County (Div. 2), April 1927.
Heaviest defeat: 0–10 v Leicester City (Div. 1), October 1928.
Best in League/Milk Cup: 5th Round 1960–61.
Pitch measurements: 116 x 72 yd.
Highest League Scorer in Single Season: Billy Haines — 40 in 1926–27 (Div. 2).
Highest transfer fee paid: £200,000 — Kevin Dillon (from Birmingham), March 1983.
Highest transfer fee received: £130,000 — Steve Foster (to Brighton), June 1979.

Port Vale

Vale Park, Burslem, Stoke-on-Trent ST6 1AW
Tel: 0782-814134   **Colours:** *White & Black*

Port Vale nearly wrote a fresh page in the history of the FA Cup in 1954. No Third Division club has reached the final, but Vale, caught up on a wave of enthusiasm which spread far beyond the Potteries, beat Queens Park Rangers away (1-0), Cardiff away (2-0), Blackpool at home (2-0) and Leyton Orient away (1-0) on their way to the semi-finals. Before a crowd of 68,221 at Villa Park, they faced their Staffordshire neighbours and famed Cup fighters, West Bromwich Albion and, incredibly, led until the second half. Albion triumphed 2-1, but as consolation Port Vale won the Third North title that season by a margin of eleven points.

A number of players have given Vale outstanding service, but none more so than local-born Roy Sproson who made 762 League appearances between 1950 and 1972. He was a member of the sides which won the Third Division (North) in 1953-54, the Fourth Division title in 1958-59 and was still an ever-present defender in the team which again won promotion to the Third Division in 1970.

They went up once more in 1983, despite having sold, at the start of that season, the coloured Chamberlain brothers, Mark and Neville, to First Division neighbours Stoke City. The fee of £150,000 for winger Mark was a Fourth Division record, and four months later he was scoring for England at Wembley.

The club have played at Vale Park since 1950, and the list of post-war managers includes such well-known names as Freddie Steele, Sir Stanley Matthews and Jackie Mudie.

Division 3 (North) Champions: 1929-30, 1953-54.
Division 4 Champions: 1958-59.
Record attendance: 50,000 v Aston Villa (FA Cup), February 1960.
Modern Capacity: 35,000. **Nickname:** 'Valiants'
Entered Football League: 1892 — Div. 2.
Biggest win: 9-1 v Chesterfield (Div. 2), September 1932.
Heaviest defeats: 0-10 v Sheffield United (Div. 2), December 1892; 0-10 v Notts County (Div. 2), February 1895.
Best in FA Cup: Semi-final 1953-54.
Best in League/Milk Cup: 2nd Round 1960-61, 1962-63, 1963-64, 1967-68, 1972-73, 1981-82, 1983-84.
Pitch measurements: 116 x 76 yd.
Highest League Scorer in Single Season: Wilf Kirkham — 38 in 1926-27 (Div 2).
Highest transfer fee paid: £40,000 — Peter Farrell (from Bury), November 1978; £40,000 — Paul Bowles (from Crewe), October 1979.
Highest transfer fee received: £150,000 — Mark Chamberlain (to Stoke), August 1982.

Preston North End

Deepdale, Preston PR1 6RU
Tel: 0772-795919   **Colours:** *White & Navy Blue*

Preston North End won the first League Championship of all in 1888–89 without losing a match, and the FA Cup the same season without conceding a goal — a 'double' without parallel.

Founder members of the League, Preston justified their title 'Invincibles' until they were relegated in 1901. They returned in 1904, continuing to move ten times up and down between the divisions until, for the first time in their history, in 1970, they found themselves in Division Three.

After being beaten by Sunderland in the 1937 FA Cup Final, Preston carried off the trophy in 1938 when George Mutch gave them a 1-0 victory over Huddersfield from the penalty spot with the last kick of Wembley's first extra-time Final.

Tom Finney, who made 433 League appearances (187 goals) and won 76 England caps, was the outstanding figure in Preston football from 1946-60.

Since the club left the First Division in 1961, they have had three spells in the Second Division and three in the Third. By February 1984, with crowds down to 3,000, the financial position at Deepdale was at crisis point; £250,000 was needed for survival, and a public appeal was launched to save one of football's most famous clubs.

It was all a far cry from the illustrious playing days of Tom Finney, OBE, JP, (now president) and the 'Proud Preston' era of the last century.

The Double (League Champions, FA Cup Winners): 1888-89.
League Champions: 1888-89, 1889-90.
Division 2 Champions: 1903-04, 1912-13, 1950-51.
Division 3 Champions: 1970-71.
FA Cup Winners: 1888-89, 1937-38.
Record attendance: 42,684 v Arsenal (League), April 1938.
Modern Capacity: 25,000.
Entered Football League: 1888 — Div. 1.
Biggest win: 26-0 v Hyde (FA Cup), October 1887.
Heaviest defeat: 0-7 v Blackpool (Div. 1), May 1948.
Best in League/Milk Cup: 4th Round 1962-63, 1965-66, 1971-72, 1980-81.
Pitch measurements: 112 x 78 yd.
Highest League Scorer in Single Season: Ted Harper — 37 in 1932-33 (Div. 2).
Highest transfer fee paid: £95,000 — Steve Elliott (from Nott'm Forest), March 1979.
Highest transfer fee received: £756,000 — Michael Robinson (to Man. City), June 1979.

Queens Park Rangers

Rangers Stadium, Shepherd's Bush, London W12 7PA
Tel: 01-743 0262   **Colours:** *Blue & White*

Rangers brought revolution to Football League pitches when, in the summer of 1981, they put down an artificial surface at their compact West London home. It cost £350,000 — a modest sum at a time when million-pound transfers were the vogue — and their enterprise was rapidly rewarded. Rangers reached their first FA Cup Final in 1982, taking Tottenham to a Wembley replay, and a year later they ran away with the Second Division by a margin of ten points.

There was little doubt that the Omniturf pitch, with its fast surface and excessive bounce, gave Rangers an advantage. That was borne out by the high percentage of home wins, but they were a good side on grass, too — their away record on the way to promotion in season 1982-83 was the best in the division. Terry Venables, team manager and managing director, had put together a 'side for all seasons', but few visiting teams (the rare winners among them) went away from Loftus Road happy about the surface.

Season 1966-67 will always be recalled as a vintage one by Rangers supporters. The club not only took the Third Division title by twelve points, but became the first outside the first two divisions to win the Football League Cup. In a thrilling decider at Wembley — the first time that venue was used for the League Cup — Rangers beat First Division opponents West Bromwich Albion 3-2 after being two down.

The magic continued under Alec Stock's managership and the following year Rangers moved up to Division One — thus emulating Charlton's feat (1935 and 1936) of climbing from Third to First Division in consecutive years.

Division 2 Champions: 1982-83.
Division 3 (South) Champions: 1947-48.
Division 3 Champions: 1966-67.
League Cup Winners: 1966-67.
Record attendance: 35,353 v Leeds (League), April 1974.
Modern Capacity: 27,000. **Entered Football League:** 1920 — Div. 3.
Biggest win: 9-2 v Tranmere Rovers (Div. 3), December 1960.
Heaviest defeats: 1-8 v Mansfield Town (Div. 3), March 1965; 1-8 v Manchester United (Div. 1), March 1969.
Best in FA Cup: Final 1981-82. **Pitch measurements:** 112 x 72 yd.
Highest League Scorer in Single Season: George Goddard — 37 in 1929-30 (Div. 3 South).
Highest transfer fee paid: £400,000 — Tony Currie (from Sheffield United), August 1979.
Highest transfer fee received: £1,250,000 — Clive Allen (to Arsenal), June 1980.

Reading

Elm Park, Reading RG3 2EF
Tel: 0734-507878 **Colours:** *Blue & White*

The Berkshire club were 100 years old in 1971, but far from celebrating their centenary in style, they were relegated to Division Four for the first time. In the last eight seasons before the war they never finished lower than sixth in Division Three (South) and twice were runners-up. When the Football League resumed in 1946 they twice more occupied second place in 1949 and 1952.

Many splendid players have served the club, among them Jack Palethorpe, who later scored in Sheffield Wednesday's Cup-winning side at Wembley in 1935; W. H. McConnell, an Ireland cap; Tony McPhee, a clever, goalscoring leader; George Marks, later Arsenal's goalkeeper; Pat McConnell, another Irish international; Maurice Edelston, an England Amateur international; and Ronnie Blackman, whose 156 League goals between 1947-54 stand as a record for the club.

A five-season stay in the Fourth Division ended in 1976, when Reading were promoted with one of the best home records in the country. They went up 50 years after their previous promotion — to the Second Division in 1926. In 1977 they slipped back into Division Four, but two years later they finished top for only the second championship success in their history.

After Reading were relegated again to Division Four in 1983, a new board spiritedly fought off a proposed amalgamation with Oxford United. Financial needs forced the departure of the Third Division's 1982-83 top marksman, Kerry Dixon, to Chelsea for £150,000 — a Reading record — and for £35,000 they replaced him with Trevor Senior, from Portsmouth. His 36 League goals helped them win immediate promotion.

Division 3 (South) Champions: 1925-26.
Division 4 Champions: 1978-79.
Record attendance: 33,042 v Brentford (FA Cup), February 1927.
Modern Capacity: 27,200. **Nickname:** 'Royals'.
Entered Football League: 1920 — Div. 3.
Biggest win: 10-2 v Crystal Palace (Div. 3 South), September 1946.
Heaviest defeat: 0-18 v Preston NE (FA Cup), 1893-94.
Best in FA Cup: Semi-final 1926-27.
Best in League/Milk Cup: 4th Round 1964-65, 1965-66, 1978-79.
Pitch measurements: 112 x 75 yd.
Highest League Scorer in Single Season: Ronnie Blackman — 39 in 1951-52 (Div. 3 South).
Highest transfer fee paid: £50,000 — Dave Shipperley (from Charlton), September 1979.
Highest transfer fee received: £150,000 — Kerry Dixon (to Chelsea), August 1983.

Rochdale

Spotland, Sandy Lane, Rochdale OL11 5DR
Tel: 0706-44648 **Colours:** *Blue & White*

Rochdale is still more famous as the birthplace of Gracie Fields than for the deeds of its football team, but it says much for the resolution and perseverance of those associated with the club that they have remained in continuous membership of the Football League since being elected to the Northern Section in 1921.

In 1931–32 they failed to win a Division Three (North) match after 7 November. They played 26 matches, lost 25 and drew one, and a total of 33 defeats that season is the worst in League football, as is the sequence of 17 consecutive losses they included.

Another lowlight on Tuesday, 5 February 1974, was the smallest crowd for any post-war League fixture. The club refused to issue an official attendance against Cambridge that afternoon, but the estimate was 450. The season ended with Rochdale relegated to Division Four, and in 1980, they found themselves applying for re-election for the eighth time in their history. In all, they have finished bottom of the Football League five times.

Rochdale made a mark in the Football League Cup as runners-up to Norwich City in 1962; no other Division Four team has reached the Final. Another of Spotland's rare big days came in January 1971, when First Division Coventry City were beaten 2–1 in the third round of the FA Cup.

A boost to club finances came in November 1974 with the £40,000 transfer of Alan Taylor, and six months later he completed a storybook climb from Fourth Division to First by scoring West Ham's FA Cup-winning goals against Fulham at Wembley.

Record attendance: 24,231 v Notts County (FA Cup), Dec. 1949.
Modern Capacity: 20,000. **Nickname:** 'Dale'.
Entered Football League: 1921 — Div. 3 (North).
Biggest win: 8–1 v Chesterfield (Div. 3 North), December 1926.
Heaviest defeat: 1–9 v Tranmere (Div. 3 North), December 1931.
Highest final League position: Runners-up Div. 3 (North) 1923–24, 1926–27.
Best in FA Cup: 4th Round 1970–71.
Best in League/Milk Cup: Runners-up 1961–62.
Pitch measurements: 110 x 72 yd.
Highest League Scorer in Single Season: Albert Whitehurst — 44 in 1926–27 (Div. 3 North).
Highest transfer fee paid: £15,000 — Malcolm Darling (from Norwich), October 1971.
Highest transfer fee received: £40,000 — David Cross (to Norwich), Oct. 1971; £40,000 — Alan Taylor (to West Ham), November 1974.

Rotherham United

Millmoor Ground, Rotherham
Tel: 0709-562434   **Colours:** *Red & White*

Fortune has certainly played some unkind tricks on Rotherham United, none more so than in 1955, when, by winning eight of the last nine games and finally beating Liverpool 6-1, they finished level on points at the top of Division Two with Birmingham City and Luton Town. Yet, despite scoring more goals than their rivals, they missed a First Division place on goal average.

In the three seasons directly after the Second World War they were runners-up in Division Three North (only the Champions gained promotion). Their points totals were 64, 59 and 62, all enough to have won the divisional title in many another season.

Rotherham slipped to sixth the following season (1949-50), but a year later their perseverance paid off. They became Champions by seven points, but 17 seasons in the Second Division ended with relegation in 1968. Five years later they fell into the Fourth for two seasons.

Rotherham, in company with other small clubs, rely heavily on finding their own players. Among the best known have been Danny Williams, a stalwart defender who made 459 League appearances between 1946-60 and Wally Ardron, whose 38 League goals in 1946-47 are still a club record.

In 1981, United put the Third Division championship on their honours list, but that latest stay in Division Two lasted only two seasons.

Division 3 (North) Champions: 1950-51.
Division 3 Champions: 1980-81.
Record attendance: 25,000 v Sheffield Wednesday (League), January 1952; 25,000 v Sheffield United (League), December 1952.
Modern Capacity: 21,000. **Nickname:** 'Millers'.
Entered Football League: 1893 — Div. 2.
Biggest win: 8-0 v Oldham Athletic (Div. 3 North), May 1947.
Heaviest defeat: 1-11 v Bradford City (Div. 3 North), August 1928.
Best in FA Cup: 5th Round 1952-53, 1967-68.
Best in League/Milk Cup: Runners-up 1960-61.
Pitch measurements: 116 x 76 yd.
Highest League Scorer in Single Season: Wally Ardron — 38 in 1946-47 (Div. 3 North).
Highest transfer fee paid: £120,000 — Ronnie Moore (from Cardiff), August 1980.
Highest transfer fee received: £100,000 — Dave Watson (to Sunderland), December 1970.

Scunthorpe United

Old Show Ground, Scunthorpe DN15 7RH
Tel: 0724-848077   **Colours:** *Claret & Sky Blue*

Scunthorpe and Lindsey United were themselves surprised by the manner in which they were elected in 1950 at the time the Football League was extending both Northern and Southern Sections of the Third Division by two clubs. When the 'North' vote was taken Scunthorpe were not even placed second. Workington and Wigan tied and there was a fresh vote. At the new count Scunthorpe and Wigan tied, and it needed a third vote before the Midland League club won election. A few years later the name Lindsey was dropped from their title.

Scunthorpe were not long in justifying their place in higher company. After finishing third in 1954, and again in 1955, they won the Northern Section in 1958.

Scunthorpe came close to providing First Division football at their picturesquely-named Old Show Ground in 1962, when finishing fourth. In 1975 Scunthorpe finished bottom of the Football League, but after a ten-year absence they returned to Division Three in 1983.

Their longest-serving player was Jack Brownsword, who made 657 League and Cup appearances between 1950–65, and was the game's first full-back to score 50 League goals. Among modern stars, goalkeeper Ray Clemence and striker Kevin Keegan were produced by Scunthorpe.

By the early eighties, the most celebrated name on the books was that of England cricketer Ian Botham, whose all-round ability extended to the role of striker or centre-back for first team or reserves.

Division 3 (North) Champions: 1957–58.
Record attendance: 23,935 v Portsmouth (FA Cup), January 1954.
Modern Capacity: 25,000. **Nickname:** 'Irons'.
Entered Football League: 1950 — Div. 3 (North).
Biggest win: 9–0 v Boston United (FA Cup), November 1953.
Heaviest defeat: 0–8 v Carlisle United (Div. 3 North), December 1952.
Best in FA Cup: 5th Round 1957–58, 1969–70.
Best in League/Milk Cup: 3rd Round 1962–63, 1968–69.
Pitch measurements: 112 x 78 yd.
Highest League Scorer in Single Season: Barrie Thomas — 31 in 1961–62 (Div. 2).
Highest transfer fee paid: £25,000 — Rick Green (from Notts County), August 1979.
Highest transfer fee received: £60,000 — Kevin Kilmore (to Grimsby), September 1979.

Sheffield United

Bramall Lane, Sheffield S2 4SU
Tel: 0742-738955   **Colours:** *Red, White & Black*

For all their long Football League history, Sheffield United achieved their greatest feats in the FA Cup, winning the trophy four times by 1925.

In 1925–26 they headed the First Division scorers with 102 goals, beating Cardiff 11-2 and Manchester City 8-3. But after brief moments of glory in the 1920s, 'The Blades' lost their cutting edge and were relegated from the First Division in 1934. Five years later they just beat their neighbours, Wednesday, for second place in the Second Division.

The summer of 1973 marked the end of an era as Yorkshire CCC played at Bramall Lane for the last time, and United erected a magnificent stand on the side where for 118 years, the cricket square had been situated.

After finishing sixth in the First Division in 1975, United suddenly slumped, and with Wednesday in even worse trouble, Sheffield suffered its deepest gloom as a soccer city in season 1975–76. At the end, United were relegated (for the fourth time since the war) with only six wins and 22 points. Three years later they fell even further, joining Wednesday in the Third Division.

In 1982, a year after falling into the Fourth Division for the first time, United played themselves back into Division Three, and 1984 brought signs of true revival in Sheffield football, as Wednesday went up to the First and United completed the promotion double in Division Three.

League Champions: 1897–98.
Division 2 Champions: 1952–53.
Division 4 Champions: 1981–82.
FA Cup Winners: 1898-99, 1901-02, 1914-15, 1924-25.
Record attendance: 68,287 v Leeds (FA Cup), February 1936.
Modern Capacity: 49,000. **Nickname:** 'The Blades'.
Entered Football League: 1892 — Div. 2.
Biggest win: 11-2 v Cardiff City (Div. 1), January 1926.
Heaviest defeat: 0–13 v Bolton Wanderers (FA Cup), February 1890.
Best in League/Milk Cup: 5th Round 1961-62, 1966-67, 1971-72.
Pitch measurements: 115 x 73 yd.
Highest League Scorer in Single Season: Jimmy Dunne — 41 in 1930–31 (Div. 1).
Highest transfer fee paid: £160,000 — Alex Sabella (from River Plate, Argentina), July 1978; £160,000 — Alan Young (from Leicester), August 1982.
Highest transfer fee received: £400,000 — Alex Sabella (to Leeds), May 1980.

Sheffield Wednesday

Hillsborough, Sheffield S6 1SW
Tel: 0742-343123 **Colours:** *Blue & White*

When Jack Charlton resigned as manager in May 1983, Howard Wilkinson (from Notts County) replaced him — the return of a real Hillsborough man. Born in Sheffield, he supported Wednesday as a boy and as a player wore their colours for four years.

Under his guidance, Wednesday made their finest start to any season (18 games unbeaten — 14 wins, 4 draws), and it ended with the club back in the First Division after 14 years — as Second Division runners-up to Chelsea.

Wednesday reached a success peak between 1929 and 1935, winning the FA Cup and two League Championships, and finishing third in the First Division on four other occasions.

Wednesday's lavish ground, with seating for 23,500, was used for World Cup matches in 1966 and has staged many an FA Cup semi-final.

One of their most celebrated players was Derek Dooley, who scored 46 goals in season 1951–52 in 30 Division Two matches. A broken leg, which had to be amputated, ended his playing career the following season. He later managed the club.

From being a First Division club in 1970, Wednesday slumped to Division Three by 1975 and a year later missed the Fourth Division by only one place but, under the management of Jack Charlton, the club returned to Division Two in 1980. During that season, on Boxing Day 1979, a new Third Division record crowd of 49,309 saw Wednesday beat their neighbours, United, 4–0.

League Champions: 1902–03, 1903–04, 1928–29, 1929–30.
Division 2 Champions: 1899–1900, 1925–26, 1951–52, 1955–56, 1958–59.
FA Cup Winners: 1895–96, 1906–07, 1934–35.
Record attendance: 72,841 v Manchester City (FA Cup), February 1934. **Modern Capacity:** 50,000. **Nickname:** 'Owls'.
Entered Football League: 1892 — Div. 1.
Biggest win: 12–0 v Halliwell (FA Cup), January 1891.
Heaviest defeat: 0–10 v Aston Villa (Div. 1), October 1912.
Best in League/Milk Cup: 5th Round 1982–83, 1983–84.
Pitch measurements: 115 x 75 yd.
Highest League Scorer in Single Season: Derek Dooley — 46 in 1951–52 (Div. 2).
Highest transfer fee paid: £200,000 — Ante Mirocevic (from Olympic Ljubijana, Yugoslavia), August 1980.
Highest transfer fee received: £110,000 — Tommy Craig (to Newcastle), December 1974.

Shrewsbury Town

Gay Meadow, Shrewsbury SY2 6AB
Tel: 0743-60111 **Colours:** *Blue & Gold*

For 64 years Shrewsbury had been in existence, but it was not until 1950 that they were elected to membership of the Football League. They spent the first season in Division Three (North) but then switched to the Southern section, where they remained until the League was reorganized in season 1958–59.

Shrewsbury moved into Division Four and promptly won promotion by finishing fourth. By the end of season 1973–74 Town were back in Division Four, but were immediately promoted as runners-up and in 1979 they advanced into the Second Division for the first time, arriving there as Third Division Champions.

Staying in Division Two on a tight budget governed by gates sometimes below 4,000 has been a remarkable achievement under Graham Turner, who joined the club as a player in January 1973.

Arthur Rowley's League scoring record of 434 goals included 152 for Shrewsbury and he holds the club's single-season record with 38 in Division Four during 1958–59.

Shrewsbury have enjoyed years of comparative success, too, in the FA Cup, progressing to the fifth rounds in 1965 and 1966 and then, in 1979, reaching the sixth round for the first time before going out to Wolves in a replay. They are also four times winners of the Welsh Cup in 1891, 1938, 1977 and 1979.

There is one unusual facility at Shrewsbury on match days. A boat is always on standby, ready to retrieve the ball if it is kicked into the River Severn that flows past Gay Meadow.

Division 3 Champions: 1978–79.
Record attendance: 18,917 v Walsall (League), April 1961.
Modern Capacity: 18,000.
Entered Football League: 1950 — Div. 3 (North).
Biggest win: 7–0 v Swindon Town (Div. 3 South), May 1955.
Heaviest defeats: 1–8 v Norwich City (Div. 3 South), September 1952; 1–8 v Coventry City (Div. 3), October 1963.
Best in FA Cup: 6th Round 1978–79, 1981–82.
Best in League/Milk Cup: Semi-final 1960–61.
Pitch measurements: 116 x 74 yd.
Highest League Scorer in Single Season: Arthur Rowley — 38 in 1958–59 (Div. 4).
Highest transfer fee paid: £100,000 — John Dungworth (from Aldershot), October 1979.
Highest transfer fee received: £250,000 — Paul Maguire (to Stoke City), August 1980.

Southampton

The Dell, Southampton SO9 4XX
Tel: 0703-39633   **Colours:** *Red & White*

A new name went on the FA Cup in 1976 when Southampton, twice losing Finalists at the beginning of the century, became the third Second Division club to win the trophy at Wembley. (West Bromwich in 1931 and Sunderland in 1973 were the others.) A solitary goal by Bobby Stokes beat 3–1 on favourites Manchester United and brought about one of the biggest shocks in Cup Final history. The players who produced it under the genial Geordie managership of Lawrie McMenemy were: Turner, Rodrigues, Peach, Holmes, Blyth, Steele, Gilchrist, Channon, Osgood, McCalliog, Stokes.

Southampton's previous highest peak was in reaching the First Division in 1966. They retained top status until 1974 when they were partners in relegation with Manchester United, the club destined to be the shock victims of Saints' first appearance at Wembley.

First Division football returned in 1978 to The Dell, which has long been a home of sensible stewardship. Since the war, Southampton have had only five managers and Lawrie McMenemy, appointed in November 1973, is football's longest-serving manager.

Down the years, Southampton teams have included a generous quota of famous names, among them Ted Drake and Tom Parker, pre-war; Alf Ramsey, Bill Ellerington, Charlie Wayman, Terry Paine, Ron Davies, Alan Ball, Peter Shilton and Mick Mills.

FA Cup Winners: 1975–76.
Division 3 (South) Champions: 1921–22.
Division 3 Champions: 1959–60.
Record attendance: 31,044 v Manchester United (League), October 1969.
Modern Capacity: 25,000. **Nickname:** 'Saints'.
Entered Football League: 1920 — Div. 3.
Biggest win: 14–0 v Newbury (FA Cup), September 1894.
Heaviest defeats: 0–8 v Tottenham (Div. 2), March 1936; 0–8 v Everton (Div. 1), November 1971.
Best in League Cup/Milk Cup: Runners-up 1978–79.
Pitch measurements: 110 x 72 yd.
Highest League Scorer in Single Season: Derek Reeves — 39 in 1959–60 (Div. 3).
Highest transfer fee paid: £600,000 — David Armstrong (from Middlesbrough), August 1981.
Highest transfer fee received: £300,000 — Mick Channon (to Manchester City), July 1977.

Southend United

Roots Hall Ground, Southend-on-Sea SS2 6NQ
Tel: 0702-40707   **Colours:** *White & Blue*

A succession of ambitious and dedicated Southend United officials have done their best to bring a higher standard of football to London's nearest seaside resort. In 1955 the club moved from Southend Stadium to a new ground at Roots Hall, Prittlewell, and three years later it looked as though Southend were heading for the Second Division.

But though they gained 54 points, they were still six points behind Brighton, the promoted club. Sammy McCrory, who won Northern Ireland honours, scored 31 of their 90 League goals that season, but by 1966 Southend had dropped to the Fourth Division, from which they climbed again six years later.

The FA Cup competition of 1951–52 produced three months of excitement when, drawn at home five times out of five, Southend fought their way into the last 16 before losing 2–1 to Sheffield United. Twenty-four years later a place in the fifth round again, followed by relegation, reflected their ups and downs.

The Fourth Division championship of 1980–81 is the only title United have ever won. In February 1984 Bobby Moore, England's World Cup winning captain of 18 years before, was made manager at Roots Hall only a few months after joining the club as executive-director. It was his first appointment in League management.

Division 4 Champions: 1980–81.
Record attendance: 31,033 v Liverpool (FA Cup), January 1979.
Modern Capacity: 27,000. **Nickname:** 'Shrimpers'.
Entered Football League: 1920 — Div. 3.
Biggest wins: 10–1 v Golders Green (FA Cup), November 1934; 10–1 v Brentwood (FA Cup), December 1968.
Heaviest defeat: 1–11 v Northampton Town (Southern League), December 1909.
Pitch measurements: 110 x 74 yd.
Highest final League position: 3rd in Div. 3 (South) 1931–32, 1949–50.
Best in FA Cup: 5th Round 1925–26, 1951–52, 1975–76.
Best in League/Milk Cup: 3rd Round 1963–64, 1964–65, 1969–70, 1979–80.
Highest League Scorers in Single Season: Jim Shankly — 31 in 1928–29 (Div. 3 South); Sammy McCrory — 31 in 1957–58 (Div. 3 South).
Highest transfer fee paid: £150,000 — Derek Spence (from Blackpool), December 1979.
Highest transfer fee received: £150,000 — Colin Morris (to Blackpool), December 1979.

Stockport County

Edgeley Park, Stockport, SK3 9DD
Tel: 061-480-8888 **Colours:** *Blue & White*

Thirteen has been a significant numeral in the story of Stockport County, the club who live closest to the two Manchester 'giants'. Only 13 people paid to watch a Football League match at Old Trafford in May 1921. This stranger-than-fiction event came about because Stockport's own ground was under suspension and they used United's pitch for their Div. 2 match against Leicester City.

Nearly 13 years later, on 6 January 1934, Stockport scored 13 times without reply against Halifax Town in a Division Three (North) match. This and Newcastle's 13-0 victory over Newport County on 5 October 1946 are the Football League record wins.

Alex Herd, who played in Manchester City's 1933 and 1934 Cup Final teams, gave Stockport splendid service. At 39, he and his 17-year-old son, David, provided a rare instance of father and son playing together in the same League side — inside-right and inside-left respectively against Hartlepools at Edgeley Park on 5 May 1951.

In November 1975, while struggling for survival, County signed 29-year-old George Best (ex-Manchester United) for a month — his third comeback attempt after two years out of the game. On his Fourth Division debut against Swansea, he more than trebled the gate at 9,240, made two goals and scored the winner (3-2), but Best's appearance was a quickly-passing phase.

A total of 18 managerial changes has reflected the club's instability since the last war, but finishing well up the Fourth Division table in 1984, on gates frequently below 2,000, was greatly to the credit of Eric Webster and his squad of 13 professionals.

Division 3 (North) Champions: 1921-22, 1936-37.
Division 4 Champions: 1966-67.
Record attendance: 27,833 v Liverpool (FA Cup), February 1950.
Modern Capacity: 16,500.
Entered Football League: 1900 — Div. 2.
Biggest win: 13-0 v Halifax Town (Div. 3 North), January 1934.
Heaviest defeat: 1-8 v Chesterfield (Div. 2), April 1902.
Best in FA Cup: 5th Round 1934-35, 1949-50.
Best in League/Milk Cup: 4th Round 1972-73.
Pitch measurements: 111 x 73 yd.
Highest League Scorer in Single Season: Alf Lythgoe — 46 in 1933-34 (Div. 3 North).
Highest transfer fee paid: £25,000 — Tony Coyle (from Albion Rovers), December 1979.
Highest transfer fee received: £88,000 — Stuart Lee (to Man. City), September 1979.

Stoke City

Victoria Ground, Stoke-on-Trent ST4 4EG
Tel: 0782-413511   **Colours:** *Red & White*

Until 1972, what success Stoke achieved in a long tradition of football had been linked with Stanley Matthews. In 1933, the young Matthews was a promising winger in the side that brought First Division football back to the Potteries after ten years.

After relegation in 1953, Stoke spent another ten-year spell in the Second Division. In 1960 Tony Waddington took over as manager and he recruited several veterans including Matthews, who returned from Blackpool, aged 46, at a bargain £3,000 fee.

Matthews and company — their average age was the highest in the four divisions — took the club back to the First Division in 1963, and the 'Wizard of Dribble', who subsequently became Sir Stanley Matthews in recognition of his outstanding services to the game, was fifty when he played his last game for the club.

One of the original twelve in 1888, they are the second-oldest League club (formed in 1863) after Notts County. Wembley 1972 brought Stoke their long-awaited first prize, the League Cup.

England's Gordon Banks, who played an outstanding part in that achievement, was City's goalkeeper for six seasons from 1967 until eye injuries received in a car crash ended his career and another of England's great 'keepers, Peter Shilton, followed Banks in the Stoke goal.

If, half a century on, a local boy named Stanley Matthews remains the club's most famous discovery, another in modern times brought Stoke their record fee — little striker Adrian Heath, transferred to Everton for £700,000 in January 1982.

League Cup Winners: 1971–72.
Division 2 Champions: 1932–33, 1962–63.
Division 3 (North) Champions: 1926–27.
Record attendance: 51,380 v Arsenal (League), March 1937.
Modern Capacity: 35,000. **Nickname:** 'Potters'.
Entered Football League: 1888 — Div. 1.
Biggest win: 10–3 v WBA (Div.1), February 1937.
Heaviest defeat: 0–10 v Preston (Div.1), September 1889.
Best in FA Cup: Semi-final 1898–99, 1970–71, 1971–72.
Pitch measurements: 116 x 75 yd.
Highest League Scorer in Single Season: Freddie Steele — 33 in 1936–37 (Div. 1).
Highest transfer fee paid: £350,000 — Sammy McIlroy (from Manchester United), February 1982.
Highest transfer fee received: £700,000 — Adrian Heath (to Everton), January 1982.

Sunderland

Roker Park, Sunderland, Tyne & Wear SR6 9SW
Tel: 0783-40332 **Colours:** *Red & White*

When Bob Stokoe was appointed manager in November 1972, Sunderland were third from bottom of the Second Division. In the months that followed, glory — and the crowds — returned to Roker Park, and after thrilling FA Cup victories Sunderland found themselves participating in Wembley's 50th birthday celebrations.

Having reached the final, they turned back the clock 42 years, for by their 1–0 triumph over Leeds the Cup went outside the First Division for the first time since West Bromwich's success in 1931.

For Sunderland, six times League Champions, this was the first prize they had won since their previous FA Cup victory in 1937.

The 1973 Cup triumph was secondary to manager Stokoe's ambition to bring First Division football back to Roker Park. Three years later Sunderland went up as Champions and the North-east rejoiced at having three First Division clubs for the first time since 1954, but within 12 months the club was back in Division Two.

In another bold promotion bid in season 1979–80, Sunderland beat their record outgoing transfer fee twice in three months. They paid neighbours Middlesbrough £300,000 for little forward Stan Cummins, and then went to South America to buy Argentina's midfield international Claudio Marangoni for £320,000. A return to Division One was the reward for their enterprise, but Marangoni went home, after only 19 League games for Sunderland.

League Champions: 1891–92, 1892–93, 1894–95, 1901–02, 1912–13, 1935–36.
Division 2 Champions: 1975–76.
FA Cup Winners: 1936–37, 1972–73.
Record attendance: 75,118 v Derby (FA Cup), March 1933.
Modern Capacity: 47,000. **Nickname:** 'Rokerites'.
Biggest win: 11–1 v Fairfield (FA Cup), 1894–95.
Heaviest defeats: 0–8 v Sheffield Wednesday (Div. 1), December 1911; 0–8 v West Ham (Div. 1), October 1968; 0–8 v Watford (Div. 1), September 1982. **Best in League/Milk Cup:** Semi-final 1962–63.
Pitch measurements: 112 x 72 yd.
Highest League Scorer in Single Season: Dave Halliday — 43 in 1928–29 (Div. 1).
Highest transfer fee paid: £320,000 — Claudio Marangoni (from San Lorenzo, Argentina), December 1979.
Highest transfer fees received: £275,000 — Dennis Tueart (to Manchester City), March 1974; £275,000 — Dave Watson (to Manchester City), June 1975.

Swansea City

Vetch Field, Swansea SA1 3SU
Tel: 0792-474114   **Colours:** *White & Black*

The rise and fall of Swansea depicts in stark reality how suddenly the fortunes of football can change. When Liverpool's John Toshack was appointed player-manager at Vetch Field in February 1978, City were in the Fourth Division. Three years later, they were playing for the Football League Championship, and in March 1982 actually topped the First Division table.

Bill Shankly said that what Toshack had achieved in such a short time entitled him to the 'manager of the century' accolade. But in an effort to stay in the top company, Swansea over-spent in the transfer market. Their decline was alarming — by October 1983, they were not only at the foot of the Second Division, but also threatened with closure.

In less than five months Toshack left the club, returned and departed again, and two years after leading the First Division, City were back in the Third.

In season 1963-64, Swansea only just avoided relegation from Division Two, yet almost reached the FA Cup Final. They won their way through to the last four with victories over First Division opponents Sheffield United, Stoke City and Liverpool before going down 2-1 to Preston in the semi-final.

The 'Swans' changed their title from Town to City in 1970 on winning promotion from Division Four. They were relegated again three years later, but the seventies ended on a most successful note, and three promotions in four seasons took the club into the First Division for the first time. Now it is all a dream.

Division 3 (South) Champions: 1924-25, 1948-49.
Record attendance: 32,796 v Arsenal (FA Cup), February 1968.
Modern Capacity: 26,000. **Nickname:** 'Swans'.
Entered Football League: 1920 — Div. 3.
Biggest win: 12-0 v Sliema, Malta (European Cup-Winners' Cup), September 1982.
Heaviest defeat: 1-8 v Fulham (Div. 2), January 1938.
Best in FA Cup: Semi-final 1925-26, 1963-64.
Best in League/Milk Cup: 4th Round 1964-65, 1976-77.
Pitch measurements: 110 x 70 yd.
Highest League Scorer in Single Season: Cyril Pearce — 35 in 1931-32 (Div. 2).
Highest transfer fee paid: £350,000 — Colin Irwin (from Liverpool), August 1981.
Highest transfer fee received: £400,000 — Alan Curtis (to Leeds), May 1979.

Swindon Town

County Ground, Swindon, Wilts. SN1 2ED
Tel: 0793-22118 **Colours:** *Red & White*

Enthusiasm reached unprecedented heights in the West Country in March 1969 when Swindon Town, managed by Danny Williams, became League Cup holders by beating Arsenal 3-1 in extra time at Wembley — and at the end of the season also gained promotion to Division Two.

Roger Smart and the flying Don Rogers (2) were the goalscoring heroes on Wembley's worst-ever pitch (ankle deep mud and sand), and the team that shocked Arsenal and put Swindon's name on the list of domestic cup-winners was: — Downsborough; Thomas, Trollope, Butler, Burrows, Harland, Heath, Smart, Smith, Noble, Rogers.

One of the club's earliest stars was Harold Fleming, an inside-forward capped nine times for England. His skills played a major part in Swindon's two FA Cup semi-final appearances in 1910 and 1912. Others of renown have included Harry Morris, who scored 47 League goals in 1926-27 and a total of 216 in eight seasons (1926-33); Norman Uprichard, Ireland's goalkeeper in the 1950s; England International Mike Summerbee and Under-23 caps Ernie Hunt and Don Rogers; Dave Mackay (ex-Tottenham and Scotland), who was player, then manager from November 1971, before moving to Nottingham Forest and Derby; and full-back John Trollope, who played for the club more than 800 times from 1960 to 1979.

There was more League Cup excitement at Swindon in season 1979-80 when they reached the semi-final before losing 4-3 on aggregate to First Division Wolves. But two years later Town dropped into the Fourth Division for the first time.

League Cup Winners: 1968-69.
Record attendance: 32,000 v Arsenal (FA Cup), January 1972.
Modern Capacity: 26,000. **Nickname:** 'Robins'.
Entered Football League: 1920 — Div. 3.
Biggest win: 10-1 v Farnham United Breweries (FA Cup), Nov. 1925.
Heaviest defeat: 1-10 v Manchester City (FA Cup), January 1930.
Highest final League position: 2nd in Div. 3 (1962-63, 1968-69).
Best in FA Cup: Semi-final 1909-10, 1911-12.
Pitch measurements: 114 x 72 yd.
Highest League Scorer in Single Season: Harry Morris — 47 in 1926-27 (Div. 3 South).
Highest transfer fee paid: £135,000 — David Peach (from Southampton), March 1980.
Highest transfer fee received: £200,000 — Alan Mayes (to Chelsea), December 1980.

Torquay United

Plainmoor, Torquay, Devon TQ1 3PS
Tel: 0803-38666 **Colours:** *Yellow & Blue*

Two local amateur clubs, Torquay Town and Babbacombe, joined forces to form the present club which became professional in 1922. In season 1927–28 the Football League clubs recognized Torquay's promise by electing them to the Southern Section of the old Division Three. Their first season ended disastrously — in bottom place — and in the years before and immediately after the Second World War they rarely rose above half-way in the table.

This applied until 1956, when they finished fifth. The following year they were runners-up, missing promotion to the Second Division only on goal average, but by the time the League was extended in 1958 they found themselves in Division Four.

Since then Torquay have alternated between Third and Fourth Divisions without achieving a title. With little money available and situated in an area of the country where League football has seldom attracted national attention, United struggle along on depressingly small gates.

When former Scottish International Bruce Rioch resigned as manager in January 1984, Torquay replaced him with David Webb, scorer of Chelsea's FA Cup-winning goal in 1970. They gave him a role to match his extrovert personality — manager, managing-director and coach combined. On attendances often below 1,500, it would not be easy even for him to make people realise that Torquay is not just a 'nice little holiday resort' in Devon.

Record attendance: 21,908 v Huddersfield Town (FA Cup), January 1955.
Modern Capacity: 20,000. **Nickname:** 'Gulls'.
Entered Football League: 1927 — Div. 3 (South).
Biggest win: 9–0 v Swindon Town (Div. 3 South), March 1952.
Heaviest defeats: 2–10 v Fulham (Div. 3 South), September 1931; 2–10 v Luton Town (Div. 3 South), September 1933.
Highest final League position: Runners-up Div. 3 (South) 1956–57.
Best in FA Cup: 4th Round 1948–49, 1954–55, 1970–71, 1982–83.
Best in League/Milk Cup: 3rd Round 1967–68, 1971–72, 1975–76, 1976–77.
Pitch measurements: 112 x 74 yd.
Highest League Scorer in Single Season: Sammy Collins — 40 in 1955–56 (Div. 3 South).
Highest transfer fee paid: £30,000 — Vince O'Keefe (from Exeter), February 1980.
Highest transfer fee received: £60,000 — Colin Lee (to Tottenham), October 1977.

Tottenham Hotspur

748 High Road, London N17 OAP
Tel: 01-801-3411   **Colours:** *White & Navy Blue*

Since the war there have been two truly great Spurs sides — Arthur Rowe's 'push and run' team, which won the Second and First Division titles in successive years (1950 and 1951) and Bill Nicholson's Tottenham. What happened on 11 October 1958, when Nicholson, former Spurs player and coach, became manager, was a pointer to the future. Tottenham beat Everton 10-4. With Danny Blanchflower, Dave Mackay, Cliff Jones and John White the corner-stones, they did the 'double' in 1960-61.

Over the next decade the club spent more than a million pounds on new players. By the time Spurs took the 1973 League Cup they had contested seven finals in four different competitions under Nicholson's command and won the lot.

Tottenham finished bottom of the Championship in 1977. They returned a year later, and 10 July 1978 was an historic date, when manager Keith Burkinshaw surprised the soccer world by paying £700,000 for two members of Argentina's World Cup-winning squad, midfield stars Ardiles and Villa.

Spurs were on the way to glory again, winning the FA Cup in successive years and the UEFA Cup in 1984. But on that triumphant note, and to the sorrow of many, manager Burkinshaw left a club that in the process of 'going public' had, it seemed, changed some of its values.

The Double (League Champions, FA Cup Winners): 1960-61.
League Champions: 1950-51, 1960-61.
Division 2 Champions: 1919-20, 1949-50.
FA Cup Winners: 1900-01, 1920-21, 1960-61, 1961-62, 1966-67, 1980-81, 1981-82.
Winners of European Cup-Winners' Cup: 1962-63.
League Cup Winners: 1970-71, 1972-73.
UEFA Cup Winners: 1971-72, 1983-84.
Record attendance: 75,038 v Sunderland (FA Cup), March 1938.
Modern Capacity: 50,000. **Nickname:** 'Spurs'.
Entered Football League: 1908 — Div. 2.
Biggest win: 13-2 v Crewe (FA Cup), February 1960.
Heaviest defeat: 2-8 v Derby (Div. 1), October 1976.
Pitch measurements: 111 x 73 yd.
Highest League Scorer in Single Season: Jimmy Greaves — 37 in 1962-63 (Div. 1).
Highest transfer fee paid: £830,000 — Steve Archibald (from Aberdeen), May 1980.
Highest transfer fee received: £250,000 — Neil McNab (to Bolton), October 1978.

Tranmere Rovers

Prenton Park, Birkenhead, Merseyside
Tel: 051-608-3677   **Colours:** *Blue & White*

If ever a club drew inspiration from its motto, it was Tranmere Rovers ('While there is faith there is light and strength') in season 1982–83. On 12 November, the little Birkenhead club that down the years produced England players like 'Dixie' Dean, 'Pongo' Waring, Roy McFarland and Steve Coppell announced that, because of dire financial problems — a £60,000 overdraft and a weekly loss of £2,500 on gates of barely 1,000 — they would be closing down two weeks later. They were bottom of the Fourth Division at that time.

Many hands were turned to help general manager Jack Butterfield and team manager Bryan Hamilton in round-the-clock survival efforts. A 'Save the Rovers' public appeal was launched; the liquidation date was delayed day by precious day; a friendly played by Manchester United at Prenton Park boosted funds by £8,000 and a similar visit by Liverpool attracted 6,000 fans.

At much later than the eleventh hour, Tranmere were finally saved by selling off part of the club car-park for £100,000 and by a £200,000 loan from Wirral Council.

Tranmere supporters fondly recall nine goals scored by 'Bunny' Bell in a 13–4 Third Division (North) victory over Oldham on Boxing Day, 1935 — the only time 17 goals have been scored in a Football League match.

Another famous Bell of Tranmere, centre-half Harold, also has a distinguished place in the records. He was ever-present for nine seasons between 1946 and 1955, playing 401 consecutive matches, a League record.

Division 3 (North) Champions: 1937–38.
Record attendance: 24,424 v Stoke City (FA Cup), February 1972.
Modern Capacity: 18,000.
Entered Football League: 1921 — Div. 3 (North).
Biggest win: 13-4 v Oldham Athletic (Div. 3 North), December 1935.
Heaviest defeat: 1–9 v Tottenham Hotspur (FA Cup), January 1953.
Best in FA Cup: 5th Round 1967–68.
Best in League/Milk Cup: 4th Round 1960–61, 1981–82.
Pitch measurements: 112 x 72 yd.
Highest League Scorer in Single Season: R. ('Bunny') Bell — 35 in 1933–34 (Div. 3 North).
Highest transfer fee paid: £15,000 — George Hudson (from Northampton), January 1967; £15,000 — Hugh McAuley (from Charlton), August 1978.
Highest transfer fee received: £130,000 — Ronnie Moore (to Cardiff), February 1979.

ANOTHER DOUBLE FOR ABERDEEN

For the second successive season Aberdeen achieved dual honours in 1984. Twelve months after their European Cup-Winners' Cup and Scottish Cup double, they won the Premier Division title and then completed a hat-trick of Scottish F.A. Cup successes. They are seen on the day the Championship went to Pittodrie for the second time in five seasons and the third in all. Back row: Neale Cooper, Jim Leighton, Peter Weir, Mark McGhee, John Hewitt, Tommy McIntyre, Eric Black, Brian Mitchell, Billy Stark. Front row: Ian Porteous, Willie Miller (captain), Doug Rougvie, Stewart McKimmie.

TRIUMPHANT FAREWELL

Keith Burkinshaw lifts the 1984 UEFA Cup after Tottenham's dramatic victory in a penalty shoot-out against the holders, Anderlecht of Belgium. Then he left the club he had taken to three Cup triumphs in four seasons – a departure that, to those outside the politics of White Hart Lane, was hard to understand.

TOP OF THE SHOTS

Liverpool's Ian Rush won both the Professional Footballers' Association and the Football Writers' 'Player of the Year' awards in season 1983–84. He was the country's highest scorer with 49 goals, comprising 32 in the First Division, 8 Milk Cup, 5 European Cup, 2 F.A. Cup and 2 for Wales.

LIVERPOOL'S 1984 TREBLE

The Milk Cup stayed with Liverpool in 1984. Then they completed only the third Championship hat-trick in the Football League's history, and won the European Cup for the fourth time, so it was not surprising that Joe Fagan was voted 'Manager of the Year' at the end of his first season in charge. Picture from Maine Road, Manchester on the night Liverpool beat next-door neighbours Everton in the Milk Cup Final replay for their fourth consecutive victory in the competition. Back row: Alan Kennedy, Michael Robinson, Bruce Grobbelaar, Ian Rush, Alan Hansen, Kenny Dalglish. Front: Sammy Lee, Graeme Souness (captain), Phil Neal, Craig Johnston, Ronnie Whelan, Mark Lawrenson.

JOY FOR EVERTON, TOO

Everton's F.A. Cup victory over Watford brought Goodison Park its first trophy for 14 years – since the 1970 League Championship. For good measure, they won the F.A. Youth Cup as well in 1984. This was how Howard Kendall's team celebrated their Wembley triumph. Back row: Derek Mountfield, John Bailey, Peter Reid, Kevin Ratcliffe (captain), Alan Harper, Andy Gray. Front: Trevor Steven, Kevin Richardson, Neville Southall, Graeme Sharp, Adrian Heath, Gary Stevens.

BRYAN ROBSON, CAPTAIN OF ENGLAND

After speculation for most of season 1983–84, Manchester United and their massive support were relieved when it became clear that Bryan Robson, captain of club and country, would not be leaving Old Trafford for Italy. Ray Wilkins went instead, in a £1·5m transfer to AC Milan. Until then, Robson had held the distinction outright as Britain's most expensive player since he joined United from West Bromwich Albion for £1·5m in October 1981.

KEVIN KEEGAN'S GLORIOUS GOODBYE

If ever one player ensured a club's promotion, it was Kevin Keegan with
Newcastle United in season 1983–84. The former England star was
their captain, top scorer, total inspiration, and folk-hero with Geordie
fans. But Keegan did not go back to the First Division with
Newcastle – at 33, the promotion goal achieved by club and player,
he retired from first-class football.

SPOTLIGHT ON KERRY DIXON

Chelsea's return to the First Division after a five-year absence brought an exciting new goalscoring talent to the Championship. In season 1982–83 Kerry Dixon was the Third Division's top League marksman with 26 goals for Reading, and in 1983–84 he led the Second Division scorers with 28. This header was his first goal towards a hat-trick in the 5–0 home win against Leeds on the day Chelsea clinched promotion. They went on to win the Second Division Championship for the first time.

Walsall

Fellows Park, Walsall WS2 9DB
Tel: 0922-22791   **Colours:** *Red & White*

Whenever the name of Walsall is mentioned someone is almost certain to remark: 'Do you recall the day they knocked Arsenal out of the FA Cup?' Few football events between the two World Wars caused a greater stir than Walsall's famous 2-0 win over Arsenal in the third round on 14 January 1933. The 'Gunners' team, then the most powerful in the land, was packed with internationals: Walsall were a Third Division (North) side of no special skills. Yet they won that afternoon on their merits, Gilbert Alsop, a centre-forward who gave the club wonderful service, getting one of the goals.

Half a century later, in the 1983-84 Milk Cup, Walsall made history by reaching the first semi-final in their 96-year existence, and on the way memories of 1933 were brought into sharp focus by another victory over Arsenal (2-1 at Highbury in Round 4).

For the semi-final first leg against the holders Liverpool, Walsall took 9,000 supporters — double their average home gate — to Anfield and played a magnificent 2-2 draw there. So hopes of a first Wembley for the little West Midlands club were high as nearly 20,000 packed Fellows Park for the return match.

The dream ended in a 2-0 defeat, and from that point the 1984 promotion bid for Division 2 also faded.

Walsall have had two spells in Division Four and, under Alan Buckley, they were promoted as runners-up in 1980. He was involved in Walsall's record transfer fee both ways at £175,000 — the figure that took him to Birmingham as a player in October 1978 and which brought him back to Fellows Park as player-manager eight months later.

Division 4 Champions: 1959–60.
Record attendance: 25,453 v Newcastle United (League), August 1961. **Modern Capacity:** 24,000. **Nickname:** 'Saddlers'.
Entered Football League: 1892 — Div. 2.
Biggest win: 10-0 v Darwen (Div. 2), March 1899.
Heaviest defeats: 0–12 v Small Heath (Div. 2), December 1892; 0–12 v Darwen (Div. 2), December 1896.
Best in FA Cup: 5th Round 1938–39, 1974–75, 1977–78.
Best in League/Milk Cup: Semi-final 1983–84.
Pitch measurements: 113 x 73 yd.
Highest League Scorer in Single Season: Gilbert Alsop — 40 in 1933–34 and 40 in 1934–35 (both in Div. 3 North).
Highest transfer fee paid: £175,000 — Alan Buckley (from Birmingham), June 1979.
Highest transfer fee received: £175,000 — Alan Buckley (to Birmingham), October 1978.

Watford

Vicarage Road, Watford, Herts. WD1 8ER
Tel: 0923-49747 **Colours:** *Yellow, Red & Black*

Watford, brilliantly managed by Graham Taylor and with their chairman, rock super-star Elton John, putting a million of his own money into the club, provide football's modern romance story. In no more than six years they climbed from the game's backwaters to the heights, promoted from the Fourth Division in 1978, from the Third in 1979 and into the First Division in 1982.

The first season in the top company was even more astonishing. Their brand of bright, entertaining, go-for-goal football earned a final place as Championship runners-up to Liverpool.

The test of Watford's nerve came early in the 1983-84. Striker Luther Blissett, with 30 goals the previous season's joint-top First Division scorer with Liverpool's Ian Rush, had been sold to AC Milan for £1m, and the combination of that with other departures and extensive injury problems, indicated a relegation battle.

But the money for Blissett was shrewdly invested in new signings, and the 'ace in the pack' proved to be Maurice Johnston, a 20-year-old ginger-haired Scottish striker bought from Partick Thistle for £200,000. He arrived unknown on the English scene, but quickly settled in the First Division, and once he started scoring — with a hat-trick in 8 minutes away to Wolves — the goals really flowed, 24 of them.

A transformed Watford reached their first Wembley and though, on the day, they were second best to Everton, it was a memorably sporting Cup Final.

Division 3 Champions: 1968-69.
Division 4 Champions: 1977-78.
Record attendance: 34,099 v Manchester United (FA Cup), February 1969. **Modern Capacity:** 28,000. **Nickname:** 'Hornets'.
Entered Football League: 1920 — Div. 3.
Biggest win: 10-1 v Lowestoft Town (FA Cup), November 1926.
Heaviest defeat: 0-10 v Wolves (FA Cup), January 1912.
Best in FA Cup: Final 1983-84.
Best in League/Milk Cup: Semi-final 1978-79.
Pitch measurements: 112 x 74 yd.
Highest League Scorer in Single Season: Cliff Holton — 42 in 1959-60 (Div 4).
Highest transfer fee paid: £200,000 — Steve Sims (from Leicester), December 1978; £200,000 — Maurice Johnston (from Partick Thistle), November 1983.
Highest transfer fee received: £1,000,000 — Luther Blissett (to AC Milan), June 1983.

West Bromwich Albion

The Hawthorns, West Bromwich, West Midlands, B71 4LF
Tel: 021-525-8888   **Colours:** *Navy Blue & White*

As FA Cup winners five times, West Bromwich Albion have a proud record, but with one exception, top League honours have eluded them throughout their history. They have appeared in ten FA Cup Finals and a record 19 semi-finals.

In 1965-66, West Bromwich made a belated entry into the League Cup and won it, they were also Finalists in 1967 and 1970. In the summer of 1971 they appointed as manager their former full-back Don Howe, under whose coaching Arsenal did the 'double' the previous season, but 1972-73 marked the end of a 24-year stay in Division One. After a poor start to season 1975-76 they snatched promotion under player-manager John Giles, signed from Leeds.

They have remained in the First Division since, without much distinction, and Giles returned to the club as manager in February 1984.

One of the highlights in Albion's history was their 1931 FA Cup Final triumph (as a Second Division team) over Birmingham. They are still the only club to have won the Cup and promotion in the same season.

West Bromwich were among the original 12 members of the Football League in 1888, but have won the Championship only once — in 1920.

In October 1981 they received the British all-time record transfer fee of £1.5m when they sold midfield star Bryan Robson to Manchester United. Remi Moses also moved to Old Trafford — as Albion manager Ron Atkinson had done four months before.

League Champions: 1919-20.
Division 2 Champions: 1901-02, 1910-11.
FA Cup Winners: 1887-88, 1891-92, 1930-31, 1953-54, 1967-68.
League Cup Winners: 1965-66.
Record attendance: 64,815 v Arsenal (FA Cup), March 1937.
Modern Capacity: 38,000. **Nickname:** 'Throstles' or 'Baggies'.
Entered Football League: 1888 — Div. 1.
Biggest win: 12-0 v Darwen (Div. 1), April 1892.
Heaviest defeat: 3-10 v Stoke City (Div. 1), February 1937.
Pitch measurements: 115 x 75 yd.
Highest League Scorer in Single Season: W. ('Ginger') Richardson — 39 in 1935-36 (Div. 1).
Highest transfer fee paid: £748,000 — Peter Barnes (from Manchester City), July 1979.
Highest transfer fee received: £1,500,000 — Bryan Robson (to Manchester United), October 1981.

West Ham United

Boleyn Ground, Green Street, Upton Park, London E13 9AZ
Tel: 01-472-2740   **Colours:** *Claret, Blue & White*

Victory over Fulham in the 1975 FA Cup Final put West Ham back on the honours list after ten years of stylish soccer without reward. The triumph climaxed a season in which Ron Greenwood became overall manager and John Lyall took charge of the team. New forwards from lower divisions contributed to that success — and Alan Taylor (£40,000 from Rochdale) scored twice in the Final.

In 1980, after two seasons back in the Second Division, Lyall again led West Ham out at Wembley to face Arsenal in the third all-London FA Cup Final, and Trevor Brooking's goal took the trophy.

When England won the World Cup in 1966, West Ham provided the captain, Bobby Moore, and two other stars — Geoff Hurst and Martin Peters. Upton Park has also produced a galaxy of well-known managers from its former players, among them Frank O'Farrell, Malcolm Allison, Dave Sexton, Noel Cantwell, Jimmy Bloomfield, John Bond and Ken Brown.

In 1923, four years after being elected to the Football League, West Ham gained promotion to the First Division and also reached the first Wembley Cup Final, which they lost 2–0 to Bolton.

They have had only six managers, and during Ron Greenwood's reign were among the most attractive sides in Britain, winning the FA Cup (1964) and the European Cup-Winners' Cup (1965).

West Ham have never finished higher than sixth in the League Championship. They made a strong effort to improve on that in 1983–84, the season marking the retirement of one of the finest players in the club's history, Trevor Brooking, but were foiled by their worst-ever injury list.

FA Cup Winners: 1963–64, 1974–75, 1979–80.
Winners of European Cup-Winners' Cup: 1964–65.
Division 2 Champions: 1957–58, 1980–81.
Record attendance: 42,322 v Tottenham (League), Oct. 1970.
Modern Capacity: 35,000. **Nickname:** 'Hammers'.
Entered Football League: 1919 — Div. 2.
Biggest win: 10–0 v Bury (Milk Cup), October 1983.
Heaviest defeat: 2–8 v Blackburn Rovers (Div.1), December 1963.
Best in League Cup/Milk Cup: Runners-up 1965–66, 1980–81.
Pitch measurements: 110 x 72 yd.
Highest League Scorer in Single Season: Vic Watson — 41 in 1929–30 (Div. 1).
Highest transfer fee paid: £800,000 — Paul Goddard (from QPR), July 1979.
Highest transfer fee received: £225,000 — Alan Curbishley (to Birmingham), June 1979.

Wigan Athletic

Springfield Park, Wigan, Lancs
Tel: 0942-44433   **Colours:** *Royal Blue & White*

From being the 'finest non-League club in the North' while in the Northern Premier League, Wigan Athletic became the Football League's newest members in June 1978 when, after a recount, they were voted in by 29–20 at the expense of Southport. In their first season as a League club, the average home gate of 6,701 was the fourth highest in the Fourth Division.

For years Wigan, the Lancashire mill and manufacturing town situated between Manchester and Liverpool, was best known for its Rugby League team. Suddenly, Wigan Athletic were challenging them for local popularity, reward for 40 years spent trying to get into the Football League. Finally, with application No 35, they were accepted.

The town had been represented in the Football League by Wigan Borough in Div. 3 (North) from 1921–31. Then, in October 1931, they went into liquidation, and the following year Wigan Athletic was formed.

In January 1980 Wigan made their mark as FA Cup fighters. Drawn away to Second Division leaders Chelsea, they won 1–0 on an icy pitch with a goal from midfield man Tommy Gore, one of six Liverpool-born members of the team. They changed into a Liverpool-style all-red strip that night, for what Scottish manager Ian McNeill described as the 'greatest win in Wigan's history'. It took them into the fourth round for the first time and an away tie with Everton. The biggest crowd of the round (51,863) saw Wigan beaten 3–0. Two years later came the next stage of progress for the club —promotion to Division Three.

Record attendance: 27,500 v Hereford United (FA Cup), December 1953.   **Modern Capacity:** 20,000. **Nickname:** 'Latics'.
Entered Football League: 1978 — Div. 4.
Biggest League win: 7–2 v Scunthorpe United (Div. 4), March 1982.
Heaviest League defeat: 2–6 v Bradford City (Div. 3), Dec. 1983.
Highest final League position: 3rd in Div. 4, 1981–82.
Best in FA Cup: 4th Round 1979–80.
Best in League/Milk Cup: 4th Round 1981–82.
Pitch measurements: 117 x 73 yd.
Highest League Scorer in Single Season: Les Bradd — 19 in 1981–82 (Div. 4).
Highest transfer fee paid: £60,000 — Eamon O'Keefe (from Everton), January 1982.
Highest transfer fee received: £150,000 — Joe Hinnigan (to Sunderland), February 1980.

Wimbledon

Durnsford Road, Wimbledon, London SW19
Tel: 01-946-6311 **Colours:** *Blue & Yellow*

Wimbledon are the yo-yo club of modern soccer. They came into the Football League (as semi-professional Southern League champions for three consecutive seasons) in 1977, replacing Workington, and in each of five successive years moved up and down between the Fourth and Third Divisions like this: 1979 promoted, 1980 relegated, 1981 promoted, 1982 relegated and 1983 promoted again — as Fourth Division champions and top scorers in the country with 96 League goals.

The Dons' goal-rush continued in 1983–84 in an exciting bid to reach the Second Division only seven years after leaving the Southern League, and they did so as runners-up to Oxford United.

Alan Cork was a consistent marksman — totalling 32 goals after missing most of the two previous seasons because of a broken leg. But for all the prolific scoring by young manager Dave Bassett's team, gates at Plough Lane were mostly below 4,000, easily the best in 1983–84 being 7,554 to see them outplay Nottingham Forest 2–0 in the 2nd Round of the Milk Cup.

In contrast, the 'house full' notices were often posted in Wimbledon's non-League days, particularly when they reached three successive Amateur Cup Finals, the last of which they won by beating Sutton United 4–2 at Wembley in 1963.

Wimbledon FC was founded in 1889 when a group of ex-pupils of Central School formed themselves into Wimbledon Old Centrals. They played on common land and used a local pub for changing-rooms. They moved to their present ground just before the First World War when it was swamp land in use as a rubbish dump.

Division 4 Champions: 1982–83.
Record attendance: 18,000 v H.M.S. Victory, FA Amateur Cup, 1935.
Modern capacity: 15,000. **Nickname:** 'Dons'.
Entered Football League: 1977 — Div. 4
Biggest win: 15–2 v Polytechnic (FA Cup) 1932–33.
Heaviest defeat: 0–8 v Everton (League Cup), August 1978.
Best in League/Milk Cup: 4th Round 1974–75, 1981–82.
Best in FA Cup: 4th Round 1974–75, 1981–82.
Pitch measurements: 110 x 72 yd.
Highest League Scorer in Single Season: Alan Cork — 28 in 1983–84 (Div. 3).
Highest transfer fee paid: £40,000 — Tommy Cunningham (from QPR), March 1979.
Highest transfer fee received: £70,000 — Steve Galliers (to Crystal Palace), October 1981.

Wolverhampton Wanderers

Molineux Grounds, Wolverhampton, W. Midlands, WV1 4QR.
Tel: 0902-712181 **Colours:** *Gold & Black*

Wolves, one of football's most famous clubs, came within three minutes of extinction in the summer of 1982. They had just been relegated and, with debts of £2.5m, the Official Receiver was called in. The Football League set a deadline at 5 pm on Friday, July 30 if the club was to be saved and, with the bulldozers poised to move in through the gates of Molineux, Derek Dougan, the club's former Irish International centre-forward, produced a consortium-type rescue that was accepted by the League at 4.57 p.m.

The 105-year-old club was saved, and Wolves celebrated survival by winning promotion nine months later. It was not a lasting success, however. They were relegated again in 1984, and clearly their problems were far from over.

Wolves began the most glamorous period in their history with a 3-1 Wembley win over Leicester City in the 1949 FA Cup Final. They went on to become League Champions in 1954, 1958 and 1959, and won the Cup again in 1960.

Billy Wright, first England player to complete a century of internationals (105 appearances), played more League and Cup games — 535 between 1946 and 1959 — than anyone for Wolves.

In 1977, a year after relegation, Wolves won the Second Division title. With a new stand proudly opened in season 1979-80, they paid £1,469,000, a British record, for Aston Villa and Scotland forward Andy Gray. He quickly repaid a large slice of that fee by scoring the winning goal in the 1980 League Cup Final.

League Champions: 1953-54, 1957-58, 1958-59.
Division 2 Champions: 1931-32, 1976-77.
Division 3 (North) Champions: 1923-24.
FA Cup Winners: 1892-93, 1907-08, 1948-49, 1959-60.
League Cup Winners: 1973-74, 1979-80.
Record attendance: 61,315 v Liverpool (FA Cup), February 1939.
Modern Capacity: 38,000. **Nickname:** 'Wolves'.
Entered Football League: 1888 — Div. 1.
Biggest win: 14-0 v Crosswell's Brewery (FA Cup), 1886-87.
Heaviest defeat: 1-10 v Newton Heath (Div. 1), October 1892.
Pitch measurements: 115 x 72 yd.
Highest League Scorer in Single Season: Dennis Westcott — 37 in 1946-47 (Div. 1).
Highest transfer fee paid: £1,469,000 — Andy Gray (from Aston Villa), September 1979.
Highest transfer fee received: £1,450,000 — Steve Daley (to Manchester City), September 1979.

Wrexham

Racecourse Ground, Mold Road, Wrexham, Clwyd
Tel: 0978-262129   **Colours:** *Red & White*

Wrexham hold the distinction of being the oldest Association football club in Wales. They were founded in 1873 and have provided a steady flow of players to the International team. Wrexham have also won the Welsh Cup 21 times, and in the 1975-76 Cup-Winners' Cup they became the first Third Division side to reach a European quarter-final.

The Racecourse Ground is an international venue, and in November 1975 was the scene of a 1-0 victory over Austria which took Wales, in their centenary season, into the European Championship quarter-finals for the first time. The scorer was 34-year-old local hero Arfon Griffiths, who later became manager.

A less auspicious occasion at Wrexham was in May 1982, when only 2,315 spectators saw Wales play Northern Ireland — the lowest attendance ever recorded at a full International in Britain being accounted for by the fact that it clashed with the Tottenham-QPR FA Cup Final replay that was shown live on TV the same night.

Wrexham provided their own FA Cup sensations in season 1973-74. They beat Second Division leaders Middlesbrough 1-0 to reach the fifth round for the first time, and did even better by winning 1-0 away to First Division Southampton. Then they were drawn away to another First Division club, Burnley, and went out by the only goal.

In 1978, Wrexham again reached the sixth round before losing 2-3 at home to Arsenal. Compensation came weeks later, when Wrexham clinched a place in the Second Division for the first time, going up as Third Division champions.

Division 3 Champions: 1977-78.
Record attendance: 34,445 v Man. United (FA Cup), January 1957.
Modern Capacity: 28,500. **Nickname:** 'Robins'.
Entered Football League: 1921 — Div. 3 (North).
Biggest win: 10-1 v Hartlepool United (Div. 4), March 1962.
Heaviest defeat: 0-9 v Brentford (Div. 3), October 1963.
Best in FA Cup: 6th Round 1973-74, 1977-78.
Best in League/Milk Cup: 5th Round 1960-61, 1977-78.
Pitch measurements: 117 x 75 yd.
Highest League Scorer in Single Season: Tommy Bamford — 44 in 1933-34 (Div. 3 North).
Highest transfer fee paid: £200,000 — Joey Jones (from Liverpool), October 1978.
Highest transfer fees received: £300,000 — Micky Thomas (to Manchester United), November 1978; £300,000 — Bobby Shinton (to Manchester City), June 1979.

York City

Bootham Crescent, York YO3 7AQ
Tel: 0904-24447 **Colours:** *Red, Navy Blue & White*

York City are one of only six Third Division clubs who have reached
the FA Cup semi-final. Millwall (1937), Port Vale (1954), Norwich
(1959), Crystal Palace (1976) and Plymouth Argyle (1984) are the
others. City startled the football world in 1955 with an extraordinary
Cup run which actually carried them further than any other Third
Division side in history; they took Newcastle United to a replay
before losing the semi-final 2–0.

York had reached the last eight in 1938 when their team, said to
have cost only £50, defeated teams from all four divisions. Some of
the club's best performances have been achieved more recently.
Four times since the League was extended in 1958 they have won
promotion to the Third Division — in 1959, 1965, 1971 and 1984.

Between October–December 1973 York equalled a 47-year-old
record (Millwall, Div. 3 South, 1926) by playing 11 consecutive
Third Division matches without conceding a goal. Such defence
played a major part in City finishing third and so reaching the
Second Division for the first time in their history.

York finished 15th on their arrival in Division Two, but were
relegated a year later, in 1976, and they dropped again to the Fourth
Division in 1977.

Twice in the next four years they had to apply for re-election, but
revival followed the appointment of Stoke centre-half Denis Smith
as player-manager in May 1982, and in 1984 York won the first
trophy in their history, running away with the Fourth Division and
totalling 101 points, a new Football League record.

Division 4 Champions: 1983–84.
Record attendance: 28,123 v Huddersfield Town (FA Cup), March
1938.
Modern Capacity: 13,800. **Nickname:** 'Minsters'.
Entered Football League: 1929 — Div. 3 (North).
Biggest win: 9–1 v Southport (Div. 3 North), February 1957.
Heaviest defeat: 0–12 v Chester (Div. 3 North), February 1936.
Best in FA Cup: Semi-final 1954–55.
Best in League/Milk Cup: 5th Round 1961–62.
Pitch measurements: 115 x 75 yd.
Highest League Scorers in Single Season: Bill Fenton — 31 in
1951–52 (Div. 3 North); Alf Bottom — 31 in 1955–56 (Div. 3 North).
Highest transfer fee paid: £18,000 — Micky Cave (from
Bournemouth), August 1974.
Highest transfer fee received: £120,000 — Gordon Staniforth (to
Carlisle), October 1979.

The Scottish League

In a controversial move aimed at revitalizing public interest, the Scottish Football League made one of the most revolutionary changes in its history at the start of season 1975–76, regrouping from two to three divisions. The Premier League consisted of ten clubs (meeting four times per season instead of twice as previously), and the First and Second Divisions each comprised 14 teams.

Aberdeen have been, by long tradition, the principal club in the north-east of Scotland, and at the start of the eighties they achieved, under Alex Ferguson, success to match the prosperity brought to the Granite City by North Sea oil.

In 1980 they became Scottish Champions for only the second time. In 1982 they won their third Scottish Cup, and kept it a year later with a repeat triumph in the Final against Rangers. But that was only half the Dons' success story of season 1982–83; ten days earlier, in Gothenburg, they beat Real Madrid 2–1 in the Final of the European Cup-Winners' Cup. Eric Black scored after seven minutes, and the winning goal was headed by his replacement, John Hewitt, in extra time.

Aberdeen thus became the first club to win both that trophy and domestic cup honours in the same season, and a further accolade was the award of the 'European Team of the Year' title for 1983. Truly, in performance as well as alphabet, that made them Scotland's No. 1 team, and they remained so by completing the double in Championship and Cup in 1984, as only the second club this century (Rangers the other) to win the Scottish Cup three years in succession.

It took Aberdeen half a century to become League Champions. After being runners-up in 1911 and 1937, they at last claimed the title in 1955. They were runners-up the following year and again in 1971 and 1972.

By 1967 Aberdeen had reached the Scottish Cup Final six times but won the trophy only once — when defeating Hibernian 2–1 in 1947. Their second FA Cup triumph came in 1970 when they beat Celtic 3–1 in the Final. They took the League Cup in its inaugural season (1945–46) and captured it for the third time in 1976–77.

Since 1969 Aberdeen have been Scotland's biggest exporters of soccer talent to England, transferring several players at six-figure fees — Tommy Craig to Sheffield Wednesday (£100,000), Jim Smith to Newcastle (£100,000), Martin Buchan to Manchester United

(£125,000), Joe Harper to Everton (£180,000) and Willie Young to Tottenham (£100,000). In 1980 they reaped Scotland's record transfer fee when striker Steve Archibald moved to Spurs for £800,000.

By the end of the seventies, Aberdeen were unique in that they had turned Pittodrie into Britain's first all-seated football stadium. The capacity is now 24,000, with everyone under cover, and manager Ferguson has produced the team worthy of such a splendid setting.

Airdrieonians climbed their highest peaks in the early 1920s when they challenged the supremacy of Rangers and Celtic. They were First Division runners-up in four successive seasons (1923–26) and won the Scottish Cup for the only time in 1924, beating Hibernian 2–0 in the Final. It was half a century before they reached the Final again (1975), and then they lost 3–1 to Celtic.

In the League during that era, Airdrie were unbeaten on their own Broomfield Park pitch for more than three years. They fielded six Scottish internationalists, the greatest of them Hughie Gallacher.

Airdrie dropped into the Second Division in 1936 and did not get back into the top class until 1947, since when they have fought an almost constant battle to stay up — or go up. As Second Division Champions in 1974 they were the only British club to top a century of League goals (102) that season.

Albion Rovers' most memorable year was 1920 when, for the only time, they reached the Scottish Cup Final, after beating mighty Rangers in the semi-final. In that Rovers team beaten 3–2 by Kilmarnock was Jock White, still their only International, who was capped with them before moving on to Hearts and Leeds. Elected to the First Division in 1919, 'Wee Albion' have had at best a see-saw existence. One of their most outstanding players, during the 1940s, was Jock Stein, later the triumphant manager of Celtic and subsequently in charge of Scotland.

Alloa Athletic's proudest achievement came in season 1921–22, when they won the Second Division Championship by a margin of 13 points. But a year later they were relegated and have not played in the top division since. They were, however, harshly affected by the outbreak of the Second World War. They were due for promotion at the end of season 1938–39, but the League was disbanded because of the war, and when it was reformed, Alloa were not elected to the First Division. They have twice won promotion to the 'modern' First Division (formerly the Second) — in 1977 and 1982.

107

Arbroath is a small Scottish coastal town famous for kippers —
and the club's 36–0 victory over Bon Accord in a first round Cup-tie
on 12 September 1885. This stands as the biggest score in a first-
class match in Britain. Bon Accord's regular goalkeeper Jimmie
Grant was unfit and replaced by wing-half Andrew Lornie. John
Petrie scored 13 against him and Arbroath totalled 55 goals in the
Cup that season before losing to Hibernian in the fourth round. The
previous year Arbroath were robbed of another place in the history
books. They beat Rangers in a fourth round Cup-tie, but after
protesting that the Gayfield pitch was smaller than regulation size,
Rangers won the replayed game 8–1 on their own ground. Arbroath
had to wait another 90 years to achieve that first win over Rangers —
a stunning 3–2 League victory on 2 February 1974. At Ibrox, too!

Ayr United entered the Scottish First Division in 1913, and have
mostly struggled. Between 1925 and 1969 they won promotion six
times — but after that last elevation they consolidated, and a final
position of seventh in 1975 ensured a place for the Somerset Park
club among the giants in the new Premier League. But they lasted
only three seasons in top company. The departure of defender
Steve Nicol, and his size 12 boots, to Liverpool in October 1981 was
a blow to whatever hopes Ayr may have had of returning to the top
class, but the fee of £300,000 was considerable consolation.

Berwick Rangers 1, Glasgow Rangers 0 will stand high on the list
of 'unbelievable' results for as long as football is played in Scotland.
The date was 28 January 1967 in the first round of the Cup, and
Shielfield Park, home of the little English border-town team of
part-timers who play in the Scottish League, was crammed with a
record 13,365 crowd.
　　Sammy Reid, a former Liverpool player, scored the historic 32nd-
minute goal, and for the rest of the game Berwick's 35-year-old
goalkeeper-manager Jock Wallace (subsequently to manage
Rangers, Leicester City, Motherwell and Rangers again), and his
defence heroically resisted ceaseless pressure to produce Scotland's
greatest 'Jock the giantkiller' story.
　　Never before had Rangers been knocked out of the Cup by
Second Division opposition . . . and it is said that many of the 7,000
fans who followed them from Glasgow to Tweedmouth that day still
refuse to believe it ever happened. A more modern highlight in
Berwick's history was the winning of the Scottish Second Division
championship in 1979.

Brechin City has the smallest population (7,000) supporting a
senior club in Britain. During the 1920s — when Brechin moved to
their present ground, Glebe Park — the town was inhabited by more

than 10,000 and attendances averaged 3,000, but after the war the population fell dramatically, and so did support for Brechin. They have never been seen in top-division football, but had the finest season in their history in 1982-83 when winning the Second Division under new player-manager Ian Fleming from Dundee.

Celtic, until the eighties arch rivals of Rangers as the top club in Scottish football, were formed in 1888 by Irish Catholics living in Glasgow, the first object being to raise money for the poor of the city's East End.

Under former captain Jock Stein (appointed manager in 1965) they reached astonishing heights, with 1966-67 their greatest season. In an historic clean sweep of four major prizes, they became the first British club to win the European Cup, defeating Inter-Milan 2-1 in the Final; they won the League Championship (scoring 111 goals and losing only one game out of 34); they took the Scottish Cup and the Scottish League Cup also went to Parkhead.

Celtic's famous green-and-white strip has long been an emblem of attacking football, and season 1971-72 brought them the Double for the fourth time in six years. A ninth *successive* League Championship (their 29th in all) in 1973-74 equalled a world record by Hungarian club MTK Budapest (1917-25) and the Bulgarians CDNA Sofia (1954-62), a feat celebrated by completion of the Double for the ninth time in their history.

Celtic have won the League title 33 times, the Scottish Cup a total of 26 times and the League Cup on nine occasions.

Of Celtic's galaxy of star players down the years, Jimmy McGrory was unquestionably the greatest goalscorer. In 378 games between 1922-39 he obtained 397 goals for them — the highest all-time total in the Scottish League — and after a playing career in which his goal aggregate reached 550, he also managed the club.

Clyde were formed in 1877 and took their name from the river and dockyards of Glasgow. Their home, Shawfield Park, is in the East End and they have constantly struggled to keep up with their big city rivals.

Although slipping out of the First Division on six occasions, they always made a rapid return to the top bracket, five times doing so at the first attempt. Clyde have never been Champions of Scotland, nor have they won the League Cup, but they have triumphed three times in the Scottish FA Cup.

After defeats in the 1910 and 1912 Finals they at last won the trophy in 1939, when they beat Motherwell 4-0 — and, with the competition suspended because of the war, it remained theirs for eight years. They were also Cup winners in 1955, defeating Celtic

1–0 in a replay, and in 1958 another single goal gave them victory over Hibernian.

Clyde won the Second Division in 1982 by a margin of nine points. The transfer of wee winger Pat Nevin to Chelsea in June 1983 brought the Shawfield club their record fee of £95,000.

Clydebank have one of the few all-seated stadiums in Britain at Kilbowie Park, and until Dumbarton (1984) were the only club to have played in all three Scottish divisions (Premier, First and Second). Formed in 1965, they spent one season in the Second Division, under the name of East Stirlingshire Clydebank, but there was a legal dispute and Clydebank became established in their own right.

In the 1920s the original Clydebank FC were a First Division club, but they resigned from the Scottish League in 1931. A team built from their remnants continued under the name of Clydebank Intermediate, but they failed to gain senior status. When the Scottish League was restructured in 1975, Clydebank found themselves in the bottom section, but they won promotion first time to Division One. They spent only one season there before climbing again to the Premier Division, but a year later they were relegated.

Cowdenbeath, after years of Second Division obscurity, won unexpected promotion in season 1969–70, and within months they were in a League Cup semi-final against Rangers — excitement unheard of at Central Park since the Second Division Championship of 1938–39. But they lasted only one more season in the top class.

Cowdenbeath won the Second Division in 1939 by 12 points, but when League football was resumed seven years later there was no place for them in the First Division.

Dumbarton produced one of the surprises in Scottish football in season 1983–84, when they won promotion to the Premier Division as First Division runners-up to Morton. They achieved their success on crowds that ranged from a lowest of 350 to a highest of 1,500, and were reported to have made a heavy loss on the way up.

Founded in 1872, Dumbarton was one of the original members of the Scottish League in 1890. They shared the first Championship title with Rangers, and won it outright the following year. They won the Cup in 1883 after losing the two previous finals. Among players they discovered and had to sell were Ian Wallace, Graeme Sharp and Murdo MacLeod.

Dundee, a First Division club for most of their history, did not win the League Championship until 1962 — after four times being runners-up. They did so under Bob Shankly, brother of the legendary Bill, and that remains their only top League title, but they were FA Cup winners in 1910, and their three League Cup successes were gained in seasons 1951–52, 1952–53 and 1973–74 (when they shocked Celtic 1–0 in the Final).

In 1963 Dundee were close to becoming the first British club to win the European Cup, losing in the semi-finals to AC Milan, who went on to win the competition.

Relegated from the Premier Division in 1976, at the end of its first season, Dundee fought their way back as First Division champions three years later, only to be relegated again in 1980. That time, they made it back to the Premier Division at the first attempt.

Dundee United achieved, in 1983, what they had always yearned to do — the right to fly the Scottish Champions' flag over Tannadice Park. In the Premier Division's tightest finish yet, they clinched the title, with only a point to spare over Celtic and Aberdeen, by winning the last match 2–1 away to neighbours Dundee, Eamonn Bannon, re-imported to Scotland from Chelsea at the club's record fee of £170,000 in November 1979, scoring the decisive goal. The season's 90 League goals (22 by David Dodds) were a record for Premier Division Champions, and United's 56 points equalled Celtic's Premier Division record in 1981.

For Jim McLean's team it was a third trophy in four seasons — United won the League Cup in 1980 and 1981 — and with Aberdeen retaining the Scottish Cup, the pendulum of club power had swung a distance to the north-east of Glasgow.

With Dundee United's name at last on the list of Scotland's Champions, only the Cup now eluded them, beaten in both their Finals of that competition (by Celtic in 1974 and by Rangers in 1981). Will their next be 'third time lucky'?

Founded in 1910, they spent years in the shadow of the club next door, Dundee. They changed from Dundee Hibernian to United on gaining entry to the Second Division in 1923. Two years later came promotion, but they led a mostly up-and-down existence until stability was brought to Tannadice in the 1960s, leading to long-overdue glory in the eighties.

Dunfermline Athletic did not 'arrive' as a top club in Scotland until the sixties, although they were formed as long ago as 1907. Their real rise began in 1960, when Jock Stein was appointed manager. The following year they reached the Scottish Cup Final for the first time, and after a goalless draw beat Celtic 2–0 in a replay. Their second FA Cup success came in 1968 when they defeated Hearts 3–1 in the Final.

After Stein left Dunfermline remained strong and were only two points from putting their name to the First Division title in 1964–65, when third to champions Kilmarnock and Hearts. They finished third again in 1968–69, but in the seventies they fell from Premier Division to Second Division. They climbed back as runners-up in 1979, but dropped again four years later.

In 1969, Dunfermline reached the semi-finals of the European Cup-Winners' Cup, eventually losing 1–2 on aggregate to Slovan Bratislava.

East Fife are unique in having won the Scottish Cup while members of the old Second Division. That highest peak came in 1938, when they beat Kilmarnock 4–2 in a Final replay after a 1–1 draw.

As a Second Division side, East Fife had sprung a surprise in 1927 by reaching the Final, but were beaten 3–0 to Rangers in 1950.

Third has been their highest final position in the Championship (in 1952 and 1953), and the League Cup has been East Fife's most successful tournament with three triumphs — in 1948, 1950 and 1954. Their 1948 achievement, as a Second Division side, makes them still the only club from outside the top division to win the League Cup.

East Stirling, in their only post-war season in the top division, 1963–64, attracted crowds of 10,000. Then, following relegation, they merged with Clydebank, but after only one season they reverted to their original identity.

Many fine players have begun their careers at Firs Park, and in 1962 Eddie McCreadie, later capped 23 times by Scotland at full-back, Tommy Knox and Jim Mulholland were all transferred to Chelsea.

Falkirk's closest bid for the Scottish League Championship was made at the start of the century when they finished runners-up to Celtic in 1908 and 1910. Since the last war they have four times been relegated to the Second Division, but they were Champions of that section in 1980.

In the Scottish FA Cup they have had two successes, beating Raith 2–0 in the 1913 Final and then, after a break of 44 years, taking the trophy again in 1957 with a replay victory by 2–1 against Kilmarnock.

Falkirk have produced many star players — for English as well as Scottish clubs — and none better than Scottish International inside-forward John White, who moved to Tottenham for £20,000 in October 1959.

Forfar Athletic, formed in 1884, did not put their name on the

Scottish honours list (Forfarshire Cup apart) until 1984. The closest they had been to glory was to reach the 1982 Scottish FA Cup semi-final, in which they held Rangers 0–0 before losing the replay 3–1.

The fact that Forfar reached their centenary was a tribute to dogged perseverance despite all the odds, and it was more than fitting that 100 years of Forfar football should be celebrated by winning the Scottish Second Division championship in 1984.

Hamilton Academical owe their derivation to the local academy at the time of their formation in 1870. No major honours, apart from the Second Division championship as long ago as 1904, have gone to Douglas Park, but Hamilton were Scottish Cup Finalists in 1911 and 1935, and a top-division team from 1906–47.

The club's best period was in the 1930s when, besides reaching the 1935 Cup Final — in which Rangers beat them 2–1 — they finished in the top eight in the old First Division five times in seven seasons.

Heart of Midlothian were among the founder-members of the Scottish League in 1890 and had never been out of the Championship Division until 1977 — a wonderful record, even if it is more than two decades since they won the last of their four major League titles (1895, 1897, 1958 and 1960).

Hearts' Scottish Cup triumphs number five (1891, 1896, 1901, 1906 and 1956) and the League Cup has been won by the famous Maroons of Tynecastle Park, close to Edinburgh's city centre, on four occasions — 1955, 1959, 1960 and 1963. The 1960 success gave them a double, because they were League Champions as well that season.

Among more than 50 Scottish internationals to represent the club, there has been no greater artist than Tommy Walker, ace inside-forward of the 1930s and beyond. After a spell with Chelsea just after the war, he returned to Tynecastle and managed Hearts through one of the most spectacular phases in their history.

At the end of the seventies and in the early eighties, Hearts moved up and down between Premier and First Divisions in five successive seasons. They were relegated in 1977, promoted as Division 1 runners-up in 1978, and relegated again in 1979. Then, in 1980, came another upward trend as Division 1 champions, but they lasted only one season back in the top grade, to which they returned yet again in 1983.

Hibernian form with Hearts the football strength in the city of Edinburgh, and although their combined records do not begin to measure up to those of the Glasgow 'big two', they have nevertheless made an invaluable contribution to Scottish soccer. Hibs' two Scottish FA Cup victories were achieved long ago, in 1887 and 1902. The first of four occasions when they have taken the League title was in 1903, the last in 1952, when they were champions for the third time in five seasons.

Apart from two seasons at the start of the thirties, they spent the whole of this century, until 1980, as members of the top division. Season 1972–73 marked Hibs' only League Cup success.

The first British team to take part in the European Cup when it was launched in 1955, Hibernian, like most Scottish clubs, have at times been forced for financial reasons to sell star players.

In February 1974 Hibs used the transfer market in the opposite way to make history — they signed Scotland striker Joe Harper from Everton for £120,000, then the highest Scottish fee ever paid to an English club.

In an effort to hold their Premier Division place, Hibs paid George Best a reputed fee of £2,000 per match in the middle of 1979–80, but apart from his presence improving gates, the club was beyond saving and went down to Division 1 after one of the most traumatic seasons in their history. Happily, they returned to the top class twelve months later.

Kilmarnock are Scotland's second-oldest club (formed in 1869, two years after Queen's Park), and no one could say that they were winning out of turn when they took the Scottish League title in 1965; they had been runners-up in four of the previous five seasons.

That remains the only major League honour to go so far to Rugby Park and the League Cup has still to be won, but Kilmarnock have had two successes in the Scottish Cup, in 1920 and 1929.

Over the years they have become almost the champion runners-up of Scottish football; besides those four 'seconds' in the championship in the early 1960s, they have been beaten FA Cup Finalists five times and three times losers of the League Cup Final.

At the start of season 1973–74 they faced the task of winning back a First Division place lost after 19 years — and achieved that objective first time. Kilmarnock were two places short of the Premier League on its inception in 1975, but within twelve months they were promoted from Division One — as runners-up, of course, as they were again in 1979 and 1982.

Meadowbank Thistle, then playing as the amateur works side Ferranti Thistle in the East of Scotland League, were surprisingly awarded the extra place when, in 1974, the Scottish League decided to recruit an additional club to make an even membership of 38. They won the vote 21–16 over Highland League team Inverness Thistle. On election, they were required to drop the commercial name and, having rented the 30,000-capacity Meadowbank Stadium from Edinburgh Corporation, the newcomers adopted the title Meadowbank Thistle. With a run of 14 consecutive defeats in League and League Cup their start did not match the impressive surroundings in which they played. In contrast, 1982–83 was their best season yet, with promotion won as Second Division runners-up in only their ninth season of League membership.

Montrose belong among the Scottish clubs never to have competed in the Championship Division, and between 1947 and 1955 they dropped into Division C. The club's most noteworthy achievements were in reaching the Cup quarter-finals in 1930 and 1948, and they were within one place of promotion to the Premier League in 1976. They slipped from First to Second Division in 1979.

Morton's only top prize is their Scottish Cup success in 1922, in which they shocked Rangers 1–0 in the Final. But they are very much part of the fabric of Scottish football with their home at Cappielow Park close to the shipyards of Clydeside.

In 1964, Morton became the first Scottish club to recruit Scandinavian talent by taking on goalkeeper Erik Sorensen, a Dane. The idea came from director-manager Hal Stewart, who took over in 1962 when they were a dying club — last but one in the Second Division with only two signed players on the staff.

Under his guidance, they reached the League Cup Final in 1963–64, and at the end of the season were Second Division Champions by the record margin of 14 points. At one stage that winter Morton won 23 games in a row (a Scottish League record). Three years later, in 1967, they were Second Division winners again with 69 points, another record.

First Division champions in 1978, they went into the Premier Division with high ambitions but the stay in the top class was never easy and ended with relegation in 1983. A year later the club were back in the 'Premier' but, sadly, Hal Stewart, for so long 'Mr. Morton', had not lived to see it.

Motherwell have achieved one success in each of the major competitions, the Championship, League Cup and Scottish FA Cup. Until season 1931–32, Celtic and Rangers had monopolized Scottish League football for 27 years, but then Motherwell came upon the scene as new Champions — a reward for the attractive football they had played for many years.

The previous season they reached the Scottish Cup Final for the first time and would have won it but for a tragic last-minute own goal allowing Celtic the chance of a replay which they won 4–2.

Motherwell had to wait another 21 years for their FA Cup Final victory which came in 1952 (4-0 against Dundee), but the year before they put their name on the League Cup (3-0 v. Hibernian).

When the Premier League was formed in 1975, Motherwell just qualified — in tenth place. They lost top-division status in 1979. David Hay took them back as First Division champions three years later and then resigned to manage a sports complex in Florida, but his plans fell through because of work permit problems in USA and he was out of football for a year until taking over at Celtic.

Partick Thistle caused the biggest sensation in Scottish football for years when on 23 October 1971, they thrashed odds-on favourites Celtic 4-1 in the League Cup Final. With an average age of 22 — and just six months after winning back their First Division place following one season in the Second —Thistle astonished a crowd of 62,740 at Hampden Park by scoring four goals in a 30-minute spell. It was their first major success in 50 years.

Thistle's only other triumph since being formed in the north-west of Glasgow in 1876 was a Cup Final victory in 1921, when they beat Rangers 1-0.

In the League Championship Partick's highest final placing has been third, three times — in 1948, 1954 and 1963. They missed a place in the new Premier Division in 1975, but qualified a year later as champions of Division 1. Relegated in 1982, they failed to win back Premier Division status in 1984 after the mid-season departure of 20-year-old striker Maurice Johnston to Watford for £200,000.

Queen of the South's most successful period was between 1933 and 1950, when they competed in the First Division. During that period they played in the Cup quarter-finals three times, and in the relegation season of 1949-50 they reached the semi-final. They were formed in 1919 when three local sides, Dumfries, the King's Own Scottish Borderers and Arrol Johnston, amalgamated. Their outstanding discovery was Hughie Gallacher — later to become one of the greatest Scottish forwards — who played two seasons for the 'Queens' before joining Airdrie on his way to a spectacular career with Newcastle, Chelsea, Derby and Scotland in the 1924-35 era.

Queen's Park, for long the only amateur club competing in Britain's big professional leagues, are unique in many other ways. From their year of formation, as Scotland's oldest club, in 1867 they went unbeaten for seven years (in the first five of which goalkeeper Jock Grant did not have a goal scored against him).

They won the Scottish Cup ten times between 1874-93 (only Celtic and Rangers stand above them on that honours list) before the Scottish FA legalized professionalism, and in addition Queen's

Park were English FA Cup Finalists in 1884 and 1885.

Except for winning the 1955–56 Second Division championship and the honour of supplying the big majority of Scotland's amateur international players, Queen's Park have no post-war claims to fame. But the great traditions, like the black-and-white hooped jerseys, survive — despite the fact that good players continue to be lost to professional rivals and that League football at Hampden Park seldom attracts more than a few hundred spectators.

Raith Rovers can claim the most goals ever scored in a league season by a British club: 142 in 34 matches when they won the Scottish Second Division championship in 1937–38. The record is unlikely to be beaten, and 108 of those Raith goals were scored by their inside trio, Gilmour, Haywood and Whitelaw.

Third in 1922, behind Celtic and Rangers, is the closest Raith have ever been to the Championship title; in knockout football they were beaten finalists in the Scottish Cup in 1913 and runners-up in the League Cup in season 1948–49.

Easily the outstanding talent produced by the Kirkcaldy club was Alex James, who became a legendary inside-forward with Preston, Arsenal and Scotland in the 1920s and 1930s. In more modern times, notable players whose careers began with the 'Fifers' included Willie McNaught, Jim Baxter and Ian Porterfield, who was destined to score Sunderland's FA-Cup-winning goal against Leeds in 1973.

Rangers have won more major honours than any other club in the world. Their total of 74 top prizes to the end of season 1983–84 comprised 37 Scottish Championship titles (four more than Celtic), 24 Cup triumphs, 12 League Cup successes and the European Cup-Winners' Cup in 1972.

They have completed the Scottish domestic treble (League, League Cup and FA Cup) four times, in 1949, 1964, 1976 and 1978. On those last two occasions they were managed by Jock Wallace, and he returned to Ibrox (via Leicester and Motherwell) to take over from John Greig after Rangers' poor start to season 1983–84.There was an immediate prize — the League Cup.

Rangers' richest phase came just after the first war with the appointment of Willie Struth as manager in 1920. In 33 years under his command — until at 79 he went on the board — Rangers won the League 18 times, the Cup ten times and the League Cup twice.

Under Struth's successor, Scot Symon, Rangers continued triumphantly until, in 1967, Celtic became predominant. Davie Whyte followed him, lasted two years and was succeeded in the managerial chair by Willie Waddell, whose first success was of double value in that it came against Celtic in the 1970–71 League Cup Final.

In European campaigns, Rangers are one of Britain's most experienced clubs. In 1961 and 1967 they were runners-up in the Cup-Winners' Cup, but season 1971–72 proved third time lucky in this particular final, with Rangers beating Moscow Dynamo 3–2 to take the trophy.

In 1975, under manager Jock Wallace, Rangers ended the nine-year Championship domination of Celtic. They reached all eight Scottish FA Cup finals (4 won, 4 lost) from 1976–83 inclusive, and a return to such glory days was clearly hoped for on the re-appointment of Wallace in November 1983.

St Johnstone, one of the sturdy provincials of Scottish football, were formed in 1884 but, apart from three times winning the Second Division championship, they made no mark for 85 years.

Then in season 1969–70 they reached the Final of the League Cup and football fever gripped the picturesque and usually quiet Tayside town of Perth. At Hampden Park, however, the mighty Celtic beat them by the only goal of a fiercely fought game.

St Johnstone's centenary season (1983–84) was launched with the club back in the Premier Division but, as in 1975–76 when the Scottish League was re-constructed, they lasted only one season in the highest company.

St Mirren spent only two seasons outside the First Division (1936–37, 1967–68) until being relegated in 1971 — a remarkable record considering the club had only once finished as high as third in the Championship, and that as long ago as 1893. They were Scottish Cup winners in 1926 and 1959.

St Mirren won back a place in the Scottish Championship in 1977, when promoted as winners of Division 1, and finished a worthy third in the Premier League in 1980.

English clubs have come to regard St Mirren as a source for transfer bargains such as Jimmy Robertson to Tottenham (£25,000), Archie Gemmill to Preston (£13,000), Gordon McQueen to Leeds (£35,000). Jim Blair to Norwich (£18,000), and two deals in 1979 that grossed more than half a million pounds — striker Frank McGarvey to Liverpool for £300,000 and midfield player Tony Fitzpatrick to Bristol City for £250,000.

Stenhousemuir have failed to win a major honour in the 100 years since their formation in 1884, and have never moved above the Second Division. But they could claim a part in Scotland's qualification for the 1974 World Cup Finals in Munich, for national team manager Willie Ormond began his playing career at Ochilview Park.

Stirling Albion owed their formation in 1945 to the miscalculations of a German bomb-aimer some five years earlier. In 1940 an enemy aircraft discharged its cargo over the town of Stirling, and the Forth Bank ground — home of King's Park FC — was destroyed. Local feeling demanded the formation of a new club and under the leadership of coal merchant Tom Fergusson, Stirling Albion was born after the war. Their ground became Annfield Park, with the dressing-rooms located in a huge mansion.

In their first season Stirling won the inaugural post-war Division C Championship. The pattern of an up-and-down existence has continued ever since, and they have been Second Division Champions five times, in 1953, 1958, 1961, 1965 and 1977.

Stranraer, situated on the south-west coast, have the smallest ground capacity (5,500) on Scotland's League club circuit. Formed in 1870, they have passed their centenary without achieving a major prize. In March 1980 the club appointed Neil Hood, from Clyde, as player-manager. Until then, Stranraer had been managerless for all but three of their 110 years, with the team selected each Monday night by a show of hands among the twelve directors.

The World Cup

THE ORIGINAL WORLD CUP
Jules Rimet Trophy

The greatest football show on earth, the most prized possession in the soccer universe, is the World Cup, staged every four years. For the first 40 years of its existence it was known as the Jules Rimet trophy, after the French lawyer who aired the idea of a world football championship among nations when he became president of FIFA in 1920.

Ten years later the dream turned to reality with the launching of the World Cup in Montevideo, Uruguay . . . but when the tenth tournament was staged in West Germany in 1974, the prize at stake was of new design and titled not the Jules Rimet Cup but the FIFA World Cup.

The reason for the change of trophy dates from the time the rules were framed for the very first tournament in 1930. Included was a clause to the effect that if any country won the Jules Rimet Cup three times, it would become theirs permanently — and Brazil's success in Mexico in 1970 was their third world conquest in the last four series. Amid unprecedented scenes of welcome and celebration, they took home to Rio the original World Cup — made of solid gold and weighing nine pounds, though standing only a foot high — to keep for ever. Or at least until January 1984, when it was stolen in Rio, melted down and the gold sold by the five-man gang for £18,000.

THE FIFA WORLD CUP
First contested in 1974

In Britain the tournament was not regarded as truly representative of world football until 1950 when, having rejoined FIFA after lengthy disagreement over amateurism and broken-time payments, the Home Countries became eligible to compete for the first time. The prize remained beyond British reach for another 16 years; then, in 1966, England became the third host country to triumph, the first since 1934. They took it from Brazil with football that was functional, disciplined and supremely efficient. In Mexico four years later Brazil, committed to all-out attack to cover their suspect defence and weakness in goal, won it back with the magic and flair of Pele, Gerson, Jairzinho and Rivelino. No country could more worthily have won the World Cup outright.

In 1974, West Germany added their name to the list of host countries who have won the World Cup, and Argentina did likewise in 1978, their triumph putting South America 6–5 ahead of Europe in the inter-continental battle for football's greatest prize. That particular tally was levelled in Spain four years later, when Italy emulated Brazil's feat by winning the trophy for the third time.

1930 World Cup: Uruguay staged and won the first World Cup. Only 13 countries took part, and all 17 matches were played in Montevideo. Because of travelling difficulties and the lengthy absence involved in a trip by sea to South America and back, Europe's representatives were restricted to France, Yugoslavia, Rumania and Belgium. Uruguay, who had trained their players in isolation for two months, and Argentina each won their semi-final by 6–1 (against USA and Yugoslavia respectively), and in the first World Cup Final, played on 30 July 1930, the host country rallied from 2–1 down at half-time to triumph 4–2, to the delight of a 90,000 crowd.

1934 World Cup: The holders, Uruguay, refused to go to Italy to defend their title, as so few European countries had participated in the first tournament. Of the 16 nations who qualified from an entry of 29, 12 were from Europe. The 'group qualifying' method up to the semi-finals was replaced by an unsatisfactory knock-out system throughout — defeat at the first attempt meant that Brazil, Argentina and USA travelled halfway across the world for only one match each. Italy kicked off with the 7–1 thrashing of USA, then beat Spain and Austria, both 1–0, to reach the Final against Czechoslovakia in Rome. There the unfancied Czechs took a surprise lead with 20 minutes left, but Italy scored a late equalizer and in extra time they squeezed home 2–1 to emulate Uruguay's feat as the second successive host nation to take the World Cup.

1938 World Cup: Now it was Argentina's turn to stay out, in protest over their request to stage the tournament being rejected. Instead, the series was again held in Europe, this time in France, and Italy impressively retained the trophy. Victories over Norway, France and Brazil carried them to the Final, in which Hungary were well beaten by 4-2. Once again Italy, under the managership of Vittorio Pozzo, had done it, and with the Second World War soon to break out, they were to hold the Cup longer than anyone before or after — until 1950.

1950 World Cup: After an interval of 12 years, the war having erased two tournaments, the world football championship was resumed in Brazil. The British Associations had rejoined FIFA in 1946, so were eligible for the first time, but only England entered; Scotland could have done so as runners-up in the Home Championship, but all along they had declared they would take part only if they were British Champions. In their first World Cup, England suffered their greatest-ever humiliation, for after beating Chile 2-0 in their opening match in Rio, they took the same eleven to Belo Horizonte on Sunday, 29 June, and ludicrously lost one-nil to the United States' part-timers. America won by a 30th-minute goal by their centre-forward Gaetjens, miraculously surviving a rearguard action that lasted all the second half. England contributed an equal part to their own destruction by missing so many chances and their elimination was complete when Spain beat them 1-0 in Rio. This was the only time that the competition was based on four qualifying groups, whose winners went into a final pool which comprised Brazil, Spain, Sweden and Uruguay (participating for the first time since the inaugural tournament). After magnificent wins against Sweden (7-1) and Spain (6-1) in the final pool, Brazil needed only to draw with Uruguay in the grand finale to be crowned World Champions for the first time, and in anticipation the all-time world record attendance of 200,000 filled the Maracana Stadium. Brazil began brilliantly and scored first, directly after half-time, but with a superbly marshalled defence Uruguay gradually wore them down, then hit them with two smoothly taken goals to triumph 2-1 and bring their World Cup record to two conquests in two attempts spanning 20 years.

1954 World Cup: The fifth World Championship, in Switzerland, established the tournament format that was to be used until 1974, with four groups each providing two qualifiers to contest the quarter-finals and beyond on a knock-out system. Hungary, with Puskas, Hidegkuti and Kocsis superb in attack, were rated 'unbeatable'. In the previous six months they had shattered England's unbeaten home record against foreign countries with an astonishing 6-3 victory at Wembley and completed the double by 7-1 in Budapest. So England were hardly in better shape to face the world than when they had left Brazil demoralized four years earlier, and after topping their group with little conviction, they went out in the quarter-final 4-2 to Uruguay, who had still to be beaten in the

World Cup after 24 years. Scotland's entry meant that Britain was doubly represented for the first time, but theirs was no more than a token appearance. In the qualifying group they failed to register a goal or a point, being humbled 7–0 by Uruguay and losing 1–0 to Austria. Meanwhile, Hungary clinched their group by slamming Korea 9–0 and Germany 8–3, and went through to the Final with 4–2 victories over both Brazil and Uruguay; but Germany countered their mastery with guile off the field and then deprived them of the World Cup on it. In their group match against Hungary, the Germans purposely fielded a weak team and did not mind losing 8–3 because they were confident that they could still qualify for the quarter-finals by beating Turkey in a play-off — and did so 7–2. Thus the easier passage to the Final was open to them, and they took it with wins by 2–0 against Yugoslavia and 6–1 against Austria. Yet, for all their strategy, Germany seemed to be heading for defeat in the Final as Puskas (playing for the first time since being injured in the group match against Germany) and Czibor gave Hungary a 2–0 lead. But skipper Fritz Walter rallied his side magnificently, and goals by Morlock and Rahn (2) earned Germany an extraordinary victory by 3–2, which made them the only country in World Cup history to win the trophy after being beaten during the final series.

1958 World Cup: In Sweden, Britain was represented for the only time by all four Home Countries, but England (apart from holding Brazil 0–0) and Scotland made no show. Surprisingly, it was the outsiders, Northern Ireland and Wales, who reached the quarter-finals. There, however, a catalogue of injuries proved insurmountable to Ireland, who lost 4–0 to France, and Brazil's one goal was too much for Wales. Hosts Sweden delighted their supporters by reaching the Final, then sent them almost delirious by scoring the first goal, but Brazil answered with one of the greatest exhibitions ever seen in a World Cup Final, devastatingly using 4–2–4 to stamp their mark on the tournament. Garrincha, Didi, Vava and a 17-year-old named Pele showed the world a new conception of attacking play, which brought them the biggest-ever World Cup Final victory by 5–2 — Vava and Pele each scored twice — and a spectacular first success in the competition.

1962 World Cup: In contrast to Sweden, Chile staged the least memorable contest for the Jules Rimet Cup since it became a truly world-wide tournament. There was a saturation of negative, defence-ridden football and England, Britain's lone representatives, went out 3–1 to Brazil in the quarter-finals. Pele was lost to Brazil through injury early in the competition, but although now an ageing side and far less impressive than four years previously, they retained the trophy, beating Czechoslovakia in the Final 3–1 after being a goal down.

1966 World Cup: Four months before they staged and won the World Cup, England literally lost it. For 36 years the solid gold cup had been in existence, and while in Italy's possession it had survived the war years hidden under the bed of Italian FA vice-president Dr Ottorino Barassi. Since 1958 it had been in the safe keeping of Brazil, and London saw it ceremonially for the first time in January 1966, at the making of the draw for the qualifying rounds of the final series. Two months later, at about midday on Sunday, 20 March, it vanished in a daring daylight theft from a padlocked cabinet while on display at a £3-million stamp exhibition at the Central Hall, Westminster. For seven days the football world was held spellbound with conjecture that the game's greatest trophy — like the FA Cup stolen in 1895 — might never be seen again. Then a black and white mongrel dog named Pickles sniffed at a parcel lying under a laurel bush in the garden of his home in Upper Norwood, London — and the World Cup was found intact! The motive for the theft had been a ransom demand for £15,000 to Football Association chairman Joe Mears. One of the accomplices, a London dock labourer, was jailed for two years, while Pickles earned some £6,000 in rewards for his owner and a medal for himself. And England, having lost and found the Jules Rimet Cup, won it at Wembley on 30 July in the most sensational World Cup Final of all.

The start of their march to glory, a 0–0 draw against Uruguay, could hardly have been less exciting for Wembley's 75,000 crowd. Then came two 2–0 wins to stir the blood a little, against Mexico (scorers Bobby Charlton and Roger Hunt) and France (Hunt 2). Argentina in the quarter-final posed the toughest problem yet, and England's World Cup hopes might have ended there had not Antonio Rattin, captain of the Argentinians, got himself sent off towards half-time for rough play and arguing with West German referee Rudolf Kreitlein. During a seven-minute hold-up before Rattin finally departed, the entire Argentine team threatened to walk off. The ten who eventually decided to stay stepped up their spoiling tactics and England struggled through 1–0 with a 77th-minute header by Geoff Hurst, replacing the injured Jimmy Greaves.

Brazil's hopes of a World Cup hat-trick dived when Pele was injured in the opening game against Bulgaria, and they failed to survive the qualifying stages. While England were playing that nasty quarter-final with Argentina at Wembley, up at Goodison Park, Portugal and rank outsiders North Korea produced a match straight out of the realms of fiction. Having shocked Italy 1–0 at Middlesbrough to qualify, Pak Doo Ik and his happy-go-lucky Korean team-mates went one . . .two . . .three up against Portugal.

But they lacked the tactical know-how to hold such an advantage, and Eusebio, striking irresistible form, scored the first four goals (two of them penalties) in Portugal's eventual victory by 5-3. At Hillsborough, Sheffield, West Germany comprehensively beat Uruguay 4-0, and in the other quarter-final at Sunderland Russia defeated Hungary 2-1.

The semi-finals provided an enormous contrast. At Goodison, West Germany scored a laborious 2-1 win against Russia (who were quickly reduced to ten fit men by injury to Sabo, and to nine when Chislenko was sent off for retaliation after a foul that injured him, too). At Wembley the following night the score was also 2-1, but this game between England and Portugal put the seal of world stature back on the competition. In terms of technique it was the finest match of the whole series in England. Bobby Charlton cracked both England goals; late on, brother Jack handled and from the spot Eusebio explosively took his only chance of the game — the first time Banks's net had been stretched in the tournament.

For only the second time, the first since 1934, the Final went to an extra half-hour. Haller shot West Germany ahead after 13 minutes, but Hurst equalized six minutes later with a splendid header from Bobby Moore's free-kick and with 13 minutes left, victory seemed assured as Martin Peters scored at close range after Hurst's shot had been blocked. But in the last seconds Weber slammed Germany level from a disputed free-kick by Emmerich, and at two-all the match went into extra-time. England found the inspiration they needed to win the game all over again in the ceaseless running of Ball. His was the centre which Hurst hammered in off the crossbar for the third goal — Swiss referee Gottfried Dienst awarded it after what seemed a timeless consultation with his Russian linesman Tofil Bakhramov — and through to the closing seconds Moore and his men clung desperately to the lead. Then, in a last-fling attack, West Germany left themselves uncovered at the back and Hurst pounded away down the left flank from halfway and finished with a lashing left-foot shot past Tilkowski from 20 yards. Moments later, England fans in their thousands swept across the Wembley pitch to acclaim the incongruously unemotional Alf Ramsey, who had fashioned the triumph with his wingless 4-3-3 tactics; to mob the three-goal hero Hurst, first man to score a hat-trick in the World Cup Final; and to salute the whole team with chants of 'Eng-land! Eng-land!' that billowed across the vast arena as Bobby Moore collected the world's greatest soccer prize.

1970 World Cup: By winning all six matches they were required to play in Mexico, Brazil worthily became the first country to take the World Cup three times and, in doing so, they won the trophy outright. Compared with the lowest-ever aggregates of 89 goals in each of the two previous tournaments, the 32-match programme now produced 95, with Brazil responsible for 19 of them. It mattered not that they had a suspect defence; their game was based on creation in midfield and a flair for all-out attack in which Pele, kicked out of the two previous World Cups, once again touched his spectacular best in this his fourth tournament. England, as indeed most of the European countries did, overcame the problems of altitude and heat better than expected. They were based at Guadalajara, and Hurst began as he had finished in 1966 — on the scoresheet. England's three group qualifying matches each produced a 1-0 result, with wins against Rumania and Czechoslovakia and defeat by Jairzinho's goal against Brazil. It was enough to take them through to the quarter-finals as group runners-up to Brazil. Then, with the venue switching to Leon, they were paired with West Germany. For an hour, England played as splendidly as they had done against them in the 1966 Final, and when Martin Peters added to Alan Mullery's first-half goal directly after half-time, a lead of 2-0 looked unassailable. But Beckenbauer put Germany back in the game with a diagonal shot that flashed under Bonetti (Banks was in bed, the victim of a stomach bug) and England were shaken again as Seeler scored with a back-header. So, again as in the Wembley Final, the sides went into extra time at 2-2, and in the second period Muller, right in front of the target, smashed in the goal that gave Germany victory by 3-2 and avenged 1966. There were inevitable question-marks — over the tactical substitution of Bobby Charlton (in his record-breaking 106th International) and Martin Peters as well as over two of the German goals — but nothing could alter the fact that the World Champions had been dethroned.

In the other quarter-finals Brazil overcame some difficult moments to beat Peru 4-2 in Guadalajara; Uruguay dismissed Russia 1-0 on a disputed goal in the last minute of extra time in Mexico City; and Italy, having scored only one goal in three matches to head their qualifying group, threw away caution, when a goal down, to the hosts Mexico in Toluca, and won 4-1.

Goals were cheap, in extra time, anyway, in the Mexico City semi-final between Italy and West Germany. Boninsegna gave Italy an early lead, and that was still the only goal as the match went into injury time. Then Schnellinger equalized, and West Germany went ahead with the first of five goals scored in the extra half-hour, which finished with Italy winners of an extraordinary match by 4-3. In the other semi-final in Guadalajara, Uruguay took a shock lead, but Brazil, albeit belatedly, turned on the full range of talents and won 3-1, with goals by Clodoaldo, Jairzinho and Rivelino.

The Azteca Stadium, home of Mexican football, did not see Brazil until the Final itself. Their performance in beating Italy 4-1 was well worth the wait. It started with Pele heading in Rivelino's cross after

18 minutes, and although Italy were level by half-time, Boninsegna punishing one of those defensive mistakes to which Brazil were prone, midfield general Gerson restored the lead with a magnificent shot from outside the penalty-area. Gerson and Pele combined to set up the third goal for Jairzinho, and the final scene was stolen by Brazil's captain, Carlos Alberto. He shot a stunning last goal from Pele's perfect pass, and three minutes later he collected the Jules Rimet Cup that was to be Brazil's to keep. Their hat-trick was an incredible achievement for Mario Zagalo, a member of the winning teams in 1958 and 1962, and now triumphant again only a few months after succeeding João Saldanha as Brazil's manager.

1974 World Cup: Helmut Schoen's West Germany, fourth host nation to win the title, also became the first country to hold the World and European Championships simultaneously. Unimpressive through the group stage, in which they were beaten 1–0 by East Germany in Hamburg, they then showed improving blend with each match and reached a peak when it mattered most — in the Final against the stylists of Holland.

For the third consecutive World Cup, the Finals opened with a goalless match, on this occasion Brazil v Yugoslovia, and by the time the competition was completed its total of 97 goals in 38 matches represented the lowest scoring average (2.55 per game) in history. The presence of unknowns such as Australia, Haiti and Zaire provided new faces; combined with the absence of such as England, Hungary, Belgium and Portugal, it ridiculed any suggestion that the world's sixteen best countries were competing in West Germany.

England, finishing with Wales behind Poland, failed to qualify for the first time, and Scotland were left to carry Britain's banner in the Finals. If there were times when Willie Ormond's players earned less than full marks for discipline off the field, they distinguished themselves as the only country not to lose a game in West Germany. In retrospect, however, their opening match, a 2–0 win against Zaire, was their undoing. One more goal in the last hour would have taken them on; instead Brazil, who failed to replace sufficient stars of the triumphant 1970 side, qualified at Scotland's expense with Yugoslavia from Group 2.

East and West Germany went through from Group 1. Holland topped Group 3 by a point from Sweden and in Group 4 Poland (conquerors of England on their way to Germany) took maximum points and most goals (12) by beating Argentina, Haiti and Italy. Two goals against both Argentina and Haiti set Polish striker Lato on the way to becoming the tournament's top scorer with a total of seven.

With quarter-finals and semi-finals discontinued, the last eight played in two groups on a league basis. More matches produced more revenue, but the knock-out element was missing. In Group A, Holland gave the most scintillating display of the whole tournament when beating Argentina 4–0 with goals by Cruyff (2), Krol and Rep. After defeating East Germany 2–0, Holland needed only to draw with the holders Brazil in their remaining qualifier to reach the Final, and they answered tough tactics that were unworthy of the reigning Champions with goals by Neeskens and Cruyff to win the group with a 100 per cent record.

On a rain-ruined pitch at Frankfurt, West Germany beat Poland by Muller's lone goal to clinch Group B with another 100 per cent record . . . and so to a dramatic Final in Munich on 7 July. Direct from the kick-off and before even one German had touched the ball, Cruyff was brought down by Hoeness. English referee Jack Taylor awarded the first penalty in the history of World Cup Finals, and Neeskens scored the fastest World Cup Final goal on record.

Twenty-five minutes later the ball was on the penalty spot again after left-winger Holzenbein was floored. Breitner scored the equalizer, and two minutes before half-time Bonhof's right-wing run led to the winner by Muller — his last goal before announcing his retirement from international football.

Individual style within the framework of brilliant team play had made Holland the most attractive team in the tournament under the managership of Rinus Michels, Barcelona and former Ajax coach. They still created second-half chances, but could not put them away, and the new FIFA World Cup was presented to Franz Beckenbauer. West Germany, twenty years after their first success, were World Champions again, and for the eighth time in ten Finals the winners had come from behind to take the crown.

1978 World Cup: For the second time in succession England failed to reach the Final series, deprived in the qualifying tournament on goal difference (15–4 to Italy's 18–4) despite winning ten points from six games. So Scotland, alone again, were left to fly the British flag in Argentina, and embarrassingly they did it. The presence of Iran, Tunisia and Mexico among the 16 finalists once again cast heavy doubts over a qualifying system that guaranteed, for reasons of sheer geography, that not all the world's strongest countries contested the finals of the world's biggest football competition.

The tradition of a goalless opening game was maintained for the fourth consecutive series, but the whistles of derision greeting West Germany and Poland that day, 1 June, turned into a tumult of frenzied jubilation 24 days later in the same Buenos Aires stadium as Argentina added their name as the fifth in the line of home countries to triumph in the World Cup.

In Group 1 of the qualifying stage, Italy beat France 2–1, Hungary

3-1 and then Argentina 1-0 for the only 100 per cent record, with Argentina finishing in second place. Poland and West Germany qualified from Group 2, Austria and Brazil from Group 3, and in Group 4 Peru surprised everyone by finishing top with five points out of a possible six, two more than Holland, who were destined to reach their second successive Final. Peru beat Scotland 3-1 in their opening match in Cordoba, then held Holland 0-0 and finally despatched Iran 4-1, with three of those goals, including two penalties, from Cubillas.

The same player's two goals had caused the downfall of Scotland, for whom the party was virtually over after the first game. Their stock plunged even lower in a 1-1 draw with Iran, and although Holland were beaten 3-2 in the final qualifier, it was too late to prevent manager Ally MacLeod's 'Tartan Army' making an early return home. They did so discredited and disgraced, quickly following the departure from Argentina of 31-year-old winger Willie Johnston who, as one of the players routine-tested after the Peru game, was found to have taken an illegal stimulant. He was banned by FIFA for a year and by Scotland for ever.

At the next stage, Holland topped group A with wins against Austria (5-1), Italy (2-1) and a 2-2 draw with West Germany, while in Group B Argentina, having beaten Poland 2-0 and drawn 0-0 with Brazil, needed to win their final game against Peru by at least four goals to proceed to the Final on goal difference at Brazil's expense. The result was Argentina 6, Peru 0, leaving Brazil in second place reflecting what might have been as the only country not to lose a match in Argentina (played 7, won 4, drawn 3). They took third place by defeating Italy 2-1.

In the Final against Holland, all ended well for Argentina, though only after their biggest fright of the tournament so nearly made extra time unnecessary. Kempes sent Argentina ahead after 38 minutes, but Nanninga equalized with eight minutes of normal time remaining. Then, in the closing moments, Rensenbrink hit a post — that was how close Holland went to becoming the first European country to win the World Cup in South America. In the extra half-hour goals by Kempes (105 minutes) and Bertoni (115) completed Argentina's first World Cup triumph and turned Buenos Aires into a city of carnival.

So Holland, their football no longer illuminated by the dazzling talent of Cruyff, finished runners-up for the second successive tournament. In 1974 West Germany had added their name to the list of host countries who have won the World Cup; now Argentina did likewise and the final memory of 'Mundial 78' was of Argentina's doleful manager Cesar Luis Menotti lighting yet another cigarette as his captain Passarella lifted the glittering prize.

1982 World Cup: Italy began dismally in Spain but, once past the first phase (in which they drew all three games and went through only on goal superiority over Cameroon), they developed into a formidable team. At the second stage they beat both South American giants — the holders Argentina 2-1 and Brazil 3-2, with the hat-trick that knocked the best footballing team out of the tournament coming from Paulo Rossi, who had only just returned to the game after a two-year ban imposed for his involvement in a bribes scandal. In the semi-final Rossi scored the two goals that beat Poland, and in the Final he launched the 3-1 victory against West Germany by which Italy, managed by Enzo Bearzot, equalled Brazil's record of three World Cup successes.

England, having qualified tenuously for Spain, made a splendid start in Bilbao with Bryan Robson scoring after only 27 seconds against France, who were beaten 3-1. With further wins against Czechoslovakia (2-0) and Kuwait (1-0), England were one of only two countries (Brazil the other) to take maximum points in the first round.

Meanwhile, West Germany had provided the shock of the opening phase by losing 2-1 to Algeria at Gijon. With Austria's coercion, however, they manipulated their way through, and were grouped with England and Spain at the next stage. A 0-0 draw with West Germany left England needing to beat Spain to stay alive but, with all to play for, Ron Greenwood, in what was to be his last match as manager, refused to gamble on the fitness of Kevin Keegan and Trevor Brooking until the later stages. Their introduction as substitutes gave England the positive approach so desperately needed, but another 0-0 result meant they were out of the tournament, though still undefeated.

Scotland found themselves drawn in an unenviable group, having to meet Brazil and Russia. After kicking off with a 5-2 win against New Zealand, Jock Stein's men crashed 4-1 to Brazil and drew 2-2 with Russia. As in Argentina, goal difference denied Scotland further progress.

From an unspectacular start, Billy Bingham's Northern Ireland had a wondrous time in Spain. After draws against Yugoslavia (0-0) and Honduras (1-1), they rocked the host country with Gerry Armstrong's goal in Valencia, and heroically held out despite Mal Donaghy being sent off early in the second half.

France ultimately ended Irish hopes (4-1) in the second round, but Bingham and his team returned home in glory. Furthermore, at 17 years 42 days, Norman Whiteside had stolen the legendary Pele's record as the youngest player to appear in the World Cup finals (the Brazilian star was aged 17 years 8 months when he played in Sweden in 1958).

The 1982 series in Spain was the biggest in World Cup history.

The qualifiers increased in number from 16 to 24, and a total of 52 matches, from opening day to Final, compared with 38 in the two previous tournaments. But greater quantity did not mean greater quality of football.

The most dramatic finish in Spain came in the semi-final between West Germany and France. Three-all after extra time, it became the first game in any World Final series to be decided on penalty-kicks, and Germany's luck held. Fortunate not to have goalkeeper Schumacher sent off for a dreadful foul on Battiston, they won the shoot-out 5-4.

But in the Final, played in Madrid's magnificent Bernabeu Stadium, they were overplayed, and Italy deservedly triumphed. Victories over the holders (Argentina), the favourites (Brazil) and the European Champions (West Germany) gave them a worthy pedigree, plus the distinction of being the first European nation to win the world crown three times.

Midway through the first half, Cabrini made his mark in the World Cup records as the first player to miss a penalty in the Final. He shot wide after Briegel brought down Conti, but it was only a temporary reprieve for the Germans.

Rossi scored after 56 minutes from a cross by Gentile, who also set up a second goal 12 minutes later by man-of-the-match Tardelli. With ten minutes left, Conti broke clear, and his long run ended with the perfect pass for substitute Altobelli to shoot past Schumacher.

Breitner's reply (82 minutes) was too late to give West Germany hope, and 40-year-old goalkeeper Dino Zoff proudly stepped forward to receive Italy's first World Cup since another goalkeeper-captain, Combi, did so in 1934. Zoff was the oldest player to earn a World Cup-winner's medal, and Rossi, with six goals, collected the Golden Boot awarded to the tournament's top scorer.

World Cup Summaries

1930 World Cup — First Tournament — in Uruguay

Winners: Uruguay. **Runners-up:** Argentina.**Third:** USA. **Entries:** 13.
Other countries taking part: Belgium, Bolivia, Brazil, Chile, France,
Mexico, Paraguay, Peru, Rumania, Yugoslavia.
All matches played in Montevideo.
Top scorer: Stabile (Argentina) 8 goals.

Final: *Uruguay* 4 (Dorado, Cea, Iriarte, Castro), *Argentina* 2
(Peucelle, Stabile)
Half-time: Uruguay 1, Argentina 2. *Attendance:* 90,000.
Uruguay: Ballesteros; Nasazzi, Mascheroni, Andrade, Fernandez,
Gestido, Dorado, Scarone, Castro, Cea, Iriarte.
Argentina: Botasso; Della Torre, Paternoster, Evaristo (J), Monti,
Suarez, Peucelle, Varallo, Stabile, Ferreira, Evaristo (M)

1934 World Cup — Second Tournament — in Italy

Winners: Italy. **Runners-up:** Czechoslovakia. **Third:** Germany.
Entries: 29 (16 qualifiers).
Other countries in final series: Argentina, Austria, Belgium, Brazil,
Egypt, France, Holland, Hungary, Rumania, Spain, Sweden,
Switzerland, USA.
Venues: Rome, Naples, Milan, Turin, Florence, Bologna, Genoa,
Trieste.
Top scorers: Schiavio (Italy), Nejedly (Czechoslovakia), Conen
(Germany), each 4 goals.

Final (Rome):
Italy 2 (Orsi, Schiavio), *Czechoslovakia* 1 (Puc). After extra time.
Half-time: Italy 0, Czechoslovakia 1. *Score after 90 minutes:* 1-1.
Attendance: 50,000.
Italy: Combi; Monzeglio, Allemandi, Ferraris, Monti, Bertolini,
Guaita, Meazza, Schiavio, Ferrari, Orsi.
Czechoslovakia: Planicka; Zenisek, Ctyroky, Kostalek, Cambal,
Krcil, Junek. Svoboda, Sobotka, Nejedly. Puc.

1938 World Cup — Third Tournament — in France

Winners: Italy. **Runners-up:** Hungary. **Third:** Brazil. **Entries:** 25 (15
qualifiers).
Other countries in final series: Belgium, Cuba, Czechoslovakia,

Dutch East Indies, France, Germany, Holland, Norway, Poland, Rumania, Sweden, Switzerland.
Venues: Paris, Marseilles, Bordeaux, Lille, Antibes, Strasbourg, Le Havre, Reims, Toulouse.
Top scorer: Leonidas (Brazil) 8 goals

Final (Paris):
Italy 4 (Colaussi 2, Piola 2), *Hungary* 2 (Titkos, Sarosi).
Half-time: Italy 3, Hungary 1. *Attendance:* 45,000;
Italy: Olivieri; Foni, Rava, Serantoni, Andreolo, Locatelli, Biavati, Meazza, Piola, Ferrari, Colaussi.
Hungary: Szabo; Polgar, Biro, Szalay, Szucs, Lazar, Sas, Vincze, Sarosi, Szengeller, Titkos.

1950 World Cup — Fourth Tournament — in Brazil

Winners: Uruguay. **Runners-up:** Brazil. **Third:** Sweden. **Entries:** 29 (13 qualifiers).
Other countries in final series: Bolivia, Chile, England, Italy, Mexico, Paraguay, Spain, Switzerland, USA, Yugoslavia.
Venues: Rio de Janeiro, Sao Paulo, Recife, Curitiba, Belo Horizonte, Porto Alegre.
Top scorer: Ademir (Brazil) 7 goals.

* Deciding Match (Rio de Janeiro):
Uruguay 2 (Schiaffino, Ghiggia). *Brazil* 1 (Friaca).
Half-time: 0–0. *Attendance:* 200,000.
Uruguay: Maspoli; Gonzales, Tejera, Gambetta, Varela, Andrade, Ghiggia, Perez, Miguez, Schiaffino, Moran.
Brazil: Barbosa; Augusto, Juvenal, Bauer, Danilo, Bigode, Friaca, Zizinho, Ademir, Jair, Chico.

* For the only time, the World Cup was decided on a Final Pool system, in which the winners of the four qualifying groups met in a six-match series. So, unlike previous and subsequent tournaments, there was no official Final as such, but Uruguay v Brazil was the deciding final match on in the Final Pool.

1954 World Cup — Fifth Tournament — in Switzerland

Winners: Germany. **Runners-up:** Hungary. **Third:** Austria. **Entries:** 35 (16 qualifiers).
Other countries in final series: Belgium, Brazil, Czechoslovakia, England, France, Italy, Korea, Mexico, Scotland, Switzerland, Turkey, Uruguay, Yugoslavia.
Venues: Berne, Zürich, Lausanne, Basle, Geneva, Lugano.

Top scorer: Kocsis (Hungary) 11 goals.

Final (Berne):
Germany 3 (Morlock, Rahn 2). *Hungary* 2 (Puskas, Czibor).
Half-time: 2-2. *Attendance:* 60,000.
Germany: Turek; Posipal, Kohlmeyer, Eckel, Liebrich, Mai, Rahn, Morlock, Walter (O), Walter (F), Schaefer.
Hungary: Grosics; Buzansky, Lantos, Boszik, Lorant, Zakarias, Czibor, Kocsis, Hidegkuti, Puskas, Toth.

1958 World Cup — Sixth Tournament — in Sweden

Winners: Brazil. **Runners-up:** Sweden. **Third:** France. **Entries:** 47 (16 qualifiers).
Other countries in final series: Argentina, Austria, Czechoslovakia, England, Hungary, Mexico, Northern Ireland, Paraguay, Russia, Scotland, Wales, West Germany, Yugoslavia.
Venues: Stockholm, Gothenburg, Malmö, Norrköping, Borås, Sandviken, Eskilstuna, Cerebro, Västeras, Hälsingborg, Halmstad.
Top scorer: Fontaine (France) 13 goals.

Final (Stockholm):
Brazil 5 (Vava 2, Pele 2, Zagalo). *Sweden* 2 (Liedholm, Simonsson).
Half-time Brazil 2, Sweden 1. *Attendance:* 50,000.
Brazil: Gilmar; Santos (D), Santos (N), Zio, Bellini, Orlando, Garrincha, Didi, Vava, Pele, Zagalo.
Sweden: Svensson; Bergmark, Axbom, Boerjesson, Gustavsson, Parling, Hamrin, Gren, Simonsson, Liedholm, Skoglund.

1962 World Cup — Seventh Tournament — in Chile

Winners: Brazil. **Runners-up:** Czechoslovakia. **Third:** Chile. **Entries:** 53 (16 qualifiers)
Other countries in final series: Argentina, Bulgaria, Colombia, England, Hungary, Italy, Mexico, Russia, Spain, Switzerland, Uruguay, West Germany, Yugoslavia.
Venues: Santiago, Vina del Mar, Rancagua, Arica.
Top scorers: Garrincha (Brazil), Vava (Brazil), Sanchez (Chile), Albert (Hungary), Ivanov (Russia), Jerkovic (Yugoslavia) each 4 goals.

Final (Santiago):
Brazil 3 (Amarildo, Zito, Vava). *Czechoslovakia* 1 (Masopust).
Half-time: 1-1. *Attendance:* 69,000.
Brazil: Gilmar; Santos (D), Mauro, Zozimo, Santos (N), Zito, Didi, Garrincha, Vava, Amarildo, Zagalo.

Czechoslovakia: Schroiff; Tichy, Novak, Pluskaj, Popluhar, Masopust, Pospichal, Scherer, Kvasniak, Kadraba, Jelinek.

1966 World Cup — Eighth Tournament — in England

Winners: England. **Runners-up:** West Germany. **Third:** Portugal. **Entries:** 53 (16 qualifiers).
Other countries in final series: Argentina, Brazil, Bulgaria, Chile, France, Hungary, Italy, Mexico, North Korea, Russia, Spain, Switzerland, Uruguay.
Venues: London (Wembley and White City), Sheffield (Hillsborough), Liverpool (Goodison Park), Sunderland, Middlesbrough, Manchester (Old Trafford), Birmingham (Villa Park).
Top scorer: Eusebio (Portugal) 9 goals.

Final (Wembley)
England 4 (Hurst 3, Peters). *West Germany* 2 (Haller, Weber). After extra time.
Half-time: 1–1. *Score after 90 minutes:* 2–2. *Attendance:* 100,000.
England: Banks; Cohen, Wilson, Stiles, Charlton (J), Moore, Ball, Hurst, Hunt, Charlton (R), Peters.
West Germany: Tilkowski; Hottges, Schnellinger, Beckenbauer, Schulz, Weber, Haller, Held, Seeler, Overath, Emmerich.

1970 World Cup — Ninth Tournament — in Mexico

Winners: Brazil. **Runners-up:** Italy. **Third:** West Germany. **Entries:** 68 (16 qualifiers).
Other countries in final series: Belgium, Bulgaria, Czechoslovakia, El Salvador, England, Israel, Mexico, Morocco, Peru, Rumania, Russia, Sweden, Uruguay.
Venues: Mexico City, Guadalajara, Leon, Puebla, Toluca.
Top scorer: Muller (West Germany) 10 goals.

Final (Mexico City):
Brazil 4 (Pele, Gerson, Jairzinho, Carlos Alberto). *Italy* 1 (Boninsegna).
Half-time: 1–1. *Attendance:* 107,000.
Brazil: Felix; Carlos Alberto, Brito, Piazza, Everaldo, Clodoalda, Gerson, Jairzinho, Tostao, Pele, Rivelino.
Italy: Albertosi; Burgnich, Facchetti, Cera, Rosato, Bertini (substitute Juliano), Domenghini, De Sisti, Mazzola, Boninsegna (substitute Rivera), Riva.

1974 World Cup — Tenth Tournament — in West Germany

Winners: West Germany. **Runners-up:** Holland. **Third:** Poland.
  Entries: 98 (16 qualifiers).
Other countries in final series: Argentina, Australia, Brazil, Bulgaria,
  Chile, East Germany, Haiti, Italy, Scotland, Sweden, Uruguay,
  Yugoslavia, Zaire.
Venues: Berlin, Hamburg, Frankfurt, Dortmund, Gelsenkirchen,
  Hanover, Dusseldorf, Stuttgart, Munich.
Top scorer: Lato (Poland) 7 goals.

Final (Munich):
West Germany: 2 (Breitner — penalty, Muller). *Holland* 1 (Neeskens
  — penalty).
Half-time: 2–1. *Attendance:* 77,833.
West Germany: Maier; Vogts, Schwarzenbeck, Beckenbauer,
  Breitner, Bonhof, Hoeness, Overath, Grabowski, Muller,
  Holzenbein.
Holland: Jongbloed; Suurbier, Rijsbergen (substitute De Jong),
  Haan, Krol, Jansen, Van Hanegem, Neeskens, Rep, Cruyff,
  Rensenbrink (substitute R. Van der Kerkhof).

1978 World Cup — Eleventh Tournament — in Argentina

Winners: Argentina. **Runners-up:** Holland. **Third:** Brazil. **Entries:**
  102 (16 qualifiers).
Other countries in final series: Austria, France, Hungary, Iran, Italy,
  Mexico, Peru, Poland, Scotland, Spain, Sweden, Tunisia, West
  Germany.
Venues: Buenos Aires, Mar del Plata, Rosario, Cordoba, Mendoza.
Top scorer: Kempes (Argentina) 6 goals.

Final (Buenos Aires):
Argentina 3 (Kempes 2, Bertoni). *Holland* 1 (Nanninga). After extra
  time.
Half-time: 1–0. *Score after 90 minutes:* 1–1. *Attendance:* 77,000.
Argentina: Fillol; Passarella, Olguin, Galvan, Tarantini, Ardiles
  (substitute Larrosa), Gallego, Ortiz (substitute Houseman),
  Bertoni, Luque, Kempes.
Holland: Jongbloed; Krol, Poortvliet, Brandts, Jansen (substitute
  Suurbier), Haan, Neeskens, Van der Kerkhof (W), Rep (substitute
  Nanninga), Van der Kerkhof (R), Rensenbrink.

1982 World Cup — Twelfth Tournament — in Spain

Winners: Italy. **Runners-up:** West Germany. **Third:** Poland. **Entries:** 109 (24 qualifiers).

Other countries in final series: Algeria, Argentina, Austria, Belgium, Brazil, Cameroon, Chile, Czechoslovakia, El Salvador, England, France, Honduras, Hungary, Kuwait, New Zealand, Northern Ireland, Peru, Russia, Scotland, Spain, Yugoslavia.

Venues: Vigo, Coruna, Gijon, Oviedo, Barcelona, Elche, Alicante, Bilbao, Valladolid, Valencia, Zaragoza, Seville, Malaga, Madrid.

Top scorer: Rossi (Italy) 6 goals.

Final (Madrid):

Italy 3 (Rossi, Tardelli, Altobelli), *West Germany* 1 (Breitner).

Half-time: 0–0. Attendance: 90,089.

Italy: Zoff; Bergomi, Scirea, Collovati, Cabrini, Oriali, Gentile, Tardelli, Conti, Rossi, Graziani (substitute Altobelli, second substitute Causio).

West Germany: Schumacher; Kaltz, Stielike, Forster (K-H), Forster (B), Dremmler (substitute Hrubesch), Breitner, Briegel, Rummenigge (substitute Muller), Fischer, Littbarski.

World Cup Final Results

1930	(Montevideo)	Uruguay	4	Argentina	2
1934	(Rome)	Italy	2	Czechoslovakia	1
		(after extra time)			
1938	(Paris)	Italy	4	Hungary	2
1950	(Rio de Janeiro)	Uruguay	2	Brazil	1
1954	(Berne)	Germany	3	Hungary	2
1958	(Stockholm)	Brazil	5	Sweden	2
1962	(Santiago)	Brazil	3	Czechoslovakia	1
1966	(Wembley)	England	4	West Germany	2
		(after extra time)			
1970	(Mexico City)	Brazil	4	Italy	1
1974	(Munich)	West Germany	2	Holland	1
1978	(Buenos Aires)	Argentina	3	Holland	1
		(after extra time)			
1982	(Madrid)	Italy	3	West Germany	1

Venue for the 1986 World Cup Finals: Mexico. 1990: Italy.

The 1986 World Cup

The Finals of the thirteenth World Cup will take place from May 31 — June 29, 1986 in Mexico, Colombia having withdrawn as the scheduled hosts. Thus, Mexico will become the first country to stage the Finals twice (previously in 1970).

As in the 1982 series in Spain, 24 countries will qualify — two of them automatically, Mexico as hosts, Italy as holders — and for the opening round they will be divided into six groups of four.

The second round will comprise 16 teams: the winners and runners-up from each section together with the four third-placed countries with the best records (to be decided on points, goal difference or goals scored) and from that stage the competition will be on a knock-out basis. This is intended to prevent the sort of 'manipulation' practised by certain countries in the last Finals in Spain.

Including the host country, Mexico, and the World Champions, Italy, there were a record 121 entries when the qualifying draw was made in Zurich on December 7, 1983 as follows:

Europe *(33 entries, 13 or 14 qualify)*

Group 1 Poland, Belgium, Greece, Albania (winner qualifies)
Group 2 West Germany, Czechoslovakia, Sweden, Portugal, Malta (winner and runner-up qualify)
Group 3 England, Northern Ireland, Rumania, Turkey, Finland (winner and runner-up qualify)
Group 4 France, Yugoslavia, East Germany, Bulgaria, Luxembourg (winner and runner-up qualify)
Group 5 Austria, Hungary, Holland, Cyprus (winner qualifies)
Group 6 Russia, Denmark, Republic of Ireland, Switzerland, Norway (winner and runner-up qualify)
Group 7 Scotland, Wales, Spain, Iceland (winner qualifies)

Italy qualify automatically as World Champions.

- Runners-up in Groups 1, 5 and 7 play off in a further section from which the winner qualifies for the Finals and the runner-up plays the winner of the Oceania group for a place in Mexico.

South America *(10 entries, 4 qualify)*

Group 1 Argentina, Peru, Colombia, Venezuela
Group 2 Uruguay, Chile, Ecuador
Group 3 Brazil, Paraguay, Bolivia

- Winner of each group qualifies; third-placed team in Group 1 and runners-up in other three sections play off for remaining place in Finals.

North-Central America/Caribbean *(18 entries, 1 qualifies – plus hosts Mexico)*

Group 1 El Salvador v Puerto Rico; Canada v Jamaica; Netherlands Antilles v USA.

Group 2 Barbados v Costa Rica; Panama v Honduras; Guatemala bye.

Group 3 Trinidad & Tobago v Grenada; Antigua v Haiti; Surinam v Guyana.

Asia *(27 entries, 2 qualify)*

Zone A — *Group 1 – Sub-group 1:* Saudi Arabia, United Arab Emirates, Oman;
Sub-group 2: Iraq, Lebanon, Qatar, Jordan.
Group 2 – Sub-group 1: Kuwait, North Yemen (Arab Republic), Syria;
Sub-group 2: Bahrain, Iran, South Yemen (Democratic Republic)

Zone B — *Group 3 – Sub-group 1:* Malaysia, Nepal, South Korea;
Sub-group 2: Thailand, India, Bangladesh, Indonesia.
Group 4 – Sub-group 1: China, Hong Kong, Macao, Brunei
Sub-group 2: Japan, Singapore, North Korea.

Oceania *(4 entries, winner to play winner of European sub-group in two-leg match for place in Finals)*

Australia, New Zealand, Taiwan, Israel.

Africa *(29 entries, 2 qualify)*

Algeria, Cameroon, Ghana — byes to second round.
First round — *Group 1:* Egypt v Zimbabwe; Kenya v Ethiopia; Mauritius v Malawi; Zambia v Uganda; Madagascar v Lesotho; Tanzania v Sudan; *Group 2:* Sierra Leone v Morocco; Libya v Niger; Benin v Tunisia; *Group 3:* Togo v Guinea; Ivory Coast v Gambia; Nigeria v Liberia; Angola v Senegal.

———————

- Qualifying matches to be completed by December 1, 1985.
  Draw for the Finals will take place in Mexico City on December 14, 1985.

Records Section

England's Complete Record
in Full Internationals

Key: WC = World Cup proper; WCQ = World Cup qualifying round; EC = European Championship proper; ECQ = European Championship qualifying round.

Date		Opponents	Venue	Result	
Season 1872-73					
Nov.	30	Scotland	Glasgow	D	0-0
Mar.	8	Scotland	Oval	W	4-2
Season 1873-74					
Mar.	7	Scotland	Glasgow	L	1-2
Season 1874-75					
Mar.	6	Scotland	Oval	D	2-2
Season 1875-76					
Mar.	4	Scotland	Glasgow	L	0-3
Season 1876-77					
Mar.	3	Scotland	Oval	L	1-3
Season 1877-78					
Mar.	2	Scotland	Glasgow	L	2-7
Season 1878-79					
Jan.	18	Wales	Oval	W	2-1
Apr.	5	Scotland	Oval	W	5-4
Season 1879-80					
Mar.	13	Scotland	Glasgow	L	4-5
Mar.	15	Wales	Wrexham	W	3-2
Season 1880-81					
Feb.	26	Wales	Blackburn	L	0-1
Mar.	12	Scotland	Oval	L	1-6
Season 1881-82					
Feb.	18	Ireland	Belfast	W	13-0
Mar.	11	Scotland	Glasgow	L	1-5
Mar.	13	Wales	Wrexham	L	3-5
Season 1882-83					
Feb.	3	Wales	Oval	W	5-0
Feb.	24	Ireland	Liverpool	W	7-0
Mar.	10	Scotland	Sheffield	L	2-3
Season 1883-84					
Feb.	23	Ireland	Belfast	W	8-1
Mar.	15	Scotland	Glasgow	L	0-1
Mar.	17	Wales	Wrexham	W	4-0

Date		Opponents	Venue	Result	
Season 1884-85					
Feb.	28	Ireland	Manchester	W	4-0
Mar.	14	Wales	Blackburn	D	1-1
Mar.	21	Scotland	Oval	D	1-1
Season 1885-86					
Mar.	13	Ireland	Belfast	W	6-1
Mar.	29	Wales	Wrexham	W	3-1
Mar.	31	Scotland	Glasgow	D	1-1
Season 1886-87					
Feb.	5	Ireland	Sheffield	W	7-0
Feb.	26	Wales	Oval	W	4-0
Mar.	19	Scotland	Blackburn	L	2-3
Season 1887-88					
Feb.	4	Wales	Crewe	W	5-1
Mar.	17	Scotland	Glasgow	W	5-0
Mar.	31	Ireland	Belfast	W	5-1
Season 1888-89					
Feb.	23	Wales	Stoke	W	4-1
Mar.	2	Ireland	Everton	W	6-1
Apr.	13	Scotland	Oval	L	2-3
Season 1889-90					
Mar.	15	Wales	Wrexham	W	3-1
Mar.	15	Ireland	Belfast	W	9-1
Apr.	5	Scotland	Glasgow	D	1-1
Season 1890-91					
Mar.	7	Wales	Sunderland	W	4-1
Mar.	7	Ireland	Wolverhampton	W	6-1
Apr.	6	Scotland	Blackburn	W	2-1
Season 1891-92					
Mar.	5	Ireland	Belfast	W	2-0
Mar.	5	Wales	Wrexham	W	2-0
Apr.	2	Scotland	Glasgow	W	4-1
Season 1892-93					
Feb.	25	Ireland	Birmingham	W	6-1
Mar.	13	Wales	Stoke	W	6-0
Apr.	1	Scotland	Richmond	W	5-2
Season 1893-94					
Mar.	3	Ireland	Belfast	D	2-2
Mar.	12	Wales	Wrexham	W	5-1
Apr.	7	Scotland	Glasgow	D	2-2
Season 1894-95					
Mar.	9	Ireland	Derby	W	9-0
Mar.	18	Wales	Kensington	D	1-1
Apr.	6	Scotland	Everton	W	3-0

Date		Opponents	Venue		Result	
		Season 1895-96				
Mar.	7	Ireland	Belfast	W	2-0
Mar.	16	Wales	Cardiff	W	9-1
Apr.	4	Scotland	Glasgow	L	1-2
		Season 1896-97				
Feb.	20	Ireland	Nottingham	W	6-0
Mar.	29	Wales	Sheffield	W	4-0
Apr.	3	Scotland	Crystal Palace	L	1-2
		Season 1897-98				
Mar.	5	Ireland	Belfast	W	3-2
Mar.	28	Wales	Wrexham	W	3-0
Apr.	2	Scotland	Glasgow	W	3-1
		Season 1898-99				
Feb.	18	Ireland	Sunderland	W	13-2
Mar.	20	Wales	Bristol	W	4-0
Apr.	8	Scotland	Birmingham	W	2-1
		Season 1899-1900				
Mar.	17	Ireland	Dublin	W	2-0
Mar.	26	Wales	Cardiff	D	1-1
Apr.	7	Scotland	Glasgow	L	1-4
		Season 1900-01				
Mar.	9	Ireland	Southampton	W	3-0
Mar.	18	Wales	Newcastle	W	6-0
Mar.	30	Scotland	Crystal Palace	D	2-2
		Season 1901-02				
Mar.	3	Wales	Wrexham	D	0-0
Mar.	22	Ireland	Belfast	W	1-0
May	3	Scotland	Birmingham	D	2-2
		Season 1902-03				
Feb.	14	Ireland	Wolverhampton	W	4-0
Mar.	2	Wales	Portsmouth	W	2-1
Apr.	4	Scotland	Sheffield	L	1-2
		Season 1903-04				
Feb.	29	Wales	Wrexham	D	2-2
Mar.	12	Ireland	Belfast	W	3-1
Apr.	9	Scotland	Glasgow	W	1-0
		Season 1904-05				
Feb.	25	Ireland	Middlesbrough	D	1-1
Mar.	27	Wales	Liverpool	W	3-1
Apr.	1	Scotland	Crystal Palace	W	1-0
		Season 1905-06				
Feb.	17	Ireland	Belfast	W	5-0
Mar.	19	Wales	Cardiff	W	1-0
Apr.	7	Scotland	Glasgow	L	1-2

142

Date		Opponents	Venue	Result	
		Season 1906-07			
Feb.	16	Ireland	Everton	W	1-0
Mar.	18	Wales	Fulham	D	1-1
Apr.	6	Scotland	Newcastle	D	1-1
		Season 1907-08			
Feb.	15	Ireland	Belfast	W	3-1
Mar.	16	Wales	Wrexham	W	7-1
Apr.	4	Scotland	Glasgow	D	1-1
June	6	Austria	Vienna	W	6-1
June	8	Austria	Vienna	W	11-1
June	10	Hungary	Budapest	W	7-0
June	13	Bohemia	Prague	W	4-0
		Season 1908-09			
Feb.	13	Ireland	Bradford	W	4-0
Mar.	15	Wales	Nottingham	W	2-0
Apr.	3	Scotland	Crystal Palace	W	2-0
May	29	Hungary	Budapest	W	4-2
May	31	Hungary	Budapest	W	8-2
June	1	Austria	Vienna	W	8-1
		Season 1909-10			
Feb.	12	Ireland	Belfast	D	1-1
Mar.	14	Wales	Cardiff	W	1-0
Apr.	2	Scotland	Glasgow	L	0-2
		Season 1910-11			
Feb.	11	Ireland	Derby	W	2-1
Mar.	13	Wales	Millwall	W	3-0
Apr.	1	Scotland	Everton	D	1-1
		Season 1911-12			
Feb.	10	Ireland	Dublin	W	6-1
Mar.	11	Wales	Wrexham	W	2-0
Mar.	23	Scotland	Glasgow	D	1-1
		Season 1912-13			
Feb.	15	Ireland	Belfast	L	1-2
Mar.	17	Wales	Bristol	W	4-3
Apr.	5	Scotland	Chelsea	W	1-0
		Season 1913-14			
Feb.	14	Ireland	Middlesbrough	L	0-3
Mar.	16	Wales	Cardiff	W	2-0
Apr.	4	Scotland	Glasgow	L	1-3
		Season 1919-20			
Oct.	25	Ireland	Belfast	D	1-1
Mar.	15	Wales	Highbury	L	1-2
Apr.	10	Scotland	Sheffield	W	5-4

Date		Opponents	Venue	Result	
Season 1920-21					
Oct.	23	Ireland	Sunderland	W	2-0
Mar.	14	Wales	Cardiff	D	0-0
Apr.	9	Scotland	Glasgow	L	0-3
May	21	Belgium	Brussels	W	2-0
Season 1921-22					
Oct.	22	Ireland	Belfast	D	1-1
Mar.	13	Wales	Liverpool	W	1-0
Apr.	8	Scotland	Aston Villa	L	0-1
Season 1922-23					
Oct.	21	Ireland	West Bromwich	W	2-0
Mar.	5	Wales	Cardiff	D	2-2
Mar.	19	Belgium	Highbury	W	6-1
Apr.	14	Scotland	Glasgow	D	2-2
May	10	France	Paris	W	4-1
May	21	Sweden	Stockholm	W	4-2
May	24	Sweden	Stockholm	W	3-1
Season 1923-24					
Oct.	20	Ireland	Belfast	L	1-2
Nov.	1	Belgium	Antwerp	D	2-2
Mar.	3	Wales	Blackburn	L	1-2
Apr.	12	Scotland	Wembley	D	1-1
May	17	France	Paris	W	3-1
Season 1924-25					
Oct.	22	Ireland	Everton	W	3-1
Dec.	8	Belgium	West Bromwich	W	4-0
Feb.	28	Wales	Swansea	W	2-1
Apr.	4	Scotland	Glasgow	L	0-2
May	21	France	Paris	W	3-2
Season 1925-26					
Oct.	24	Ireland	Belfast	D	0-0
Mar.	1	Wales	Crystal Palace	L	1-3
Apr.	17	Scotland	Manchester	L	0-1
May	24	Belgium	Antwerp	W	5-3
Season 1926-27					
Oct.	20	Ireland	Liverpool	D	3-3
Feb.	12	Wales	Wrexham	D	3-3
Apr.	2	Scotland	Glasgow	W	2-1
May	11	Belgium	Brussels	W	9-1
May	21	Luxembourg	Luxembourg	W	5-2
May	26	France	Paris	W	6-0
Season 1927-28					
Oct.	22	Ireland	Belfast	L	0-2
Nov.	28	Wales	Burnley	L	1-2
Mar.	31	Scotland	Wembley	L	1-5

144

Date		Opponents	Venue		Result	
May	17	France	Paris		W	5-1
May	19	Belgium	Antwerp		W	3-1
		Season 1928-29				
Oct.	22	Ireland	Everton		W	2-1
Nov.	17	Wales	Swansea		W	3-2
Apr.	13	Scotland	Glasgow		L	0-1
May	9	France	Paris		W	4-1
May	11	Belgium	Brussels		W	5-1
May	15	Spain	Madrid		L	3-4
		Season 1929-30				
Oct.	19	Ireland	Belfast		W	3-0
Nov.	20	Wales	Chelsea		W	6-0
Apr.	5	Scotland	Wembley		W	5-2
May	10	Germany	Berlin		D	3-3
May	14	Austria	Vienna		D	0-0
		Season 1930-31				
Oct.	20	Ireland	Sheffield		W	5-1
Nov.	22	Wales	Wrexham		W	4-0
Mar.	31	Scotland	Glasgow		L	0-2
May	14	France	Paris		L	2-5
May	16	Belgium	Brussels		W	4-1
		Season 1931-32				
Oct.	17	Ireland	Belfast		W	6-2
Nov.	18	Wales	Liverpool		W	3-1
Dec.	9	Spain	Highbury		W	7-1
Apr.	9	Scotland	Wembley		W	3-0
		Season 1932-33				
Oct.	17	Ireland	Blackpool		W	1-0
Nov.	16	Wales	Wrexham		D	0-0
Dec.	7	Austria	Chelsea		W	4-3
Apr.	1	Scotland	Glasgow		L	1-2
May	13	Italy	Rome		D	1-1
May	20	Switzerland	Berne		W	4-0
		Season 1933-34				
Oct.	14	Ireland	Belfast		W	3-0
Nov.	15	Wales	Newcastle		L	1-2
Dec.	6	France	Tottenham		W	4-1
Apr.	14	Scotland	Wembley		W	3-0
May	10	Hungary	Budapest		L	1-2
May	16	Czechoslovakia	Prague		L	1-2
		Season 1934-35				
Sept.	29	Wales	Cardiff		W	4-0
Nov.	14	Italy	Highbury		W	3-2
Feb.	6	Ireland	Everton		W	2-1

Date		Opponents	Venue	Result	
Apr.	6	Scotland	Glasgow	L	0-2
May	18	Holland	Amsterdam	W	1-0

Season 1935-36

Oct.	19	Ireland	Belfast	W	3-1
Dec.	4	Germany	Tottenham	W	3-0
Feb.	5	Wales	Wolverhampton	L	1-2
Apr.	4	Scotland	Wembley	D	1-1
May	6	Austria	Vienna	L	1-2
May	9	Belgium	Brussels	L	2-3

Season 1936-37

Oct.	17	Wales	Cardiff	L	1-2
Nov.	18	Ireland	Stoke	W	3-1
Dec.	2	Hungary	Highbury	W	6-2
Apr.	17	Scotland	Glasgow	L	1-3
May	14	Norway	Oslo	W	6-0
May	17	Sweden	Stockholm	W	4-0
May	20	Finland	Helsinki	W	8-0

Season 1937-38

Oct.	23	Ireland	Belfast	W	5-1
Nov.	17	Wales	Middlesbrough	W	2-1
Dec.	1	Czechoslovakia	Tottenham	W	5-4
Apr.	9	Scotland	Wembley	L	0-1
May	14	Germany	Berlin	W	6-3
May	21	Switzerland	Zürich	L	1-2
May	26	France	Paris	W	4-2

Season 1938-39

Oct.	22	Wales	Cardiff	L	2-4
Oct.	26	FIFA	Highbury	W	3-0
Nov.	9	Norway	Newcastle	W	4-0
Nov.	16	Ireland	Manchester	W	7-0
Apr.	15	Scotland	Glasgow	W	2-1
May	13	Italy	Milan	D	2-2
May	18	Yugoslavia	Belgrade	L	1-2
May	24	Rumania	Bucharest	W	2-0

Season 1946-47

Sept.	28	Ireland	Belfast	W	7-2
Sept.	30	Rep. Ireland	Dublin	W	1-0
Nov.	13	Wales	Manchester	W	3-0
Nov.	27	Holland	Huddersfield	W	8-2
Apr.	12	Scotland	Wembley	D	1-1
May	3	France	Highbury	W	3-0
May	18	Switzerland	Zürich	L	0-1
May	25	Portugal	Lisbon	W	10-0

Date		Opponents	Venue	Result	
		Season 1947-48			
Sept.	21	Belgium	Brussels	W	5-2
Oct.	18	Wales	Cardiff	W	3-0
Nov.	5	Ireland	Everton	D	2-2
Nov.	19	Sweden	Highbury	W	4-2
Apr.	10	Scotland	Glasgow	W	2-0
May	16	Italy	Turin	W	4-0
		Season 1948-49			
Sept.	26	Denmark	Copenhagen	D	0-0
Oct.	9	Ireland	Belfast	W	6-2
Nov.	10	Wales	Villa Park	W	1-0
Dec.	2	Switzerland	Highbury	W	6-0
Apr.	9	Scotland	Wembley	L	1-3
May	13	Sweden	Stockholm	L	1-3
May	18	Norway	Oslo	W	4-1
May	22	France	Paris	W	3-1
		Season 1949-50			
Sept.	21	Rep. Ireland	Everton	L	0-2
Oct.	15	Wales	Cardiff	W	4-1 WCQ
Nov.	16	Ireland	Manchester	W	9-2 WCQ
Nov.	30	Italy	Tottenham	W	2-0
Apr.	15	Scotland	Glasgow	W	1-0 WCQ
May	14	Portugal	Lisbon	W	5-3
May	18	Belgium	Brussels	W	4-1
June	25	Chile	Rio de Janeiro	W	2-0 WC
June	29	USA	Belo Horizonte	L	0-1 WC
July	2	Spain	Rio de Janeiro	L	0-1 WC
		Season 1950-51			
Oct.	7	Ireland	Belfast	W	4-1
Nov.	15	Wales	Sunderland	W	4-2
Nov.	22	Yugoslavia	Highbury	D	2-2
Apr.	14	Scotland	Wembley	L	2-3
May	9	Argentina	Wembley	W	2-1
May	19	Portugal	Everton	W	5-2
		Season 1951-52			
Oct.	3	France	Highbury	D	2-2
Oct.	20	Wales	Cardiff	D	1-1
Nov.	14	Ireland	Villa Park	W	2-0
Nov.	28	Austria	Wembley	D	2-2
Apr.	5	Scotland	Glasgow	W	2-1

Date		Opponents	Venue	Result	
May	18	Italy	Florence	D	1-1
May	25	Austria	Vienna	W	3-2
May	28	Switzerland	Zürich	W	3-0

Season 1952-53

Oct.	4	Ireland	Belfast	D	2-2
Nov.	12	Wales	Wembley	W	5-2
Nov.	26	Belgium	Wembley	W	5-0
Apr.	18	Scotland	Wembley	D	2-2
May	17	Argentina	Buenos Aires		0-0
		(Abandoned after 23 min. — rain)			
May	24	Chile	Santiago	W	2-1
May	31	Uruguay	Montevideo	L	1-2
June	8	USA	New York	W	6-3

Season 1953-54

Oct.	10	Wales	Cardiff	W	4-1 WCQ
Oct.	21	FIFA	Wembley	D	4-4
Nov.	11	Ireland	Everton	W	3-1 WCQ
Nov.	25	Hungary	Wembley	L	3-6
Apr.	3	Scotland	Glasgow	W	4-2 WCQ
May	16	Yugoslavia	Belgrade	L	0-1
May	23	Hungary	Budapest	L	1-7
June	17	Belgium	Basle	D	4-4 WC
June	20	Switzerland	Berne	W	2-0 WC
June	26	Uruguay	Basle	L	2-4 WC

Season 1954-55

Oct.	2	Ireland	Belfast	W	2-0
Nov.	10	Wales	Wembley	W	3-2
Dec.	1	Germany	Wembley	W	3-1
Apr.	2	Scotland	Wembley	W	7-2
May	15	France	Paris	L	0-1
May	18	Spain	Madrid	D	1-1
May	22	Portugal	Oporto	L	1-3

Season 1955-56

Oct.	2	Denmark	Copenhagen	W	5-1
Oct.	22	Wales	Cardiff	L	1-2
Nov.	2	Ireland	Wembley	W	3-0
Nov.	30	Spain	Wembley	W	4-1
Apr.	14	Scotland	Glasgow	D	1-1
May	9	Brazil	Wembley	W	4-2
May	16	Sweden	Stockholm	D	0-0

Date		Opponents	Venue	Result	
May	20	Finland	Helsinki	W	5-1
May	26	Germany	Berlin	W	3-1

Season 1956-57

Oct.	6	Ireland	Belfast	D	1-1	
Nov.	14	Wales	Wembley	W	3-1	
Nov.	28	Yugoslavia	Wembley	W	3-0	
Dec.	5	Denmark	Wolverhampton	W	5-2	WCQ
Apr.	6	Scotland	Wembley	W	2-1	
May	8	Rep. Ireland	Wembley	W	5-1	WCQ
May	15	Denmark	Copenhagen	W	4-1	WCQ
May	19	Rep. Ireland	Dublin	D	1-1	WCQ

Season 1957-58

Oct.	19	Wales	Cardiff	W	4-0	
Nov.	6	Ireland	Wembley	L	2-3	
Nov.	27	France	Wembley	W	4-0	
Apr.	19	Scotland	Glasgow	W	4-0	
May	7	Portugal	Wembley	W	2-1	
May	11	Yugoslavia	Belgrade	L	0-5	
May	18	Russia	Moscow	D	1-1	
June	8	Russia	Gothenburg	D	2-2	WC
June	11	Brazil	Gothenburg	D	0-0	WC
June	15	Austria	Boras	D	2-2	WC
June	17	Russia	Gothenburg	L	0-1	WC

Season 1958-59

Oct.	4	Ireland	Belfast	D	3-3
Oct.	22	Russia	Wembley	W	5-0
Nov.	26	Wales	Villa Park	D	2-2
Apr.	11	Scotland	Wembley	W	1-0
May	6	Italy	Wembley	D	2-2
May	13	Brazil	Rio de Janeiro	L	0-2
May	17	Peru	Lima	L	1-4
May	24	Mexico	Mexico City	L	1-2
May	28	USA	Los Angeles	W	8-1

Season 1959-60

Oct.	17	Wales	Cardiff	D	1-1
Oct.	28	Sweden	Wembley	L	2-3
Nov.	18	Ireland	Wembley	W	2-1
Apr.	9	Scotland	Glasgow	D	1-1
May	11	Yugoslavia	Wembley	D	3-3
May	15	Spain	Madrid	L	0-3
May	22	Hungary	Budapest	L	0-2

Date		Opponents	Venue	Result	
Season 1960-61					
Oct.	8	Ireland	Belfast	W	5-2
Oct.	19	Luxembourg	Luxembourg	W	9-0 WCQ
Oct.	26	Spain	Wembley	W	4-2
Nov.	23	Wales	Wembley	W	5-1
Apr.	15	Scotland	Wembley	W	9-3
May	10	Mexico	Wembley	W	8-0
May	21	Portugal	Lisbon	D	1-1 WCQ
May	24	Italy	Rome	W	3-2
May	27	Austria	Vienna	L	1-3
Season 1961-62					
Sept.	28	Luxembourg	Highbury	W	4-1 WCQ
Oct.	14	Wales	Cardiff	D	1-1
Oct.	25	Portugal	Wembley	W	2-0 WCQ
Nov.	22	Ireland	Wembley	D	1-1
Apr.	4	Austria	Wembley	W	3-1
Apr.	14	Scotland	Glasgow	L	0-2
May	9	Switzerland	Wembley	W	3-1
May	20	Peru	Lima	W	4-0
May	31	Hungary	Rancagua	L	1-2 WC
June	2	Argentina	Rancagua	W	3-1 WC
June	7	Bulgaria	Rancagua	D	0-0 WC
June	10	Brazil	Vina del Mar	L	1-3 WC
Season 1962-63					
Oct.	3	France	Sheffield	D	1-1 ECQ
Nov.	20	Ireland	Belfast	W	3-1
Nov.	21	Wales	Wembley	W	4-0
Feb.	27	France	Paris	L	2-5 ECQ
Apr.	6	Scotland	Wembley	L	1-2
May	8	Brazil	Wembley	D	1-1
May	29	Czechoslovakia	Bratislava	W	4-2
June	2	East Germany	Leipzig	W	2-1
June	5	Switzerland	Basle	W	8-1
Season 1963-64					
Oct.	12	Wales	Cardiff	W	4-0
Oct.	23	FIFA	Wembley	W	2-1
Nov.	20	Ireland	Wembley	W	8-3
Apr.	11	Scotland	Glasgow	L	0-1
May	6	Uruguay	Wembley	W	2-1
May	17	Portugal	Lisbon	W	4-3
May	24	Rep. Ireland	Dublin	W	3-1

Date		Opponents	Venue	Result	
May	27	USA	New York	W	10-0
May	30	Brazil	Rio de Janeiro	L	1-5
June	4	Portugal	Sao Paulo	D	1-1
June	6	Argentina	Rio de Janeiro	L	0-1

Season 1964-65

Oct.	3	Ireland	Belfast	W	4-3
Oct.	21	Belgium	Wembley	D	2-2
Nov.	18	Wales	Wembley	W	2-1
Dec.	9	Holland	Amsterdam	D	1-1
Apr.	10	Scotland	Wembley	D	2-2
May	5	Hungary	Wembley	W	1-0
May	9	Yugoslavia	Belgrade	D	1-1
May	12	West Germany	Nuremberg	W	1-0
May	16	Sweden	Gothenburg	W	2-1

Season 1965-66

Oct.	2	Wales	Cardiff	D	0-0
Oct.	20	Austria	Wembley	L	2-3
Nov.	10	Ireland	Wembley	W	2-1
Dec.	8	Spain	Madrid	W	2-0
Jan.	5	Poland	Everton	D	1-1
Feb.	23	West Germany	Wembley	W	1-0
Apr.	2	Scotland	Glasgow	W	4-3
May	4	Yugoslavia	Wembley	W	2-0
June	26	Finland	Helsinki	W	3-0
June	29	Norway	Oslo	W	6-1
July	3	Denmark	Copenhagen	W	2-0
July	5	Poland	Chorzow	W	1-0
July	11	Uruguay	Wembley	D	0-0 WC
July	16	Mexico	Wembley	W	2-0 WC
July	20	France	Wembley	W	2-0 WC
July	23	Argentina	Wembley	W	1-0 WC
July	26	Portugal	Wembley	W	2-1 WC
July	30	West Germany	Wembley	W	4-2 WC

Season 1966-67

Oct.	22	Ireland	Belfast	W	2-0 ECQ
Nov.	2	Czechoslovakia	Wembley	D	0-0
Nov.	16	Wales	Wembley	W	5-1 ECQ
Apr.	15	Scotland	Wembley	L	2-3 ECQ
May	24	Spain	Wembley	W	2-0
May	27	Austria	Vienna	W	1-0

Date		Opponents	Venue	Result	
		Season 1967-68			
Oct.	21	Wales	Cardiff	W	3-0 ECQ
Nov.	22	Ireland	Wembley	W	2-0 ECQ
Dec.	6	Russia	Wembley	D	2-2
Feb.	24	Scotland	Glasgow	D	1-1 ECQ
Apr.	3	Spain	Wembley	W	1-0 EC
May	8	Spain	Madrid	W	2-1 EC
May	22	Sweden	Wembley	W	3-1
June	1	West Germany	Hanover	L	0-1
June	5	Yugoslavia	Florence	L	0-1 EC
June	8	Russia	Rome	W	2-0 EC
		Season 1968-69			
Nov.	6	Rumania	Bucharest	D	0-0
Dec.	11	Bulgaria	Wembley	D	1-1
Jan.	15	Rumania	Wembley	D	1-1
Mar.	12	France	Wembley	W	5-0
May	3	Ireland	Belfast	W	3-1
May	7	Wales	Wembley	W	2-1
May	10	Scotland	Wembley	W	4-1
June	1	Mexico	Mexico City	D	0-0
June	8	Uruguay	Montevideo	W	2-1
June	12	Brazil	Rio de Janeiro	L	1-2
		Season 1969-70			
Nov.	5	Holland	Amsterdam	W	1-0
Dec.	10	Portugal	Wembley	W	1-0
Jan.	14	Holland	Wembley	D	0-0
Feb.	25	Belgium	Brussels	W	3-1
Apr.	18	Wales	Cardiff	D	1-1
Apr.	21	Ireland	Wembley	W	3-1
Apr.	25	Scotland	Glasgow	D	0-0
May	20	Colombia	Bogota	W	4-0
May	24	Ecuador	Quito	W	2-0
June	2	Rumania	Guadalajara	W	1-0 WC
June	7	Brazil	Guadalajara	L	0-1 WC
June	11	Czechoslovakia	Guadalajara	W	1-0 WC
June	14	West Germany	Leon	L	2-3 WC
		Season 1970-71			
Nov.	25	East Germany	Wembley	W	3-1
Feb.	3	Malta	Valletta	W	1-0 ECQ
Apr.	21	Greece	Wembley	W	3-0 ECQ
May	12	Malta	Wembley	W	5-0 ECQ

152

Date		Opponents	Venue	Result	
May	15	Ireland	Belfast	W	1-0
May	19	Wales	Wembley	D	0-0
May	22	Scotland	Wembley	W	3-1

Season 1971-72

Oct.	13	Switzerland	Basle	W	3-2 ECQ
Nov.	10	Switzerland	Wembley	D	1-1 ECQ
Dec.	1	Greece	Athens	W	2-0 ECQ
Apr.	29	West Germany	Wembley	L	1-3 EC
May	13	West Germany	Berlin	D	0-0 EC
May	20	Wales	Cardiff	W	3-0
May	23	Ireland	Wembley	L	0-1
May	27	Scotland	Glasgow	W	1-0

Season 1972-73

Oct.	11	Yugoslavia	Wembley	D	1-1
Nov.	15	Wales	Cardiff	W	1-0 WCQ
Jan.	24	Wales	Wembley	D	1-1 WCQ
Feb.	14	Scotland	Glasgow	W	5-0
May	12	Ireland	Everton	W	2-1
May	15	Wales	Wembley	W	3-0
May	19	Scotland	Wembley	W	1-0
May	27	Czechoslovakia	Prague	D	1-1
June	6	Poland	Chorzow	L	0-2 WCQ
June	10	Russia	Moscow	W	2-1
June	14	Italy	Turin	L	0-2

Season 1973-74

Sept.	26	Austria	Wembley	W	7-0
Oct.	17	Poland	Wembley	D	1-1 WCQ
Nov.	14	Italy	Wembley	L	0-1
Apr.	3	Portugal	Lisbon	D	0-0
May	11	Wales	Cardiff	W	2-0
May	15	Ireland	Wembley	W	1-0
May	18	Scotland	Glasgow	L	0-2
May	22	Argentina	Wembley	D	2-2
May	29	East Germany	Leipzig	D	1-1
June	1	Bulgaria	Sofia	W	1-0
June	5	Yugoslavia	Belgrade	D	2-2

Season 1974-75

Oct.	30	Czechoslovakia	Wembley	W	3-0 ECQ
Nov.	20	Portugal	Wembley	D	0-0 ECQ
Mar.	12	West Germany	Wembley	W	2-0
Apr.	16	Cyprus	Wembley	W	5-0 ECQ

Date		Opponents	Venue	Result	
May	11	Cyprus	Limassol	W	1-0 ECQ
May	17	Ireland	Belfast	D	0-0
May	21	Wales	Wembley	D	2-2
May	24	Scotland	Wembley	W	5-1
Season 1975-76					
Sept.	3	Switzerland	Basle	W	2-1
Oct.	29	Czechoslovakia	Bratislava		0-0 ECQ
		(Abandoned after 17 min. — fog)			
Oct.	30	Czechoslovakia	Bratislava	L	1-2 ECQ
Nov.	19	Portugal	Lisbon	D	1-1 ECQ
Mar.	24	Wales	Wrexham	W	2-1
May	8	Wales	Cardiff	W	1-0
May	11	Ireland	Wembley	W	4-0
May	15	Scotland	Glasgow	L	1-2
May	23	Brazil	Los Angeles	L	0-1
May	28	Italy	New York	W	3-2
June	13	Finland	Helsinki	W	4-1 WCQ
Season 1976-77					
Sept.	8	Rep. Ireland	Wembley	D	1-1
Oct.	13	Finland	Wembley	W	2-1 WCQ
Nov.	17	Italy	Rome	L	0-2 WCQ
Feb.	9	Holland	Wembley	L	0-2
Mar.	30	Luxembourg	Wembley	W	5-0 WCQ
May	28	Ireland	Belfast	W	2-1
May	31	Wales	Wembley	L	0-1
June	4	Scotland	Wembley	L	1-2
June	8	Brazil	Rio de Janeiro	D	0-0
June	12	Argentina	Buenos Aires	D	1-1
June	15	Uruguay	Montevideo	D	0-0
Season 1977-78					
Sept.	7	Switzerland	Wembley	D	0-0
Oct.	12	Luxembourg	Luxembourg	W	2-1 WCQ
Nov.	16	Italy	Wembley	W	2-0 WCQ
Feb.	22	W. Germany	Munich	L	1-2
Apr.	19	Brazil	Wembley	D	1-1
May	13	Wales	Cardiff	W	3-1
May	16	Ireland	Wembley	W	1-0
May	20	Scotland	Glasgow	W	1-0
May	24	Hungary	Wembley	W	4-1
Season 1978-79					
Sept.	20	Denmark	Copenhagen	W	4-3 ECQ
Oct.	25	Rep. Ireland	Dublin	D	1-1 ECQ
Nov.	29	Czechoslovakia	Wembley	W	1-0
Feb.	7	Ireland	Wembley	W	4-0 ECW
May	19	Ireland	Belfast	W	2-0

Date		Opponents	Venue	Result	
May	23	Wales	Wembley	D	0-0
May	26	Scotland	Wembley	W	3-1
June	6	Bulgaria	Sofia	W	3-0 ECQ
June	10	Sweden	Stockholm	D	0-0
June	13	Austria	Vienna	L	3-4

Season 1979-80

Sept.	12	Denmark	Wembley	W	1-0 ECQ
Oct.	17	Ireland	Belfast	W	5-1 ECQ
Nov.	22	Bulgaria	Wembley	W	2-0 ECQ
Feb.	6	Rep. Ireland	Wembley	W	2-0 ECQ
Mar.	26	Spain	Barcelona	W	2-0
May	13	Argentina	Wembley	W	3-1
May	17	Wales	Wrexham	L	1-4
May	20	Ireland	Wembley	D	1-1
May	24	Scotland	Glasgow	W	2-0
May	31	Australia	Sydney	W	2-1
June	12	Belgium	Turin	D	1-1 EC
June	15	Italy	Turin	L	0-1 EC
June	18	Spain	Naples	W	2-1 EC

Season 1980-81

Sept.	10	Norway	Wembley	W	4-0 WCQ
Oct.	15	Rumania	Bucharest	L	1-2 WCQ
Nov.	19	Switzerland	Wembley	W	2-1 WCQ
Mar.	25	Spain	Wembley	L	1-2
Apr.	29	Rumania	Wembley	D	0-0 WCQ
May	12	Brazil	Wembley	L	0-1
May	20	Wales	Wembley	D	0-0
May	23	Scotland	Wembley	L	0-1
May	30	Switzerland	Basle	L	1-2 WCQ
June	6	Hungary	Budapest	W	3-1 WCQ

Season 1981-82

Sept.	9	Norway	Oslo	L	1-2 WCQ
Nov.	18	Hungary	Wembley	W	1-0 WCQ
Feb.	23	Ireland	Wembley	W	4-0
Apr.	27	Wales	Cardiff	W	1-0
May	25	Holland	Wembley	W	2-0
May	29	Scotland	Glasgow	W	1-0
June	2	Iceland	Reykjavik	D	1-1
June	3	Finland	Helsinki	W	4-1
June	16	France	Bilbao	W	3-1 WC
June	20	Czechoslovakia	Bilbao	W	2-0 WC
June	25	Kuwait	Bilbao	W	1-0 WC

Date		Opponents	Venue	Result	
June	29	West Germany	Madrid	D	0-0 WC
July	5	Spain	Madrid	D	0-0 WC

Season 1982-83

Date		Opponents	Venue	Result	
Sept.	22	Denmark	Copenhagen	D	2-2 ECQ
Oct.	13	West Germany	Wembley	L	1-2
Nov.	17	Greece	Salonika	W	3-0 ECQ
Dec.	15	Luxembourg	Wembley	W	9-0 ECQ
Feb.	23	Wales	Wembley	W	2-1
Mar.	30	Greece	Wembley	D	0-0 ECQ
Apr.	27	Hungary	Wembley	W	2-0 ECQ
May	28	Ireland	Belfast	D	0-0
June	1	Scotland	Wembley	W	2-0
June	12	Australia	Sydney	D	0-0
June	15	Australia	Brisbane	W	1-0
June	19	Australia	Melbourne	D	1-1

Season 1983-84

Date		Opponents	Venue	Result	
Sept.	21	Denmark	Wembley	L	0-1 ECQ
Oct.	12	Hungary	Budapest	W	3-0 ECQ
Nov.	16	Luxembourg	Luxembourg	W	4-0 ECQ
Feb.	29	France	Paris	L	0-2
Apr.	4	Ireland	Wembley	W	1-0
May	2	Wales	Wrexham	L	0-1
May	26	Scotland	Glasgow	D	1-1

Football League Champions
and their Records

Season	Champions	P	W	D	L	F	A	Pts
1888-89	Preston NE	22	18	4	0	74	15	40
1889-90	Preston NE	22	15	3	4	71	30	33
1890-91	Everton	22	14	1	7	63	29	29
1891-92	Sunderland	26	21	0	5	93	36	42
1892-93	Sunderland	30	22	4	4	100	36	48
1893-94	Aston Villa	30	19	6	5	84	42	44
1894-95	Sunderland	30	21	5	4	80	37	47
1895-96	Aston Villa	30	20	5	5	78	45	45
1896-97	Aston Villa	30	21	5	4	73	38	47
1897-98	Sheffield Utd	30	17	8	5	56	31	42
1898-99	Aston Villa	34	19	7	8	76	40	45
1899-1900	Aston Villa	34	22	6	6	77	35	50
1900-01	Liverpool	34	19	7	8	59	35	45
1901-02	Sunderland	34	19	6	9	50	35	44
1902-03	Sheffield Wed.	34	19	4	11	54	36	42
1903-04	Sheffield Wed.	34	20	7	7	48	28	47
1904-05	Newcastle Utd	34	23	2	9	72	33	48
1905-06	Liverpool	38	23	5	10	79	46	51
1906-07	Newcastle Utd	38	22	7	9	74	46	51
1907-08	Manchester Utd	38	23	6	9	81	48	52
1908-09	Newcastle Utd	38	24	5	9	65	41	53
1909-10	Aston Villa	38	23	7	8	84	42	53
1910-11	Manchester Utd	38	22	8	8	72	40	52
1911-12	Blackburn Rov.	38	20	9	9	60	43	49
1912-13	Sunderland	38	25	4	9	86	43	54
1913-14	Blackburn Rov.	38	20	11	7	78	42	51
1914-15	Everton	38	19	8	11	76	47	46
1915-1919	No competition — First World War							
1919-20	West Brom. Albion	42	28	4	10	104	47	60
1920-21	Burnley	42	23	13	6	79	36	59
1921-22	Liverpool	42	22	13	7	63	36	57
1922-23	Liverpool	42	26	8	8	70	31	60
1923-24	Huddersfield Town	42	23	11	8	60	33	57
1924-25	Huddersfield Town	42	21	16	5	69	28	58
1925-26	Huddersfield Town	42	23	11	8	92	60	57
1926-27	Newcastle Utd	42	25	6	11	96	58	56
1927-28	Everton	42	20	13	9	102	66	53
1928-29	Sheffield Wed.	42	21	10	11	86	62	52
1929-30	Sheffield Wed.	42	26	8	8	105	57	60

Season	Champions	P	W	D	L	F	A	Pts
1930-31	Arsenal	42	28	10	4	127	59	66
1931-32	Everton	42	26	4	12	116	64	56
1932-33	Arsenal	42	25	8	9	118	61	58
1933-34	Arsenal	42	25	9	8	75	47	59
1934-35	Arsenal	42	23	12	7	115	46	58
1935-36	Sunderland	42	25	6	11	109	74	56
1936-37	Manchester City	42	22	13	7	107	61	57
1937-38	Arsenal	42	21	10	11	77	44	52
1938-39	Everton	42	27	5	10	88	52	59
1939-46	No competition — Second World War							
1946-47	Liverpool	42	25	7	10	84	52	57
1947-48	Arsenal	42	23	13	6	81	32	59
1948-49	Portsmouth	42	25	8	9	84	42	58
1949-50	Portsmouth	42	22	9	11	74	38	53
1950-51	Tottenham Hotspur	42	25	10	7	82	44	60
1951-52	Manchester Utd	42	23	11	8	95	52	57
1952-53	Arsenal	42	21	12	9	97	64	54
1953-54	Wolverhampton W.	42	25	7	10	96	56	57
1954-55	Chelsea	42	20	12	10	81	57	52
1955-56	Manchester Utd	42	25	10	7	83	51	60
1956-57	Manchester Utd	42	28	8	6	103	54	64
1957-58	Wolverhampton W.	42	28	8	6	103	47	64
1958-59	Wolverhampton W.	42	28	5	9	110	49	61
1959-60	Burnley	42	24	7	11	85	61	55
1960-61	Tottenham Hotspur	42	31	4	7	115	55	66
1961-62	Ipswich Town	42	24	8	10	93	67	56
1962-63	Everton	42	25	11	6	84	42	61
1963-64	Liverpool	42	26	5	11	92	45	57
1964-65	Manchester Utd	42	26	9	7	89	39	61
1965-66	Liverpool	42	26	9	7	79	34	61
1966-67	Manchester Utd	42	24	12	6	84	45	60
1967-68	Manchester City	42	26	6	10	86	43	58
1968-69	Leeds United	42	27	13	2	66	26	67
1969-70	Everton	42	29	8	5	72	34	66
1970-71	Arsenal	42	29	7	6	71	29	65
1971-72	Derby County	42	24	10	8	69	33	58
1972-73	Liverpool	42	25	10	7	72	42	60
1973-74	Leeds United	42	24	14	4	66	31	62
1974-75	Derby County	42	21	11	10	67	49	53
1975-76	Liverpool	42	23	14	5	66	31	60
1976-77	Liverpool	42	23	11	8	62	33	57
1977-78	Nottingham Forest	42	25	14	3	69	24	64
1978-79	Liverpool	42	30	8	4	85	16	68
1979-80	Liverpool	42	25	10	7	81	30	60

Season	Champions	P	W	D	L	F	A	Pts
1980-81	Aston Villa	42	26	8	8	72	40	60
1981-82	Liverpool	42	26	9	7	80	32	87
1982-83	Liverpool	42	24	10	8	87	37	82
1983-84	Liverpool	42	22	14	6	73	32	80

Summary of League Champions

Liverpool	15	Huddersfield	3	Preston	2
Arsenal	8	Wolves	3	Tottenham	2
Aston Villa	7	Blackburn Rov.	2	Chelsea	1
Everton	7	Burnley	2	Ipswich	1
Manchester Utd	7	Derby County	2	Nott'm Forest	1
Sunderland	6	Leeds	2	Sheffield Utd	1
Newcastle	4	Manchester City	2	West Bromwich	1
Sheffield Wed.	4	Portsmouth	2		

FA Cup Winners

Cup Final Venues:

1872-92	Kennington Oval (except 1873 — at Lillie Bridge, London)	1895-1914	Crystal Palace
		1915	Old Trafford, Manchester
1893	Fallowfield, Manchester	1920-22	Stamford Bridge
1894	Anfield, Liverpool	1923 to date	Wembley

* = Replay; † = After extra time

Season	Winners	Runners-up	Result	Attendance
1871-72	Wanderers	Royal Engineers	1-0	2,000
1872-73	Wanderers	Oxford University	2-0	3,000
1873-74	Oxford University	Royal Engineers	2-0	2,500
1874-75	Royal Engineers	Old Etonians	*2-0 (after 1-1 draw)	3,000
1875-76	Wanderers	Old Etonians	*3-0 (after 0-0 draw)	4,000
1876-77	Wanderers	Oxford University	†2-0	3,000
1877-78	Wanderers	Royal Engineers	3-1	5,000

Season	Winners	Runners-up	Result	Attend-ance
1878-79	Old Etonians	Clapham Rovers	1-0	5,000
1879-80	Clapham Rovers	Oxford University	1-0	6,000
1880-81	Old Carthusians	Old Etonians	3-0	4,000
1881-82	Old Etonians	Blackburn R.	1-0	7,000
1882-83	Blackburn Olympic	Old Etonians	†2-1	8,000
1883-84	Blackburn R.	Queen's Park, Glasgow	2-1	4,000
1884-85	Blackburn R.	Queen's Park, Glasgow	2-0	12,500
1885-86	Blackburn R.	W.B.A.	*2-0	15,000
(Replay at Derby – after 0-0 draw; att: 12,000)				
1886-87	Aston Villa	WBA	2-0	16,000
1887-88	WBA	Preston NE	2-1	19,000
1888-89	Preston NE	Wolves	3-0	22,000
1889-90	Blackburn R.	Sheffield Wed.	6-1	20,000
1890-91	Blackburn R.	Notts County	3-1	23,000
1891-92	WBA	Aston Villa	3-0	25,000
1892-93	Wolves	Everton	1-0	45,000
1893-94	Notts County	Bolton W.	4-1	37,000
1894-95	Aston Villa	WBA	1-0	42,500
1895-96	Sheffield Wed.	Wolves	2-1	49,000
1896-97	Aston Villa	Everton	3-2	66,000
1897-98	Nott'm Forest	Derby County	3-1	62,000
1898-99	Sheffield Utd	Derby County	4-1	74,000
1899-1900	Bury	Southampton	4-0	69,000
1900-01	Tottenham H.	Sheffield Utd.	*3-1	30,000
(Replay at Bolton – after 2-2 draw, att: 110,820)				
1901-02	Sheffield Utd	Southampton	*2-1	33,000
(Replay at Crystal Palace – after 1-1 draw, att: 77,000)				
1902-03	Bury	Derby County	6-0	63,000
1903-04	Manchester C.	Bolton W.	1-0	61,000
1904-05	Aston Villa	Newcastle U.	2-0	101,000
1905-06	Everton	Newcastle U.	1-0	76,000
1906-07	Sheffield Wed.	Everton	2-1	84,500
1907-08	Wolves	Newcastle U.	3-1	75,000
1908-09	Manchester U.	Bristol City	1-0	68,000
1909-10	Newcastle U.	Barnsley	*2-0	69,000
(Replay at Goodison Park, Everton – after 1-1 draw, att: 78,000)				

160

Season	Winners	Runners-up	Result	Attend-ance
1910-11	Bradford City	Newcastle U.	*1-0	58,000
(Replay at Old Trafford, Manchester – after 0-0 draw, att: 69,000)				
1911-12	Barnsley	WBA	†*1-0	38,500
(Replay at Bramall Lane, Sheffield – after 0-0 draw, att: 54,500)				
1912-13	Aston Villa	Sunderland	1-0	120,000
1913-14	Burnley	Liverpool	1-0	73,000
1914-15	Sheffield U.	Chelsea	3-0	50,000
1915-19	No competition — First World War			
1919-20	Aston Villa	Huddersfield T.	†1-0	50,000
1920-21	Tottenham H.	Wolves	1-0	73,000
1921-22	Huddersfield T.	Preston NE	1-0	53,000

Results, with scorers, since the FA Cup Final has been played at Wembley

Season	Winners	Runners-up	Result	Attend-ance
1922-23	Bolton W. *(Jack, J.R. Smith)*	West Ham U.	2-0	126,047
1923-24	Newcastle U. *(Harris, Seymour)*	Aston Villa	2-0	92,000
1924-25	Sheffield Utd. *(Tunstall)*	Cardiff City	1-0	92,000
1925-26	Bolton W. *(Jack)*	Manchester C.	1-0	91,500
1926-27	Cardiff City *(Ferguson)*	Arsenal	1-0	91,000
1927-28	Blackburn R. *(Roscamp 2, McLean)*	Huddersfield T. *(Jackson)*	3-1	92,000
1928-29	Bolton W. *(Butler, (Blackmore)*	Portsmouth	2-0	92,500
1929-30	Arsenal *(James, Lambert)*	Huddersfield T.	2-0	92,500
1930-31	WBA *(W.G. Richardson 2)*	Birmingham *(Bradford)*	2-1	92,500
1931-32	*Newcastle U. (Allen 2)*	Arsenal *(John)*	2-1	92,000
1932-33	Everton *(Stein, Dean, Dunn)*	Manchester City	3-0	93,000

Season	Winners	Runners-up	Result	Attend-ance
1933-34	Manchester C. (Tilson 2)	Portsmouth (Rutherford)	2-1	93,500
1934-35	Sheffield Wed. (Rimmer 2, Palethorpe, Hooper)	WBA (Boyes, Sandford)	4-2	93,000
1935-36	Arsenal (Drake)	Sheffield Utd.	1-0	93,500
1936-37	Sunderland (Gurney, Carter, Burbanks)	Preston NE (F. O'Donnell)	3-1	93,500
1937-38	Preston NE (Mutch – pen.)	Huddersfield T.	†1-0	93,500
1938-39	Portsmouth (Parker 2, Barlow, Anderson.)	Wolves (Dorsett)	4-1	99,000
1939-45	No competition — Second World War			
1945-46	Derby County (H. Turner own goal, Doherty, Stamps 2)	Charlton A. (H. Turner)	† 4-1	98,000
1946-47	Charlton A. (Duffy)	Burnley	†1-0	98,000
1947-48	Manchester U. (Rowley 2, Pearson, Anderson.)	Blackpool (Shimwell – pen. Mortensen)	4-2	99,000
1948-49	Wolves (Pye 2, Smyth)	Leicester City (Griffiths)	3-1	100,000
1949-50	Arsenal (Lewis 2)	Liverpool	2-0	100,000
1950-51	Newcastle U. (Milburn 2)	Blackpool	2-0	100,000
1951-52	Newcastle U. (G. Robledo)	Arsenal	1-0	100,000
1952-53	Blackpool (Mortensen 3, Perry)	Bolton W. (Lofthouse, Moir, Bell)	4-3	100,000

Season	Winners	Runners-up	Result	Attend-ance
1953-54	WBA (Allen 2-1 pen., Griffin)	Preston NE (Morrison, Wayman)	3-2	100,000
1954-55	Newcastle U. (Milburn, Mitchell, Hannah)	Manchester C. (Johnstone)	3-1	100,000
1955-56	Manchester C. (Hayes, Dyson, Johnstone)	Birmingham C. (Kinsey)	3-1	100,000
1956-57	Aston Villa (McParland 2)	Manchester U. (Taylor)	2-1	100,000
1957-58	Bolton W. (Lofthouse 2)	Manchester U.	2-0	100,000
1958-59	Nott'm Forest (Dwight, Wilson)	Luton Town (Pacey)	2-1	100,000
1959-60	Wolves (McGrath own goal, Deeley 2)	Blackburn R.	3-0	100,000
1960-61	Tottenham H. (Smith, Dyson)	Leicester C.	2-0	100,000
1961-62	Tottenham H. (Greaves, Smith, Blanchflower – pen.)	Burnley (Robson)	3-1	100,000
1962-63	Manchester U. (Law, Herd 2)	Leicester C. (Keyworth)	3-1	100,000
1963-64	West Ham U. (Sissons, Hurst, Boyce)	Preston NE (Holden, Dawson)	3-2	100,000
1964-65	Liverpool (Hunt, St. John)	Leeds United (Bremner)	†2-1	100,000
1965-66	Everton (Trebilcock 2, Temple)	Sheffield Wed. (McCalliog, Ford)	3-2	100,000
1966-67	Tottenham H. (Robertson, Saul)	Chelsea (Tambling)	2-1	100,000
1967-68	WBA (Astle)	Everton	†1-0	100,000

Season	Winners	Runners-up	Result	Attend-ance
1968-69	Manchester C. *(Young)*	Leicester City.	1-0	100,000
1969-70	Chelsea	Leeds United	*†2-1	62,000

(Replay at Old Trafford, Manchester – after † 2-2 draw at Wembley — att: 100,000)

Scorers at Wembley Chelsea: *Houseman, Hutchinson*
Leeds: *Charlton, Jones.*

Scorers in replay Chelsea:*Osgood, Webb.* Leeds: *Jones.*

Season	Winners	Runners-up	Result	Attend-ance
1970-71	Arsenal *(Kelly, George)*	Liverpool *(Heighway)*	†2-1	100,000
1971-72	Leeds United *(Clarke)*	Arsenal	1-0	100,000
1972-73	Sunderland *(Porterfield)*	Leeds United	1-0	100,000
1973-74	Liverpool *(Keegan 2, Heighway)*	Newcastle U.	3-0	100,000
1974-75	West Ham U. *(A. Taylor 2)*	Fulham	2-0	100,000
1975-76	Southampton *(Stokes)*	Manchester U.	1-0	100,000
1976-77	Manchester U. *(Pearson, Greenhoff, J.)*	Liverpool *(Case)*	2-1	100,000
1977-78	Ipswich Town *(Osborne)*	Arsenal	1-0	100,000
1978-79	Arsenal *(Talbot, Stapleton, Sunderland)*	Manchester U. *McQueen, McIlroy)*	3-2	100,000
1979-80	West Ham U. *(Brooking)*	Arsenal	1-0	100,000
1980-81	Tottenham H.	Manchester C.	*3-2	92,000

(Replay at Wembley — after †1-1 draw at Wembley — att: 100,000)
Scorers – first match – Tottenham: Hutchison own goal.
Man. City: *Hutchison.*
Scorers – second match – Tottenham: Villa 2, Crooks.
Man. City: *Mackenzie, Reeves – pen.*

Season	Winners	Runners-up	Result	Attend-ance
1981-82	Tottenham H.	QPR	*1-0	90,000

(Replay at Wembley — after †1-1 draw at Wembley — att: 100,000)
Scorers – first match – Tottenham: Hoddle. QPR: Fenwick.
Scorer – second match – Tottenham: Hoddle – pen.

Season	Winners	Runners-up	Result	Attend-ance
1982-83	Manchester U.	Brighton HA	* 4-0	92,000

(Replay at Wembley — after †2-2 draw at Wembley — att: 100,000)

Scorers – first match – Man. Utd: Stapleton, Wilkins.
Brighton: Smith, Stevens.

Scorers – second match – Man. Utd: Robson 2, Whiteside,
Muhren – pen.

1983-84	Everton (Sharp, Gray)	Watford	2-0	100,000

Summary of FA Cup Winners

Aston Villa	7	West Ham Utd	3	Charlton	1
Tottenham	7	Bury	2	Chelsea	1
Blackburn	6	Liverpool	2	Clapham Rovers	1
Newcastle	6	Nottingham F.	2	Derby	1
Arsenal	5	Old Etonians	2	Huddersfield	1
Manchester U.	5	Preston	2	Ipswich Town	1
Wanderers	5	Sunderland	2	Leeds Utd	1
West Bromwich	5	Barnsley	1	Notts. Co.	1
Bolton	4	Blackburn Olympic	1	Old Carthusians	1
Everton	4	Blackpool	1	Oxford Univ.	1
Manchester City	4	Bradford C.	1	Portsmouth	1
Sheffield Utd.	4	Burnley	1	Royal Engineers	1
Wolves	4	Cardiff	1	Southampton	1
Sheffield Wed.	3				

League Cup/Milk Cup Winners

For the first 6 seasons, before the fixture was taken to Wembley, the Football League Cup Final was played on a home-and-away basis. The first sponsored Final, as the Milk Cup, was in 1982, and in 1984 the final was played for the first time on a Sunday and televised 'live' on ITV.

Season	Winners	Runners-up	Aggre-gate	Home	Away
1960-61	Aston Villa	Rotherham U.	3-2	3-0	0-2
1961-62	Norwich City	Rochdale	4-0	1-0	3-0
1962-63	Birmingham C	Aston Villa	3-1	3-1	0-0
1963-64	Leicester C	Stoke City	4-3	3-2	1-1
1964-65	Chelsea	Leicester C	3-2	3-2	0-0
1965-66	WBA	West Ham U	5-3	4-1	1-2

Results, with scorers, of Finals at Wembley

Season	Winners	Runners-up	Result	Attendance
1966-67	QPR (R. Morgan, Marsh, Lazarus)	WBA (Clark 2)	3-2	97,952
1967-68	Leeds United (Cooper)	Arsenal	1-0	97,887
1968-69	Swindon T. (Rogers 2, Smart)	Arsenal (Gould)	†3-1	98,189
1969-70	Man. City (Doyle, Pardoe)	WBA (Astle)	†2-1	97,963
1970-71	Tottenham (Chivers 2)	Aston Villa	2-0	100,000
1971-72	Stoke City (Conroy, Eastham)	Chelsea (Osgood)	2-1	100,000
1972-73	Tottenham H. (Coates)	Norwich City	1-0	100,000
1973-74	Wolves (Hibbitt, Richards)	Man. City (Bell)	2-1	100,000

Season	Winners	Runners-up	Result	Attendance
1974-75	Aston Villa (Graydon)	Norwich City	1-0	100,000
1975-76	Man. City (Barnes, Tueart)	Newcastle U. (Gowling)	2-1	100,000
1976-77	Aston Villa (Little 2, Nicholl)	Everton (Latchford, Lyons)	*†3-2	54,749 (at Man. Utd)

* After Aston Villa 0, Everton 0, Wembley, 100,000; and † Aston Villa 1 (Kenyon, o.g.), Everton 1 (Latchford), Sheffield Wed., 55,000.

1977-78	Nott'm F. (Robertson)	Liverpool	*1-0	54,375 (at Man. Utd)

* After Nott'm F. 0, Liverpool 0 (extra time): Wembley, 100,000.

1978-79	Nott'm F. (Birtles 2, Woodcock)	Southampton (Peach, Holmes)	3-2	100,000
1979-80	Wolves (Gray)	Nott'm F.	1-0	100,000
1980-81	Liverpool (Dalglish, Hansen)	West Ham U. (Goddard)	2-1	36,693 (at Villa Park)

* After Liverpool 1 (A. Kennedy), West Ham 1 (Stewart — pen.), (extra time), Wembley, 100,000 (0-0, 90 minutes).

1981-82	Liverpool (Whelan 2, Rush)	Tottenham H. (Archibald)	†3-1	100,000 (1-1, 90 minutes)
1982-83	Liverpool (Kennedy, Whelan)	Manchester U. (Whiteside)	†2-1	100,000
1983-84	Liverpool (Souness)	Everton	*1-0	52,089 (at Man. City)

* After Liverpool 0, Everton 0 (extra time): Wembley, 100,000.

(† = After extra time)

Summary of League Cup/Milk Cup Winners

Liverpool	4	Wolves	2	Norwich	1
Aston Villa	3	Birmingham	1	QPR	1
Manchester City	2	Chelsea	1	Stoke	1
Nott'm Forest	2	Leeds	1	Swindon	1
Tottenham	2	Leicester	1	West Bromwich	1

Scottish League Champions

Season		Points	Season		Points
1890-91	Rangers	29	1933-34	Rangers	66
	Dumbarton		1934-35	Rangers	55
1891-92	Dumbarton	37	1935-36	Celtic	66
1892-93	Celtic	29	1936-37	Rangers	61
1893-94	Celtic	29	1937-38	Celtic	61
1894-95	Hearts	31	1938-39	Rangers	59
1895-95	Celtic	30	1939-46	No competition	
1896-97	Hearts	28	1946-47	Rangers	46
1897-98	Celtic	33	1947-48	Hibernian	48
1898-99	Rangers	36	1948-49	Rangers	46
1899-			1949-50	Rangers	50
1900	Rangers	32	1950-51	Hibernian	48
1900-01	Rangers	35	1951-52	Hibernian	45
1901-02	Rangers	28	1952-53	Rangers	43
1902-03	Hibernian	37	1953-54	Celtic	43
1903-04	Third Lanark	43	1954-55	Aberdeen	49
1904-05	Celtic	41	1955-56	Rangers	52
1905-06	Celtic	49	1956-57	Rangers	55
1906-07	Celtic	55	1957-58	Hearts	62
1907-08	Celtic	55	1958-59	Rangers	50
1908-09	Celtic	51	1959-60	Hearts	54
1909-10	Celtic	54	1960-61	Rangers	51
1910-11	Rangers	52	1961-62	Dundee	54
1911-12	Rangers	51	1962-63	Rangers	57
1912-13	Rangers	53	1963-64	Rangers	55
1913-14	Celtic	65	1964-65	Kilmarnock	50
1914-15	Celtic	65	1965-66	Celtic	57
1915-16	Celtic	67	1966-67	Celtic	58
1916-17	Celtic	64	1967-68	Celtic	63
1917-18	Rangers	56	1968-69	Celtic	54
1918-19	Celtic	58	1969-70	Celtic	57
1919-20	Rangers	71	1970-71	Celtic	56
1920-21	Rangers	76	1971-72	Celtic	60
1921-22	Celtic	67	1972-73	Celtic	57
1922-23	Rangers	55	1973-74	Celtic	53
1923-24	Rangers	59	1974-75	Rangers	56
1924-25	Rangers	60	1975-76	Rangers	54
1925-26	Celtic	58	1976-77	Celtic	54
1926-27	Rangers	56	1977-78	Rangers	55
1927-28	Rangers	60	1978-79	Celtic	48
1928-29	Rangers	67	1979-80	Aberdeen	48
1929-30	Rangers	60	1980-81	Celtic	56
1930-31	Rangers	60	1981-82	Celtic	55
1931-32	Motherwell	66	1982-83	Dundee Utd	56
1932-33	Rangers	62	1983-84	Aberdeen	57

Summary of Scottish League Champions

Rangers	*37	Aberdeen	3	Kilmarnock	1
Celtic	33	Dumbarton	*2	Motherwell	1
Hearts	4	Dundee	1	Third Lanark	1
Hibernian	4	Dundee Utd.	1		

(* Includes one shared title)

168

Scottish FA Cup Winners

(* = Replay)

Season	Winners	Runners-up	Result
1873-74	Queen's Park	Clydesdale	2-0
1874-75	Queen's Park	Renton	3-0
1875-76	Queen's Park	Third Lanark	*2-0
			(after 1-1 draw)
1876-77	Vale of Leven	Rangers	*3-2
			(after 0-0, 1-1 draws)
1877-78	Vale of Leven	Third Lanark	1-0
1878-79	Vale of Leven *(Rangers did not appear for replay after 1-1 draw)*		
1879-80	Queen's Park	Thornlibank	3-0
1880-81	Queen's Park	Dumbarton	3-1
1881-82	Queen's Park	Dumbarton	*4-1
			(after 2-2 draw)
1882-83	Dumbarton	Vale of Leven	*2-1
			(after 2-2 draw)
1883-84	Queen's Park *(Vale of Leven did not appear for Final)*		
1884-85	Renton	Vale of Leven	*3-1
			(after 0-0 draw)
1885-86	Queen's Park	Renton	3-1
1886-87	Hibernian	Dumbarton	2-1
1887-88	Renton	Cambuslang	6-1
1888-89	Third Lanark	Celtic	2-1
1889-90	Queen's Park	Vale of Leven	*2-1
			(after 1-1 draw)
1890-91	Hearts	Dumbarton	1-0
1891-92	Celtic	Queen's Park	5-1
1892-93	Queen's Park	Celtic	2-1
1893-94	Rangers	Celtic	3-1
1894-95	St Bernard's	Renton	2-1
1895-96	Hearts	Hibernian	3-1
1896-97	Rangers	Dumbarton	5-1
1897-98	Rangers	Kilmarnock	2-0
1898-99	Celtic	Rangers	2-0
1899-1900	Celtic	Queen's Park	4-3
1900-01	Hearts	Celtic	4-3
1901-02	Hibernian	Celtic	1-0
1902-03	Rangers	Hearts	*2-0
			(after 0-0, 1-1 draws)

Season	Winners	Runners-up	Result
1903-04	Celtic	Rangers	3-2
1904-05	Third Lanark	Rangers	*3-1
			(after 0-0 draw)
1905-06	Hearts	Third Lanark	1-0
1906-07	Celtic	Hearts	3-0
1907-08	Celtic	St Mirren	5-1
1908-09	*Cup withheld because of riot following two drawn games (2-2, 1-1) between Celtic and Rangers.*		
1909-10	Dundee	Clyde	*2-1
			(after 2-2, 0-0 draws)
1910-11	Celtic	Hamilton	*2-0
			(after 0-0 draw)
1911-12	Celtic	Clyde	2-0
1912-13	Falkirk	Raith Rovers	2-0
1913-14	Celtic	Hibernian	*4-1
			(after 0-0 draw)
1914-19	*No competition*	First World War	
1919-20	Kilmarnock	Albion Rovers	3-2
1920-21	Partick Thistle	Rangers	1-0
1921-22	Morton	Rangers	1-0
1922-23	Celtic	Hibernian	1-0
1923-24	Airdrieonians	Hibernian	2-0
1924-25	Celtic	Dundee	2-1
1925-26	St Mirren	Celtic	2-0
1926-27	Celtic	East Fife	3-1
1927-28	Rangers	Celtic	4-0
1928-29	Kilmarnock	Rangers	2-0
1929-30	Rangers	Partick Thistle	*2-1
			(after 0-0 draw)
1930-31	Celtic	Motherwell	*4-2
			(after 2-2 draw)
1931-32	Rangers	Kilmarnock	*3-0
			(after 1-1 draw)
1932-33	Celtic	Motherwell	1-0
1933-34	Rangers	St Mirren	5-0
1934-35	Rangers	Hamilton	2-1
1935-36	Rangers	Third Lanark	1-0
1936-37	Celtic	Aberdeen	2-1
1937-38	East Fife	Kilmarnock	*4-2
			(after 1-1 draw)
1938-39	Clyde	Motherwell	4-0
1939-46	*No competition*	Second World War	
1946-47	Aberdeen	Hibernian	2-1

Season	Winners	Runners-up	Result
1947-48	Rangers	Morton	*1-0
			(after 1-1 draw)
1948-49	Rangers	Clyde	4-1
1949-50	Rangers	East Fife	3-0
1950-51	Celtic	Motherwell	1-0
1951-52	Motherwell	Dundee	4-0
1952-53	Rangers	Aberdeen	*1-0
			(after 1-1 draw)
1953-54	Celtic	Aberdeen	2-1
1954-55	Clyde	Celtic	*1-0
			(after 1-1 draw)
1955-56	Hearts	Celtic	3-1
1956-57	Falkirk	Kilmarnock	*2-1
			(after 1-1 draw)
1957-58	Clyde	Hibernian	1-0
1958-59	St Mirren	Aberdeen	3-1
1959-60	Rangers	Kilmarnock	2-0
1960-61	Dunfermline	Celtic	*2-0
			(after 0-0 draw)
1961-62	Rangers	St Mirren	2-0
1962-63	Rangers	Celtic	*3-0
			(after 1-1 draw)
1963-64	Rangers	Dundee	3-1
1964-65	Celtic	Dunfermline	3-2
1965-66	Rangers	Celtic	*1-0
			(after 0-0 draw)
1966-67	Celtic	Aberdeen	2-0
1967-68	Dunfermline	Hearts	3-1
1968-69	Celtic	Rangers	4-0
1969-70	Aberdeen	Celtic	3-1
1970-71	Celtic	Rangers	*2-1
			(after 1-1 draw)
1971-72	Celtic	Hibernian	6-1
1972-73	Rangers	Celtic	3-2
1973-74	Celtic	Dundee United	3-0
1974-75	Celtic	Airdrieonians	3-1
1975-76	Rangers	Hearts	3-1
1976-77	Celtic	Rangers	1-0
1977-78	Rangers	Aberdeen	2-1
1978-79	Rangers	Hibernian	*3-2
			(after 0-0, 0-0 draws)
1979-80	Celtic	Rangers	1-0
1980-81	Rangers	Dundee United	*4-1
			(after 0-0 draw)
1981-82	Aberdeen	Rangers	4-1

Season	Winners	Runners-up	Result
1982-83	Aberdeen	Rangers	1-0
1983-84	Aberdeen	Celtic	2-1

Summary of Scottish FA Cup Winners

Celtic	26	Falkirk	2	Dumbarton	1
Rangers	24	Hibernian	2	Dundee	1
Queen's Park	10	Kilmarnock	2	East Fife	1
Aberdeen	5	Renton	2	Morton	1
Hearts	5	Third Lanark	2	Motherwell	1
Clyde	3	St Mirren	2	Partick	1
Vale of Leven	3	Airdrieonians	1	St Bernard's	1
Dunfermline	2				

Scottish League Cup Winners

(* = Replay)

Season	Winners	Runners-up	Result
1945-46	Aberdeen	Rangers	3-2
1946-47	Rangers	Aberdeen	4-0
1947-48	East Fife	Falkirk	*4-1
			(after 1-1 draw)
1948-49	Rangers	Raith Rovers	2-0
1949-50	East Fife	Dunfermline	3-0
1950-51	Motherwell	Hibernian	3-0
1951-52	Dundee	Rangers	3-2
1952-53	Dundee	Kilmarnock	2-0
1953-54	East Fife	Partick Thistle	3-2
1954-55	Hearts	Motherwell	4-2
1955-56	Aberdeen	St Mirren	2-1
1956-57	Celtic	Partick Thistle	*3-0
			(after 0-0 draw)
1957-58	Celtic	Rangers	7-1
1958-59	Hearts	Partick Thistle	5-1
1959-60	Hearts	Third Lanark	2-1
1960-61	Rangers	Kilmarnock	2-0
1961-62	Rangers	Hearts	*3-1
			(after 1-1 draw)
1962-63	Hearts	Kilmarnock	1-0
1963-64	Rangers	Morton	5-0
1964-65	Rangers	Celtic	2-1

Season	Winners	Runners-up	Result
1965-66	Celtic	Rangers	2-1
1966-67	Celtic	Rangers	1-0
1967-68	Celtic	Dundee	5-3
1968-69	Celtic	Hibernian	6-2
1969-70	Celtic	St Johnstone	1-0
1970-71	Rangers	Celtic	1-0
1971-72	Partick Thistle	Celtic	4-1
1972-73	Hibernian	Celtic	2-1
1973-74	Dundee	Celtic	1-0
1974-75	Celtic	Hibernian	6-3
1975-76	Rangers	Celtic	1-0
1976-77	Aberdeen	Celtic	2-1
1977-78	Rangers	Celtic	2-1
1978-79	Rangers	Aberdeen	2-1
1979-80	Dundee United	Aberdeen	*3-0
			(after 0-0 draw)
1980-81	Dundee United	Dundee	3-0
1981-82	Rangers	Dundee United	2-1
1982-83	Celtic	Rangers	2-1
1983-84	Rangers	Celtic	3-2

Summary of Scottish League Cup Winners

Rangers	12	Aberdeen	3	Hibernian	1
Celtic	9	Dundee	3	Motherwell	1
Hearts	4	East Fife	3	Partick Thistle	1
		Dundee Utd	2		

All-Time Records

Goalscoring

British record for first-class match: Arbroath 36, Bon Accord 0 (Scottish Cup — 1st Round, 1885)

Football League: Stockport County 13, Halifax Town 0 (Div. 3 North, 1934); Newcastle United 13, Newport County 0 (Div. 2, 1946)

Highest Football League aggregate: 17 goals Tranmere Rovers 13, Oldham Athletic 4 (Div. 3 North, 1935)

Scottish League Championship: Celtic 11, Dundee 0 (1895).

FA Cup: Preston North End 26, Hyde United 0 (1st Round, 1887)

League/Milk Cup: West Ham United 10, Bury 0 (2nd Round, 2nd. Leg, 1983)

England: 13-0 v Ireland (1882). **Scotland:** 11-0 v Ireland (1901).

Ireland: 7-0 v Wales (1930). **Wales:** 11-0 v Ireland (1888)

Individual Match Scoring

13 by John Petrie in Arbroath 36, Bon Accord 0 (Scottish Cup — 1st Round, 1885); 10 by Joe Payne in Luton Town 12, Bristol Rovers 0 (Div. 3 South, 1936); 9 by Ted MacDougall in Bournemouth 11, Margate 0 (FA Cup — 1st Round, 1971); 9 by 'Bunny' Bell in Tranmere Rovers 13, Oldham Athletic 4 (Div. 3 North, 1935).

First Division: 7 by James Ross in Preston North End 7, Stoke City 0 (1888); 7 by Ted Drake in Aston Villa 1, Arsenal 7 (1935).

Second Division: 7 by Tommy Briggs in Blackburn Rovers 8, Bristol Rovers 3 (1955); 7 by Tim Coleman in Stoke City 8, Lincoln City 0 (1957) — all-time record for a winger.

Third Division: 5 by Barrie Thomas in Scunthorpe United 8, Luton Town 1 (1965); 5 by Keith East in Swindon Town 6, Mansfield Town 2 (1965); 5 by Steve Earle in Halifax Town 0, Fulham 8 (1969); 5 by Alf Wood in Shrewsbury Town 7, Blackburn Rovers 1 (1971); 5 by Tony Caldwell in Bolton 8, Walsall 1 (1983).

Fourth Division: 6 by Bert Lister in Oldham 11, Southport 0 (1962).

Football League Cup: 5 by Derek Reeves in Southampton 5, Leeds United 4 (4th Round, 1960-61); 5 by Alan Wilks in Queens Park Rangers 5, Oxford United 1 (3rd Round, 1967-68).

Scottish League (Championship): 8 by Jimmy McGrory in Celtic 9, Dunfermline Athletic 0 (1928).

England: 5 by Steve Bloomer v Wales (9-1, 1896; 5 by G. O. Smith v Ireland (13-2, 1899); 5 by Willie Hall v Ireland (7-0, 1938); 5 by Malcolm Macdonald v Cyprus (5-0, 1975).

Ireland: 6 by Joe Bambrick v Wales (7-0, 1930).

Scotland: 5 by Charles Heggie v Ireland (7-2, 1886).

Wales: 4 by Jimmy Price v Ireland (7-1, 1882); 4 by John Doughty v Ireland (11-0, 1888); 4 by Mel Charles v Ireland (4-0, 1962).

Most Goals by Clubs in League Season

Football League — Div. 1: 128 by Aston Villa (1930-31); **Div. 2:** 122 by Middlesbrough (1926-27); **Div. 3:** 111 by Queens Park Rangers (1961-62); **Div. 4:** 134 by Peterborough United (1960-61); **Div. 3 South:** 127 by Millwall (1927-28); **Div. 3 North:** 128 by Bradford City (1928-29).

Scottish League Championship — Div. 1: 132 by Heart of Midlothian (1957-58): **Div. 2:** 142 by Raith Rovers (1937-38).

Most Individual League Goals in Season

Football League — Div.1: 60 by W.R. ('Dixie') Dean (Everton, 1927-28); **Div. 2:** 59 by George Camsell (Middlesbrough, 1926-27); **Div. 3:** 39 by Derek Reeves (Southampton, 1959-60); **Div. 4:** 52 by Terry Bly (Peterborough United, 1960-61); **Div. 3 South:** 55 by Joe Payne (Luton Town, 1936-37); **Div. 3 North:** 55 by Ted Harston (Mansfield Town, 1936-37).

Scottish League Championship — Div. 1: 52 by Willie McFadyen (Motherwell 1931-32); **Div.2:** 66 by Jim Smith (Ayr United, 1927-28).

Most League Goals in Career

Football League: 434 by Arthur Rowley, 1946-65 (4 for West Bromwich Albion, 27 for Fulham, 251 for Leicester City, 152 for Shrewsbury Town).

Scottish League: 410 by Jimmy McGrory, 1922-38 (397 for Celtic, 13 for Clydebank).

Most League Appearances in Career

Football League: *824 – Terry Paine*, 1957-77 (Southampton 713, Hereford Utd. 111); *777 – Alan Oakes*, 1959-84 (Man. City 565, Chester 211, Port Vale 1); *770 – John Trollope*, 1960-80 (Swindon Town — record for single club); *764 – Jimmy Dickinson*, 1946-64 (Portsmouth); *762 – Roy Sproson*, 1950-72 (Port Vale).
Record for *consecutive* League appearances: *401 – Harold Bell* for Tranmere Rovers in Div. 3 North, 1946-55.

Scottish League: 626 appearances by Bob Ferrier for Motherwell (1918-37).

International Appearances and Goals
(To May 27, 1984)

Appearances
England: 108 by Bobby Moore
Ireland: 105 by Pat Jennings
Scotland: 93 by Kenny Dalglish
Wales: 68 by Ivor Allchurch

Goals
England: 49 by Bobby Charlton
Ireland: 13 by Billy Gillespie
Scotland: 30 by Denis Law
Wales: 23 by Trevor Ford

Most Points in Season — Football League

(A) under old system of 2 points for win:
Div. 1 68 by Liverpool, 1978-79; **Div. 2** 70 by Tottenham Hotspur, 1919-20; **Div. 3** 70 by Aston Villa, 1971-72; **Div. 4** 74 by Lincoln City, 1975-76; **Div. 3 South** 70 by Nottingham Forest 1950-51; 70 by Bristol City, 1954-55; **Div. 3 North** 72 by Doncaster Rovers, 1946-47.

(B) Since 3 points for win introduced in season 1981-82:
Div. 1 87 by Liverpool, 1981-82; **Div. 2** 88 by Luton Town, 1981-82; 88 by Chelsea & Sheffield Wednesday, 1983-84; **Div. 3** 95 by Oxford United, 1983-84; **Div. 4** 101 by York City, 1983-84.
Scottish League Championship 76 by Rangers, 1920-21.

Record Crowds

World: 200,000 Brazil v Uruguay (World Cup Final, Rio de Janeiro, 1950).
Britain: 149,547 Scotland v England (Hampden Park, Glasgow, 1937).
England: 126,047 Bolton Wanderers v West Ham United (FA Cup Final, Wembley, 1923)
European Cup: 135,826 Celtic v Leeds United (semi-final, Hampden Park, Glasgow, 1970).
Biggest Football League crowd: 82,950 Manchester United v Arsenal (Maine Road, Manchester, 1948).
Record attendance for English club ground: 84,569 Manchester City v Stoke City (FA Cup — 6th Round, 1934)
Football League record season's attendance aggregate: 41,271,424 in season 1948-49.
Football League highest single-day aggregate: 1,269,934 on 27 December 1949.
Smallest League match attendance: 13 for Stockport County v Leicester City (Div. 2) played at Old Trafford, Manchester, on 7 May 1921.
Smallest League attendance since the 2nd World War: 450 for Rochdale v Cambridge United (Div. 3) on 5 February 1974.

The European Championship

Originally known as the Henri Delaunay Cup, after its French founder, later as the Nations Cup, and now as the European Championship, it was introduced in 1958. The tournament takes two years to complete, with the Final scheduled to take place exactly halfway between one World Cup and the next. The first five European Championships were won by different countries, and West Germany became the first nation to take the title twice when they beat Belgium in the 1980 Final in Rome.

1958-60: in France
Semi-finals: Yugoslavia 5, France 4 (Paris); Russia 3, Czechoslovakia 0 (Marseilles).
Final (Paris): *Russia* 2, Yugoslavia 1 (after extra time).

1962-64: in Spain
Semi-finals: Russia 3, Denmark 0 (Barcelona); Spain 2, Hungary 1 (Madrid)
Final (Madrid): *Spain* 2, Russia 1.

1966-68: in Italy
Semi-finals: Yugoslavia 1, England 0 (Florence); Italy 0, Russia 0 (Naples) after extra time — Italy won on toss.
Final (Rome): *Italy* 2, Yugoslavia 0 in replay after 1-1 draw.

1970-72: in Belgium
Semi-finals: Russia 1, Hungary 0 (Brussels); West Germany 2, Belgium 1 (Antwerp).
Final (Brussels); *West Germany* 3, Russia 0.

1974-76 in Yugoslavia
Semi-finals: Czechoslovakia 3, Holland 1 (Zagreb); West Germany 4, Yugoslavia 2 (Belgrade)
Final (Belgrade): *Czechoslovakia* 2, West Germany 2 (Czechoslovakia won 5-3 on penalties)

1978-80: in Italy
Third place match (no semi-finals): Italy 1, Czechoslovakia 1 (Naples) — Czechoslovakia won 9-8 on penalties.
Final (Rome): *West Germany* 2, Belgium 1.

1982-84: in France
Britain failed to provide a qualifier for the Finals played in France in the summer of 1984 (after this publication went to press). The host nation qualified automatically, and the eight countries were drawn into two sections. The tournament began on June 12, with the Final in Paris on June 27.
Group 1: France, Denmark, Belgium, Yugoslavia.
Group 2: West Germany (European Champions), Portugal, Rumania, Spain.

The European Cup

The European Cup has presented a standard of international club football that could hardly have been imagined when it was launched in 1955. The idea was conceived by French soccer journalist Gabriel Hanot, a former international player, and developed rapidly after a meeting which he and the proprietors of his newspaper, *L'Equipe*, called in Paris in the spring of 1955 among all the leading European clubs. Six months later the dream became reality, and so began a contest bringing together the champions of all the European countries and now long established as football's greatest club tournament.

In 1949 Hanot had been a prominent figure in the introduction of the Latin Cup, featuring the champion clubs of France, Spain, Italy and Portugal. As long ago as 1927 a similar competition, the Mitropa Cup, had been started in Central Europe among the principal clubs of Austria, Czechoslovakia, Hungary, Italy and Yugoslavia. By combining those two tournaments, and inviting the champion teams of North and Western Europe to participate, Hanot found the formula for the European Cup.

The champions of 17 countries entered the opening tournament in season 1955-56, but Chelsea subsequently withdrew under pressure from the Football League, who saw the new venture as a threat to their own competition. A year later Manchester United, disregarding the Establishment, took part. Fittingly, in 1968, they became the first English club to win the trophy — ten years after a European Cup journey had decimated the Old Trafford club with the Munich air disaster.

Ironically, although France was the birthplace of the European Cup and the first final was staged in Paris, no French club has taken the prize. St Etienne have been closest, as losing finalists in 1976.

Real Madrid's Domination

With bewildering football, Spanish champions Real Madrid initially made the competition their own, winning it for the first five years (1956–60). In the last of that astonishing sequence of finals, they beat the German champions, Eintracht Frankfurt, by 7–3 at Hampden Park, Glasgow, with one of the most dazzling displays in the game's history. Outshining all others in a magnificent team performance were Real's legendary strikers Ferenc Puskas, who scored four goals, and Alfredo di Stefano, who got the other three. Real Madrid appeared in eight of the first eleven European Cup Finals and won the trophy on six of those occasions. Either as its holders or as champions of Spain, they took part in the first 15 seasons of the competition and the following year (1970–71) reached the final of the European Cup-Winners' Cup.

Until the inception of the European Cup, Real Madrid were little known outside Spain. Suddenly they found themselves the centre of world-wide acclaim — and if Real Madrid made the European Cup, it can also be said that the 'European Coupe des Clubs Champions' made Real. Their vast profits from the competition were invested in a permanent monument to their triumphs with the construction of the 120,000-capacity Bernabeu Stadium in the Chamartin suburb of Madrid.

For the first 11 years the European Cup was the 'Latins' Cup', with Spanish, Portuguese and Italian clubs dominating the tournament. During that period its winners came exclusively from three cities: Madrid, Lisbon and Milan.

Celtic Break Latin Grip

Britain, through the medium of Glasgow Celtic, finally broke the Latin grip in 1967. Entering the competition for the first time, they had a comfortable passage through the rounds against Zürich, Nantes, Vojvodina and Dukla. The final, in Lisbon, brought them opposition of the strongest calibre in Inter-Milan, and after falling behind to an early penalty, Celtic saved the tie with Gemmell's second-half equalizer and, five minutes from the end, won it with a goal by Chalmers.

Thus Jock Stein's magnificent Celtic put Britain's hand on the European Cup for the first time. They won four major trophies that season, also completing the domestic treble at home. At Wembley a year later England took possession of Europe's principal club prize from Scotland with a wonderful extra-time victory by Manchester United against Benfica. Three times before — in 1957, 1958 and 1966 — Matt Busby's men had been foiled at the semi-final stage. Now, in 1968, they beat their bogey, winning the first leg against Real Madrid by Best's only goal at Old Trafford and storming back from 3–1 down with 18 minutes left to draw the return match in Madrid 3–3, so winning the 4–3 on aggregate.

The Final, on 29 May 1968, produced an emotional occasion which approached England's 1966 World Cup triumph. Remembering how close Manchester United had been to European success in the past, unable to forget how the European Cup had destroyed the famous 'Busby Babes' in the snows of Munich Airport in 1958, everyone, it seemed, was willing them to victory over Benfica, the Eagles of Lisbon.

Charlton's dipping header early in the second half looked to be sufficient when, with 11 minutes left, that was still the only goal. Then Graca smashed Benfica level, and Stepney miraculously held Eusebio's shot to earn extra time. It was a save that lifted the hearts of United and, with fresh wind in their sails, they moved majestically to victory. Aston demoralized Benfica's right defensive flank, and from the moment Best beat one man, then dribbled the 'keeper to put United back in front, the European Cup was destined for Old Trafford, the margin stretching to 4–1 as Kidd celebrated his 19th birthday by heading in a crossbar rebound and Charlton himself shooting the final goal.

A year later AC Milan took the European Cup back to Italy, thus sharing four successes in the competition for that country equally with Inter-Milan. In 1970 Celtic were finalists again, and following Arsenal's victory in the Fairs Cup and Manchester City's success in the Cup-Winners' Cup, there was the prospect of a clean sweep by Britain in three European tournaments.

In anticipation, 25,000 fanatical Celtic supporters travelled to Milan — the biggest following any British team has ever had abroad — for the final against Dutch 'outsiders' Feyenoord. In the semi-final Celtic had twice beaten Leeds United, in Milan full-back Gemmell shot them ahead after half an hour and the Cup seemed to be heading for Glasgow again. But Feyenoord equalized, dominated the second half, and deservedly triumphed.

In 1971 Wembley staged its third European Champion Clubs' Final, in which Ajax (Amsterdam) kept the prize in Dutch possession by beating Panathinaikos, of Greece, 2–0. Ajax retained the trophy in 1972 and 1973, again without conceding a goal in either Final, and so became the first club to win the European Cup in three successive seasons since Real Madrid in the competition's early years.

Ajax's reign as European Champions ended with the departure of ace forward Johan Cruyff to Barcelona, and in 1974 Bayern Munich earned West Germany the trophy for the first time. Yet with barely a minute left in the final in Brussels, the prize seemed destined for Atletico Madrid (who had dealt brutally with Celtic in a goalless semi-final first leg in Glasgow and won the return 2–0). Justice was done, however, when Bayern centre-back Schwarzenbeck equalized in the closing seconds, and in the first replayed final in European Cup history the German champions switched to all-out attack and triumphed 4–0, with two goals apiece from Hoeness and Muller.

In 1975 Leeds United became only the second English club to reach the final — a remarkable end to a season which began with Don Revie gone from Elland Road to manage England, his successor Brian Clough lasting for only 44 turbulent days, and Jimmy Armfield arriving from Bolton to restore stability to the camp.

En route to the final at the Parc des Princes, Leeds beat Zürich 5-3 on aggregate. Hungary's Ujpest Dozsa 5-1, Belgian champions Anderlecht 4-0 and, in the semi-final, Barcelona (Cruyff, Neeskens and all) 3-2. Then, in Paris, Leeds faced the holders, Bayern Munich, who were also under new management, Udo Lattek having been replaced by Dettmar Cramer.

But a final rich in promise was, in reality, one of the poorest in the history of the competition. A contributing factor was the first Leeds tackle, which put defender Andersson out of the match, and the necessary team reshuffle heightened Bayern's defensive resolve. Leeds had two first-half penalty claims against Beckenbauer rejected, and what looked a perfectly valid goal by Lorimer after 67 minutes was disallowed for offside by French referee Kitabdjian.

European Ban for Leeds

When Roth and Muller scored late goals for Bayern, it was too much for Leeds' followers behind Maier's goal. They smashed seats and hurled the wreckage over the wire fencing onto the pitch, then greeted Bayern's lap of honour with a further barrage of cushions and debris. British football was disgraced in the eyes of the world, and the sequel was a European ban on Leeds.

By defeating French club St Etienne 1-0 in a splendid 1976 final at Hampden Park, Bayern Munich emulated European Cup hat-tricks previously performed by Real Madrid and Ajax Amsterdam.

Britain's prestige was restored in Rome in May 1977 when Liverpool fans behaved impeccably and their favourites became only the second English club to win the trophy, beating Moenchengladbach by three goals to one. Liverpool played superbly with goals coming from Terry McDermott, Tommy Smith and Phil Neal (penalty). But without doubt the star of the match was Kevin Keegan, subsequently transferred to SV Hamburg for £500,000.

Twelve months later, in Wembley's fourth European Cup Final, Liverpool became the first British club to win the trophy in successive years, beating Belgian champions FC Bruges by the only goal. It was scored by Kenny Dalglish, the replacement for Keegan, and thus was brought to Anfield another top prize for Bill Shankly's successor in the managerial seat, Bob Paisley.

Compared with earlier round matches against Dynamo Dresden, Benfica and Borussia Moenchengladbach, the final fell well below expectations, mainly due to Bruges' lack of initiative. From the kick-off, the height of their ambitions seemed to be a 0-0 draw and then the 50-50 chance of getting a decision on penalties.

In 1979 England completed a European Cup hat-trick, not through Liverpool this time, but Nottingham Forest. They began by knocking out Liverpool in the preliminary round in September, and then comfortably disposed of AEK Athens and Switzerland's Grasshoppers.

Forest appeared to have lost their chance when only drawing the semi-final first leg 3-3 (from two goals down at one stage) at home to FC Cologne, who were quarter-final conquerors of Glasgow Rangers, but Ian Bowyer scored the only goal of the second leg in Germany and Forest were through to the final in Munich. There, Trevor Francis repaid a handsome slice of his £1 million transfer from Birmingham by heading the only goal, from John Robertson's centre a minute before half-time against negative Malmo, champions of Sweden. Victory completed a season's double for Brian Clough's men who, two months earlier, had beaten Southampton 3-2 at Wembley to lift the Football League Cup.

Forest went on to emulate Liverpool by keeping the European Cup in England for a second year, beating Hamburg in the 1980 Final in Madrid by Robertson's 20th-minute shot. With Francis out through injury, Clough settled for a largely defensive formation, which, allied to Peter Shilton's goalkeeping, was always too good for the Germans.

A year later, the trophy went back to Anfield. Alan Kennedy, Liverpool's attacking left-back, scored the only goal of the Final against Real Madrid in Paris. That made Liverpool European Cup-holders for the third time and gave them a double cup success in 1981, for they had won the League Cup at the start of their monopoly of that tournament too.

In 1982 the fourth Football League club etched their name on the European Cup when Tony Barton's Aston Villa triumphed against Bayern Munich in Rotterdam. Once again, a solitary goal did it — scorer Peter Withe — and for a sixth successive season the trophy stayed in England.

The sequence ended with its return to West Germany in 1983. Hamburg more than compensated for defeat twelve months earlier in the UEFA Cup Final, beating the favourites Juventus in Athens by the now usual European Cup Final score, 1-0. The prize was Hamburg's from the moment Magath sent an early shot past Zoff.

A year later the tournament was decided on penalties for the first time. For the 67th and last match of Joe Fagan's first season as manager, Liverpool went back to Rome, where they first won the trophy in 1977, and faced Roma on their own pitch. Phil Neal scored after 14 minutes, but just on half-time Pruzzo equalised and, with the score still 1-1 after extra time, the match turned into a lottery. A week before, Tottenham had won the UEFA Cup in a similar shoot-out, and now Liverpool, already League Champions and Milk Cup winners in 1984, completed the treble as, with the final kick of the night, Alan Kennedy gave Anfield its fourth European Cup in seven years, 4–2 on penalties.

Results of European Cup Finals

Year	Venue	Winners	Runners-up	Score
1956	Paris	Real Madrid	Reims	4–3
1957	Madrid	Real Madrid	Fiorentina	2–0
1958	Brussels	Real Madrid	AC Milan	3–2
1959	Stuttgart	Real Madrid	Reims	2–0
1960	Glasgow	Real Madrid	Eintracht	7–3
1961	Berne	Benfica	CF Barcelona	3–2
1962	Amsterdam	Benfica	Real Madrid	5–3
1963	Wembley	AC Milan	Benfica	2–1
1964	Vienna	Inter-Milan	Real Madrid	3–1
1965	Milan	Inter-Milan	Benfica	1–0
1966	Brussels	Real Madrid	Partizan	2–1
1967	Lisbon	Celtic	Inter-Milan	2–1
1968	Wembley	Manchester United	Benfica	4–1
1969	Madrid	AC Milan	Ajax Amsterdam	4–1
1970	Milan	Feyenoord	Celtic	2–1
1971	Wembley	Ajax Amsterdam	Panathinaikos	2–0
1972	Rotterdam	Ajax Amsterdam	Inter-Milan	2–0
1973	Belgrade	Ajax Amsterdam	Juventus	1–0
1974	Brussels	Bayern Munich	Atletico Madrid	4–0
		(After 1–1 draw also in Brussels)		
1975	Paris	Bayern Munich	Leeds United	2–0
1976	Glasgow	Bayern Munich	St Etienne	1–0
1977	Rome	Liverpool	M'Gladbach	3–1
1978	Wembley	Liverpool	FC Bruges	1–0
1979	Munich	Nottingham F.	Malmo	1–0
1980	Madrid	Nottingham F.	SV Hamburg	1–0
1981	Paris	Liverpool	Real Madrid	1–0
1982	Rotterdam	Aston Villa	Bayern Munich	1–0
1983	Athens	SV Hamburg	Juventus	1–0
1984	Rome	Liverpool	AS Roma	1–1
		(Liverpool won 4–2 on penalties)		

European Cup-Winners' Cup

Staged for the first time in season 1960-61, the Cup-Winners' Cup is the youngest of the three European club tournaments, but in prestige it stands second to the Champions' Cup and British teams have done much to popularize it. In nine seasons between 1963 and 1971 the Cup of Cups was won by Football League clubs no fewer than four times, with Tottenham, West Ham, Manchester City and Chelsea all using victory in the FA Cup one year as the passport to European success the following season, and in 1972 Rangers became the first Scottish name on the list of winners — compensation for being beaten finalists in 1961 and 1967.

The enormous success of the Champions' Cup clearly indicated scope for another European competition, and in 1959 the organizers of the Mitropa Cup succeeded in their campaign to launch a knock-out competition for national cup-winners.

It started the following year with only ten entries, the initial problem being that in few Continental countries was the domestic cup greeted with the same enthusiasm and regarded with the same seriousness as the FA and Scottish Cups. For instance, Spain played their FA Cup at the end of the season, Italy in midweek (like the Football League Cup), France on neutral grounds and Portugal on a home-and-away basis.

By the third season (1962-63), however, 24 clubs took part in the Cup-Winners' Cup and there is now a regular entry of 32 teams. Not only has the Cup of Cups grown to full maturity; its development boosted the national cup competitions in many countries, because success brought prospects of a lucrative campaign in Europe.

After the first final, in which Fiorentina triumphed for Italy by beating Rangers home and away, UEFA took over the competition and one of their first decisions was to do away with two-leg finals. But two matches were still needed to decide the 1962 winners — Atletico Madrid, who held the holders Fiorentina 1-1 in Glasgow and, four months later, triumphed 3-0 in Stuttgart.

Tottenham Win in Style

In 1963 Tottenham Hotspur put themselves, and the Cup-Winners' Cup, truly on the European map. At the Feyenoord Stadium in Rotterdam a capacity 65,000 crowd saw them take the trophy from Atletico in tremendous style by 5–1, scorers Greaves (2), Dyson (2) and White.

The following year Sporting Lisbon won the cup for Portugal, but in 1965 it was back in England, with Wembley housing the first 100,000 crowd in the history of the competition and West Ham celebrating the occasion by 2–0 against TSV Munich (scorer Sealey, 2).

Britain also supplied a finalist in each of the next two seasons, but twice West German opposition proved too powerful. Liverpool losing 2–1 to Borussia Dortmund in Glasgow in 1966 and a year later Rangers going down by the only goal to Bayern Munich in Nuremberg.

Season 1965–66, the year following West Ham's success, may not have retained the trophy for Britain, but a record was established by providing three of the semi-finalists: Liverpool, West Ham and Celtic. In 1970 the Cup-Winners' Cup did return to England . . . and stayed for two seasons.

Manchester City's 2–1 victory over the Polish mining team Gornik Zabrze in Vienna was earned with goals from Young and Lee, who celebrated his 25th birthday with what proved to be the winner from the penalty spot. Thus City completed a spectacular cup double, for they had already won the Football League Cup that season.

Chelsea's Replay Triumph

On the night they lifted the Cup-Winners' Cup in the rain-lashed Prater Stadium in Vienna, Chelsea were in Manchester, winning the FA Cup in the replayed final against Leeds United — a success that paved the way for them to take over the Cup of Cups from Manchester City in 1971.

Some 4,000 supporters journeyed to Athens to cheer Chelsea in the final against the old masters of Europe, Real Madrid. Osgood's lone goal looked all over the winner until, in the most dramatic climax to any European final, Zoco equalized with the last kick of normal time. Webb's goal-line clearance kept Chelsea alive in extra time, and two nights later in the same Karaiskaki Stadium it began all over again.

This time Chelsea, putting the emphasis on attack from the start, took a two-goal lead through Dempsey and Osgood, and although Real Madrid replied 15 minutes from the end, the experience and tradition of eight previous European finals was not enough to save them. So Chelsea won their first European prize.

The 1971–72 tournament ended with Rangers giving Scotland its first sight of the Cup-Winners' Cup. They beat Moscow Dynamo 3–2 in the final in Barcelona, but the Russians protested that their players had been handicapped by the pitch invasions of supporters from Glasgow. It was several weeks before Rangers' victory was confirmed by UEFA, but because of their supporters' misconduct they were barred from European football for two years — a ban subsequently reduced to one season.

Leeds United justifiably claimed that local Greek referee Michas cost them the 1973 final against AC Milan, who were themselves beaten in the final a year later, when FC Magdeburg put East Germany's name on a European trophy for the first time. In 1975 Dynamo Kiev did likewise for Russia. Their team was also chosen to represent the Soviet Union internationally in the European Championship.

In 1976 West Ham became England's seventh finalists in this tournament. As in the earlier rounds, they left behind dismal League form and scored first against Anderlecht in Brussels, but in a fine match they were defeated 4–2. It was Belgium's first success in a European competition.

Anderlecht also reached the next two finals, losing 2–0 to SV Hamburg in Amsterdam (1977), and beating Austria Vienna 4–0 in Paris (1978). In 1979 the Cup-Winners' Cup went to Spain for only the second time, Barcelona defeating Fortuna Dusseldorf 4–3 in Basle. It was gripping, entertaining, at times rough — and seven goals represented a record aggregate for any final in this tournament.

In contrast, none was scored after two hours in the 1980 Final in Brussels, where Valencia kept the trophy in Spain by beating Arsenal 5–4 on penalties. It was the first European Final to be decided in such a way and Arsenal, despite being unbeaten in the competition, were the victims.

In the next two years the Cup-Winners' Cup went to Russia (Dinamo Tbilisi) and back to Spain, where 100,000 saw Barcelona win 2–1 on their home ground against Standard Liege.

Aberdeen Supreme

Then, in 1983, the 'Cup of Cups' returned to Britain, and to Scotland for the first time since Rangers' victory in 1972. There have been no more deserved or popular winners than Alex Ferguson's Aberdeen. On the way they knocked out Sion (Switzerland), Dinamo Tirana (Albania), Lech Poznan (Poland), then the powerful Bayern Munich (0–0 away, followed by a magnificent 3–2 at Pittodrie) and, in the semi-final, a 5–2 aggregate score against Waterschei, of Belgium.

On a dramatic night in rainswept Gothenburg, 19-year-old Eric Black put Aberdeen ahead with six minutes, but Real Madrid, playing their eleventh European Final compared with Aberdeen's first, drew level from Juanito's penalty after goalkeeper Jim Leighton brought down Santillana.

Three minutes before normal time ended, Black limped off, and only eight minutes of extra time remained when his replacement, 20-year-old John Hewitt, met Mark McGhee's cross with a far-post header (his fifth goal in the competition). The greatest victory in Aberdeen's 80-year history made them the sixth British winners of the Cup-Winners' Cup. They then came home to take the Scottish Cup again.

Results of European Cup-Winners' Cup Finals

Year	Venue	Winners	Runners-up	Score
1961	—	Fiorentina	Rangers	4-1
				aggregate
(Fiorentina won first leg 2-0 in Glasgow, second leg 2-1 in Florence)				
1962	Stuttgart	Atletico Madrid	Florentina	3-0
	(In replay after 1-1 draw in Glasgow)			
1963	Rotterdam	Tottenham Hotspur	Atletico Madrid	5-1
1964	Antwerp	Sporting Lisbon	MTK Budapest	1-0
	(In replay after 3-3 draw in Brussels)			
1965	Wembley	West Ham United	TSV Munich	2-0
1966	Glasgow	Borussia Dortmund	Liverpool	2-1
1967	Nuremberg	Bayern Munich	Rangers	1-0
1968	Rotterdam	AC Milan	Hamburg	2-0
1969	Basle	Slovan Bratislava	CF Barcelona	3-2
1970	Vienna	Manchester City	Gornik Zabrze	2-1
1971	Athens	Chelsea	Real Madrid	2-1
	(In replay after 1-1 draw, also in Athens)			
1972	Barcelona	Rangers	Dynamo Moscow	3-2
1973	Salonika	AC Milan	Leeds United	1-0
1974	Rotterdam	FC Magdeburg	AC Milan	2-0
1975	Basle	Dynamo Kiev	Ferencvaros	3-0
1976	Brussels	Anderlecht	West Ham	4-2
1977	Amsterdam	SV Hamburg	Anderlecht	2-0
1978	Paris	Anderlecht	Austria Vienna	4-0
1979	Basle	Barcelona	Fortuna Dusseldorf	4-3
1980	Brussels	Valencia	Arsenal	0-0
	(Valencia won 5-4 on penalties)			
1981	Dusseldorf	Dinamo Tbilisi	Carl Zeiss Jena	2-1
1982	Barcelona	Barcelona	Standard Liege	2-1
1983	Gothenburg	Aberdeen	Real Madrid	2-1
1984	Basle	Juventus	FC Porto	2-1

The UEFA Cup

Season 1971–72 marked the innovation of the UEFA Cup in succession to the European Fairs Cup, which was originally known as the European Inter-City Industrial Fairs Cup. This was the forerunner of the three major European football competitions, although in Britain at least it is ranked No. 3 behind the European Cup and Cup-Winners' Cup.

For many years before the Fairs Cup was launched in 1955 matches were played between cities on the Continent, but it was not until 1950 that Ernst B. Thommen, of Switzerland, suggested a tournament for cities regularly holding industrial and trade fairs.

The competition got off the ground largely through the initiative of FIFA president Sir Stanley Rous, and until 1971 it ran independently of UEFA under an organizing committee.

Some cities (e.g. London) at first entered representative teams but others preferred to nominate club sides, and as the competition grew in prestige and popularity, club sides took over.

Although the first Fairs Cup tournament began in 1955, it was not completed until 1958. The reason for staggering the schedule was to avoid a clash with long-standing domestic fixtures. But interest could not be sustained over such a long period, and the competition almost ground to a halt. The organizers, recognising this weakness, staged the second series over two years, and since season 1960–61 it has been an annual event.

Spain Win Five of First Six

Spain provided five of the first six winners, starting with two triumphs for Barcelona. They won the drawn-out 1955–58 series, beating a representative London side 6–0 in Barcelona and by what was to remain the record aggregate of 8–2. In the 1958–60 series Barcelona went through the finals without losing a game and won the trophy again by defeating Birmingham City 5–2 on aggregate.

Birmingham were also the losing finalists in the 1960–61 series, when they held AS Roma to a 2-2 draw at home but lost 2-0 in Rome.

Valencia were the high-scoring winners in 1961-62, defeating Barcelona 7-3 on aggregate. They won the trophy again the following season and went close to completing a hat-trick in 1963-64, when for the first time a one-match final was played on a neutral ground. In an all-Spanish decider they lost 2-1 to Real Zaragoza in Barcelona.

But single-leg finals were not a success and after Ferencvaros had beaten Juventus 1-0 in Turin in 1965 — Hungary's first Fairs Cup conquest — the 1965-66 final reverted to two matches. It was held over until the following season and when it was eventually played Barcelona became the first team to win the Fairs Cup three times, beating their Spanish rivals Real Zaragoza after losing the home leg.

Leeds went down 2-0 on aggregate to Dynamo Zagreb in the 1967 final, but a year later they became the first British winners of the trophy. In the first leg they gained a slender 1-0 lead and then held Ferencvaros to a goalless draw in Budapest.

Honours for Newcastle

In the last competition under the title of Inter-Cities Fairs Cup, another British team took the prize — Newcastle United in season 1968-69. It was Newcastle's first venture into Europe, and the Geordies' theme song, 'Blaydon Races' rang out as the crowds thronged St James's Park to see the Tynesiders beat crack Continental clubs Feyenoord, Sporting Lisbon, Real Zaragoza and Vitoria Setubal.

There was an all-British semi-final between Newcastle and Rangers. United fought a rearguard action to hold Rangers 0-0 at Ibrox and then won 2-0 at St James's Park. With their team two down in the second leg, Rangers followers invaded the field intent on getting the game abandoned and play was held up for 18 minutes. There were 31 arrests, 60 spectators were taken to hospital and the match was played out with 1,000 police surrounding the pitch.

In the final, Newcastle beat the Hungarians Ujpest Dozsa 3-0 in the home leg, but even that margin began to look inadequate when Ujpest quickly pulled back two goals in the return game in Budapest. A storming rally by Newcastle, however, produced three goals and an impressive 6-2 victory on aggregate.

In 1970 Arsenal scored a dramatic victory over Belgium's Anderlecht which kept the Fairs Cup in England for the third successive season. They lost the first leg of the final 3-1 in Brussels, but the second match was won 3-0, and a 51,000 Highbury crowd went wild at Arsenal's first success for 17 years.

A year later Leeds United became the first British club to win the competition twice. In what was the last European Fairs Cup tournament, they were its first winners on the 'away goals', rule, drawing 2–2 against Juventus in Turin and 1–1 at Elland Road.

Season 1971–72 produced the first all-British final in any European contest. Tottenham beating Wolves 3–2 on aggregate, and by the same score Liverpool defeated Borussia Moenchengladbach in the 1973 final.

Spurs were finalists in 1974, losing this time to Feyenoord, who thus ended England's six-year grip on the competition. Borussia Moenchengladbach's success in 1975 meant that, combined with Bayern Munich's European Cup, West German clubs held two European trophies, but a year later Liverpool brought England the prize again, defeating Bruges after conceding two early goals in the home leg of the final and then clinging on for a draw in Belgium to repeat their League Championship — UEFA Cup double of 1973.

That victory marked the end of England's long spell of domination in this competition, the prize going in the next four years to Juventus (Italy), the attractive Dutch side PSV Eindhoven, to Borussia Moenchengladbach again, and then staying in West Germany, with Eintracht Frankfurt beating Moenchengladbach on away goals for their first European success.

Glory for Ipswich

After an interval of five years, the UEFA Cup returned to England in 1981 when, for the first time, a European trophy won by a British side went to a town, not a city. Bobby Robson's Ipswich were the team to do it. Along the way, they had to beat opponents like Widzew Lodz (Poland), St. Etienne (France) and FC Cologne (West Germany), and in the two-leg Final they met the Dutch club, AZ Alkmaar. Goals at Portman Road by John Wark (penalty), Frans Thijssen — scoring against his fellow countrymen — and Paul Mariner gave them a good lead to take to Holland. It was enough, but only just, supplemented by further goals by Thijssen and Wark, so although Ipswich lost the second leg 4–2, they won the Final 5–4 on aggregate.

The Swedish club IFK Gothenburg, produced a real surprise in the 1982 Final, winning 4–0 (1–0 at home, then convincingly 3–0 away) against SV Hamburg — the first time Scandinavia had taken a European trophy.

A new name went on the UEFA Cup for the fourth successive time in 1983, when Anderlecht added to two previous European successes — in the Cup-Winners' Cup — with a 2–1 aggregate win against Benfica. It was an embarrassing tournament for England's four participants, Arsenal, Ipswich, Manchester United and Southampton. Not one of them survived the first round.